WEYMOUTH

Overleaf: Weymouth from the air
(Crown Copyright)

WEYMOUTH

An Illustrated History

Maureen Boddy and Jack West

Maureen Boddy

Jack A. C. West

THE DOVECOTE PRESS LTD

Summertime at Weymouth

WOULDST THOU ENJOY HEALTH, CONTEMPLATION, EASE,
SALUBRIOUS WATERS, AND A PURER BREEZE;
CAN FRIENDSHIP CHARM THEE, OR CAN EASE EXCITE,
PHILANDER HASTE, FAIR WEYMOUTH'S SCENES INVITE.

William Holloway, 1798

First published in 1983 by The Dovecote Press Ltd
Stanbridge, Wimborne, Dorset

ISBN 0 946159 13 0 (casebound)
ISBN 0 946159 14 9 (paperback)

Photoset in English Times
Printed and bound in Great Britain by
Biddles Ltd, Guildford, Surrey

Contents

Introduction

Not so very many years ago, the study of local history was the specialised interest of a few worthies, most of whom were classified by their contemporaries as 'antiquarians' and then left alone to enjoy their eccentricity. Today, the study of the story of one's own town or village finds a regular place in school curricula for all ages and there is a wide general interest as well as a never ending search for the most precise detail.

Using the wide range of material now preserved at Weymouth Library and at the Local History Museum, we have attempted to set out this new 'History of Weymouth'. It is partly our own interpretation of well-established facts, and partly new material not published before, at least in a general history, all brought together in the hope of interesting a new generation of readers. Whilst we have benefited by the availability of so much material, we have also faced the same problem which must have confronted the earlier local historians – what to include and what to leave out. If we have omitted the very facts which you wished to know, we are sorry, but to include it all would have resulted in a multi-volume publication which no one would have had time to read, and which, to be accurate, we would never have found time to write.

This book could never have been written but for the pioneer work done by others during the past two hundred years. We have tried to list every book consulted in the Bibliography, but much of our information and many of our ideas have come as the result of the hundreds of discussions we have had with others interested in Weymouth's long history.

The majority of the illustrations have been provided by the Dorset County Library and the Weymouth Local History Museum, without whose co-operation it would have been impossible to produce this book. In addition we wish to thank Eric Ricketts for his maps specially drawn for this book; Mrs. Kynaston Thompson for the historic photographs of Weymouth Railway Station, the Royal Baths, the Town Bridge and Ferrybridge; H.M.S. Osprey Photographic Section, Portland, for the modern aerial photographs; and David Attwooll, Graham Herbert and W. G. (Bill) Macey for providing pictures of present day Weymouth.

We are grateful to The Bodley Head Ltd., for an extract from *Dorset Essays* by Llewelyn Powys, and David and Charles (Publishers) Ltd., for extracts from the *Memoirs and Diary of Sir Daniel Gooch,* edited by Roger Burdett Wilson. We owe a special debt to David Burnett, our publisher, for his guidance in reducing our manuscript to a reasonable length, and to all those who have contributed in their own way to this book we say a very sincere thank you.

Finally we must express our gratitude to the members of our families, whose lives have been more than a little affected during the final months when this record took shape.

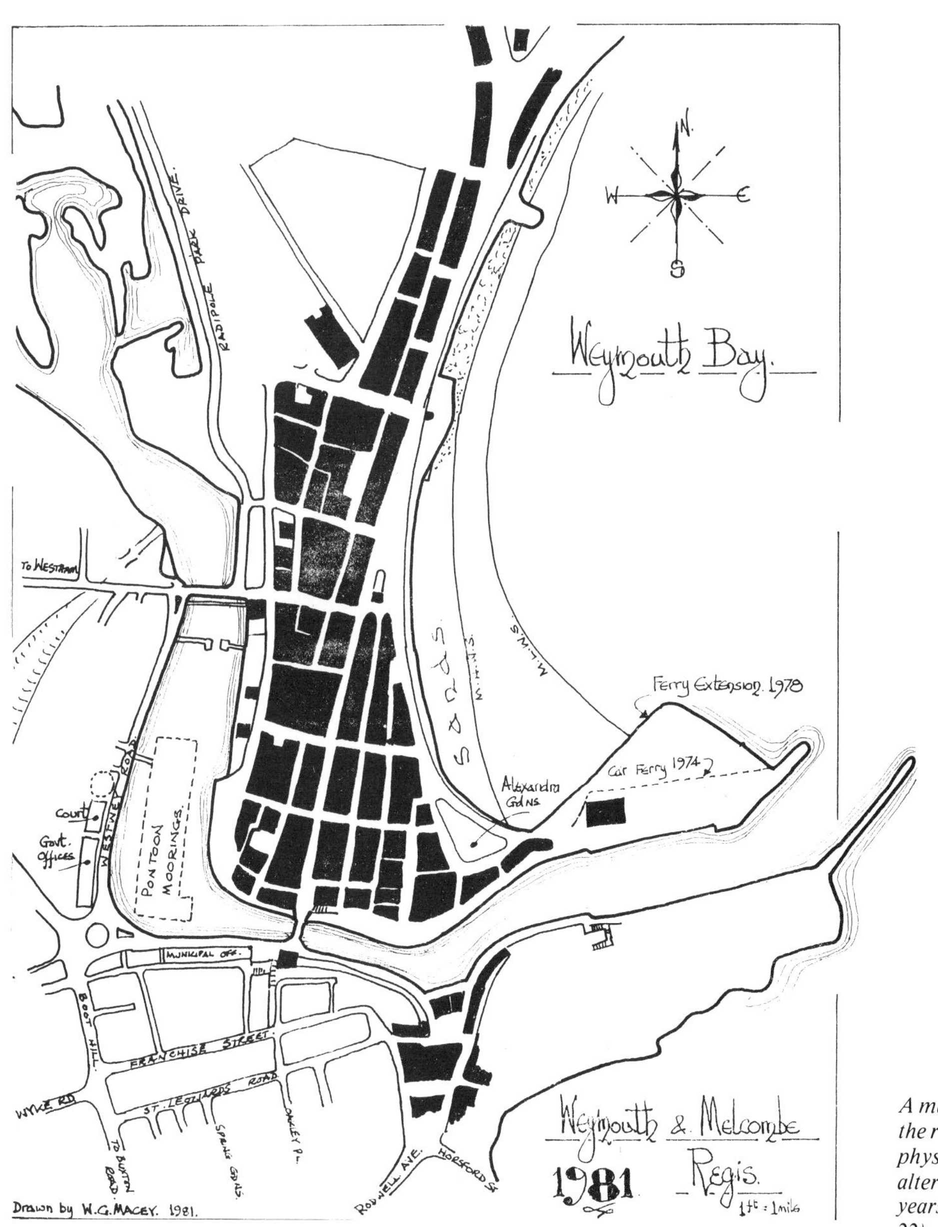

A map of modern Weymouth. As the result of land reclamation, the physical shape of the town has altered over the past five hundred years. (Compare to the map on page 22).

ONE

Beginnings

Chesil Beach and The Fleet, with Portland in the background. The natural barrier of Chesil Beach has protected Weymouth and its hinterland since prehistoric times. (Crown Copyright)

In AD 43 the Second Roman Legion under Vespasian stormed the great fortified hill fort at Maiden Castle near Dorchester, and although Weymouth's history did not begin with this attack, it does mark the first local event that can be accurately dated.

Prior to the arrival of the Romans, evidence of settlement in the area is sparse and uncertain. Weymouth's site must have encouraged occupation, for its recorded history begins with the small communities that eked out a living along the banks of the River Wey. The river is short, rising at Upwey and flowing for three miles before entering Radipole Lake, then narrowing prior to entering the sea. Stone tools have been recovered from the Lake, whilst along the shores of the Fleet, the slender tidal lagoon that divides the Chesil Beach from the mainland, evidence has been found of a simple stone industry in scrapers, awls and knives, mostly in Portland chert.

Finds such as these date from the Stone Age, and were probably used when fishing or wildfowling, and those early huntsmen would have looked out on a landscape which has changed little. Vast earth movements millions of years ago had created the limestone mass of the Island of Portland, and this then acted as an anchor for the eastern end of the Chesil Beach. Eventually, long before man settled in the area, the Beach took up the position which it occupies today.

The shaping of the local landscape is still continuing, for wind, tide and man have all left their mark on it. The coastal marshes of Radipole Lake and Lodmoor owe their origins to a period when the shoreline of Weymouth Bay was lower than it is now and the sea could wash over them. Since then, a sand and shingle spit has formed, barring the ancient drowned valley of Radipole Lake and continuing across the edge of Lodmoor to the foot of Furzy Cliff and Bowleaze Cove. Against this bank a true storm beach has developed, facing the open sea between White Nothe and the Nothe Headland on the southern side of the entrance to Weymouth Harbour. Before the construction of the Portland Breakwaters in the 19th century, the natural action of the sea drove the pebbles north-east and simultaneously accumulated the sand at Melcombe Regis. The Breakwaters, and to some extent the reclamation of land at the southern end of Weymouth Bay have caused a slight deflection of the wave fronts. Consequently during the last hundred years the shingle has tended to extend southwards, driving the sands before it, reducing the length but not the quantity of Weymouth Sands.

Weymouth Esplanade and sands about 1890. Today the small breakwater in the foreground of the picture is covered by sand, a visible reminder of the way in which Melcombe Spit has continued to build up over the past century.

The steep cliffs on the south side of the Harbour are the result of river erosion, a process which would have continued if man had not built quays and walls along this final stretch of river, thus stabilizing the cliff-face. In the same way, although river deposits gradually led to the silting up of Lodmoor and Radipole Lake, the process was accelerated in Radipole Lake following the construction of Westham Bridge Dam in 1921. The sea's action has also caused erosion at the northern end of Weymouth Bay, where between 1860 and 1890 the Preston Beach Road was moved back some sixty feet, and despite the construction of extensive sea defences, the landward drive of this shingle beach remains a constant source of concern.

Such problems did not trouble Weymouth's first settlers. Stone Age man preferred to live on the high land, where he could grow cereals and graze his livestock, and traces have been found of a Neolithic occupation site just south of the road running along the summit of Ridgeway Hill.

Stone gave way to bronze some 4000 years ago, encouraging new settlers and cross-Channel trade with the continent. Bronze swords have twice been dredged from Weymouth Backwater, suggesting that it was in use long before the arrival of the Romans. A Bronze Age burial barrow once stood alongside the main Dorchester road at Redlands, and when excavated was found to contain the remains of a cremation, some skeletons and fragments of a bronze dagger.

With the beginning of the Iron Age in about 450 BC the evidence of occupation in the area dramatically increases. The first Iron Age invaders came ashore near Lulworth Cove, building the vast earthwork crowning Bindon Hill to protect their beach-head. Over the next five hundred years the various hill-forts which so dominate the Dorset landscape were either built or enlarged, one being at Chalbury on the outskirts of modern Weymouth. Others are at Abbotsbury, at the Verne on Portland, and, by far the largest and most important, at Maiden Castle, just west of the modern road linking Weymouth to Dorchester. Excavations at Chalbury have revealed hut sites and sufficient fragments of pottery to indicate their continued use after the coming of the Romans, but evidence of pottery outside the forts is scarce. Traces of a pottery and salt-workings have been found on the shores of the Fleet at Wyke Regis, whilst an almost perfect bowl was dug up near Wyke

The River Wey at Radipole, as it enters Radipole Lake. Craft of the prehistoric and Roman periods could have sailed up as far as here to make a sheltered landing.

In the early 19th century the remains of a Roman villa were uncovered at Preston in the valley of the River Jordan, but the fine mosaic pavement shown here was not protected and can no longer be seen.

Church. Perhaps most interesting is the Iron Age cemetery at Jordan Hill, Preston, and a large collection of the finds from it can be seen at the Dorset County Museum.

By the date of the Roman invasion the Durotriges were the dominant tribe, and Maiden Castle was their tribal capital. Despite its massive earthworks, Maiden Castle was soon taken, initiating some four hundred years of Roman rule. Sadly, the legacy left behind by those years is tantalisingly slight. Much has been destroyed, and detailed knowledge of the Roman occupation in the Weymouth area is confined to scattered remains excavated during the past one-hundred-and-fifty years.

The Roman town of Dorchester dates from soon after the Conquest. It was sited at the crossing of the River Frome on the new Roman road heading west from Badbury Rings. With the coast so close, landing facilities for Roman galleys must have soon been established. There is clear evidence of a Roman road running south from Dorchester towards Weymouth, crossing Ridgeway Hill above Upwey, and descending the slope by what is still known as the 'Old Roman Road'. At the eastern end of Upwey it disappears, and from then on its exact route is uncertain. It may well have followed the general route of the modern road from Upwey to Weymouth, but there is no firm evidence to confirm this.

The Romans would have found a very different Weymouth from that of today, for the inland area had probably yet to be cleared of forest and scrub. Radipole Lake would have been an open stretch of water, protected on the seaward side by sand and shingle and the high ground north of modern Greenhill. As the river swung eastwards past the end of the Melcombe sandbank it would have been sheltered to the south by what is now Chapelhay. A futher inlet in the vicinity of Hope Square led to a valley rising along the line of modern Rodwell Avenue, and beyond it lay the Nothe Headland, projecting seawards well beyond the end of the sandbank on the other side of the river mouth. Only to the west was the landscape similar, with higher ground in the Southill, Field Barn and Goldcroft areas, and marshes running inland in the areas of Chafey's Lake and Weymouth Marsh.

Sufficient remains have been found to suggest that the Romans used

An artist's impression of how the Roman Temple above Bowleaze Cove might have looked.

Radipole Lake as a harbour, sailing their galleys up-river and beaching them at a spot on the northern shore of the lake. Roman burials have been uncovered near the highest part of Spa Road, Radipole, but it is difficult to pin-point an exact landing place. The fact that they did use the River Wey is confirmed by the dredging up of a fine wine amphora from Radipole Lake and a smaller one from Weymouth Bay.

It is known that a Roman villa once stood south of the Harbour in what is today Newberry Road, and a section of the mosaic pavement from it can be seen in Weymouth Museum. The villa's site is ideal, in a sheltered valley, close to the sea, and with easy access to the river. Curiously, a Saxon coin was uncovered on the pavement, indicating a possible use into a much later period in Weymouth's history.

To reach the villa it would have been necessary to travel down to the west of Radipole Lake, for it seems unlikely that the Roman base south of the river mouth was large enough to justify a road along the exposed Melcombe sand spit and a ferry across the harbour. This raises the possibility that a Roman road once skirted the west side of Radipole Lake, linking with the site on the south side of the river and perhaps even with Wyke and Portland.

At Preston, the foundations of a small Roman temple have been found above Bowleaze Cove. Despite being regarded as a temple, there is a faint possibility that it was an early lighthouse for guiding ships into the Cove. In 1969 the nearby foundations of a second building were uncovered on the edge of the cliff, and the two buildings may have been associated in some way. It was certainly not a military installation as there were no defences, and it was too large for purely domestic use.

All these scattered remains confirm a general occupation of the Weymouth area throughout the Roman period, with villas at Rodwell and Preston, cemeteries at Wyke, Southill and Radipole, and a major find of over 4000 Roman coins from near the summit of Jordan Hill. The greatest mystery remains the route of the road from Dorchester, for if it could be traced we would have a much clearer idea of how Weymouth's first residents developed the area.

TWO

Growth and Rivalry

If uncertainty surrounds Weymouth's contribution to Roman Britain, the same is true of the Saxons. We do know however that the Saxon King Athelstan, grandson of King Alfred and founder of Middleton (Milton) Abbey in 934 conveyed to it 'All the water within the shore of Waimouie (Weymouth) and half of the stream of Waimouie out at sea'. This grant was made as a penance for the death of his brother, Prince Edwin, and as it grants only 'half' the stream at Weymouth, it does indicate that there was already some form of community on the Melcombe side of the river.

It is also known that three Danish ships raided Portland in the year 982, during the reign of Ethelred II, and it was Ethelred who in 988 granted to his minister Atsere a certain part of land in the place called by the inhabitants 'Wyck' (Wyke Regis). This charter still exists and the boundaries of 'Wyck' are described as follows:

> From the West Sea to Saggeloth—
> from Saggeloth to Muleditch, (millditch?)
> from Muleditch to Blackstone,
> from Blackstone to Goldcroft,
> from Goldcroft to Sorediche,
> from Sorediche to Lodmore,
> and from Lodmore to the East Sea.

The place-name Lodemor appears in a charter dated 1297, and this document was quoted in 1582 in an effort to settle disputes between Weymouth and Melcombe Regis. The place name Gold Croft Farm appears about the middle of the 19th century, but it is not necessarily the Goldcroft of 988.

It was during the closing years of the Saxon period that Edward the Confessor accused his mother Emma of adultery with the Bishop of Winchester. To prove her chastity, the queen walked barefoot and blindfolded over nine red-hot ploughshares in Winchester Cathedral—a drastic test, but Edward paid his penance in 1042 by giving nine manors to the Church at Winchester. These included the Manors of Portelond (Portland), Wikes (Wyke Regis), Hellwell (Elwell near Upwey) and Waimuth (Weymouth).

Much the most interesting information about the Saxon period immediately prior to the Norman Conquest comes from the Domesday Survey of 1086. In Weymouth's case, this is sadly not so. There are no less than eight manors or holdings named either 'Wai' or 'Waia' listed in the Dorset Domesday, far too many for them all to be sited along the banks of the River Wey. As a result, there is no general agreement on which is the forerunner of Weymouth, although two can be identified as 'Broadwey' and 'Upwey'. Another is thought to be local because it lists saltpans—mentioned in the grant by Athelstan in 934 and in a later grant of 1665. The saltpans appear to be in the vicinity of either Radipole Lake or the Weymouth Marsh.

There are two local holdings on which there is complete agreement.

Radipole is listed as 'Retpole' or 'Retpola' and full details are given, these being taken to include the area which we know today as Melcombe Regis. The second one is the very small community of 'Brige', the site of which was in the vicinity of Wyke Regis. Its main claim to fame is that it is one of only two communities listed in the Dorset Domesday which includes fishermen in its return. Bridge Farm of today, (SY 653777) is a logical site for Brige, close to the Fleet and the Chesil Beach.

The entries in Domesday offer a lively portrait of feudal society, and the hierarchy it supported. The following is the entry for Radipole:

The abbot (of St Peter of Cerne) has 1 manor which is called Retpola, which paid geld T.R.E. (in the time of King Edward) for 3 hides (about 180 acres). Three ploughs can plough these. Thence the abbot has 1½ hide and 1 plough in demesne and the villeins 1½ hide and 2 ploughs. There he had 1 villein and 5 bordars and 1 serf and 1 pack-horse and 20 pigs and 100 sheep and 10 acres of meadow and 5 furlongs of pasture and it renders 40s. a year.

From Domesday and from records dating from the reign of Henry I, it is obvious that William the Conqueror refused to recognise the grant made by Edward the Confessor in 1042 and declared the manors of Wyke, Weymouth, Portland and Elwell to be royal possessions. On the accession of Henry I in 1100, the Church of St Swithun at Winchester sued the King for the return of these manors, Henry agreeing to the request, and in about 1110 we find the following grant:

Henry gives to the Prior and Convent of St Swithun of Winchester, the ports of Waimuth and Melecumb, with all its appurtenances, together with the manors of Wike and Portelond, which King Edward gave them, and that they might enjoy all the liberties, wrecks, and all free customs, by sea and by land, as they had ever enjoyed them.

Some sixty years later, Henry II renewed this grant, using almost the same words, but with some interesting changes:

King Henry renews to the Prior and Convent of St Swithun of Winton, the Port of Waimue (Weymouth) and the lands of Melecumbe (Melcombe), which belongs to the manor of Wyk (Wyke Regis), that they might have and hold all their liberties, wrecks, and all free customs, by sea and by land, freely, quietly, justly and honorably, the same as they were wont to do in St Edward's time.

The notable change is that only Weymouth is referred to as a 'port' but that both Weymouth and Melcombe belong to the Manor of Wyke. There can be little doubt that the villages of Radipole and Wyke are of very much older foundation than the settlements of Weymouth and Melcombe, and that the latter were almost certainly founded by settlers moving to the river mouth from the villages in the area. Although there was no recognisable mention of Melcombe in Domesday, it is interesting to find that only a little over twenty years later it was being associated with Weymouth as a 'port', only to lose this appellation sixty years later when the charter of Henry II mentions merely 'the lands of Melcombe'. In neither of these grants is Melcombe linked in any way with the Manor of Radipole, and yet its ties with Radipole existed, as will be seen later.

A distant view of Melcombe Regis from the Wyke Road, based on a drawing by Samuel Grimm made in 1790. In the bottom corner is the fragment of a fair cross which has survived since the 13th century. It stands today in front of a block of flats in Faircross Avenue.

As Lord of the Manor of Wyke, the Prior of St Swithun's at Winchester was responsible for its administration. Authority to hold fairs and markets was first given in 1221. By chance a possible link with this first fair was discovered in about 1880 when the base and part of the upright of an ancient fair cross were found in a ditch on the Wyke Road about half-way between Wyke and Weymouth. The discovery of this fragment of the cross must not be taken as definite proof that the annual fair was held near here, but it does seem a logical site, half-way between the village of Wyke and the growing township on the southern bank of the harbour.

By the 13th century there is clear evidence of the growing importance of Weymouth as a port, and of Melcombe's steady growth on the opposite side of the river. Other local place-names begin to appear in various records. Prestone, or Priest's Town is recorded in 1226 as having provided the prebend or provender of one of the canons of Salisbury Cathedral. The courtesy still survives and the present Prebendary of Preston has a stall in the Cathedral choir. There are definite traces of Norman work in the church of St. Andrew at Preston. Brodeway (Broadwey) appears in 1243, but opinions differ as to whether the 'broad' applies to the flooding of the river at this point or to the fact that it stands on a main highway. 'Kingeswik' is used in the year 1242, although the modern form of Wyke Regis does not appear until 1407. Nottington, which was not listed in Domesday, appears as 'Notinton' in 1212 and as Notington in 1234.

Account rolls for the manor of Wyke covering the years 1242-1243 have survived, and they give a clear indication of the wages paid to the men who farmed its narrow strip fields overlooking the Chesil. The senior member of the workforce was the hayward, who received 6s.8d. (33p) for a year's work, next came the carter and the shepherd, who each received 5s.0d. (25p). Two ploughmen were paid 4s. (20p), the dairywoman 3s. (15p) and the lowest paid of all was the cowherd, who did his year's toil for 2s.8d. (13p).

The total rents collected amounted to £8.10s.9d. (£8.54). Anselm, a priest, paid an annual rent of 4d. (1½p) for a piece of land reclaimed from the sea at the port of Weymouth, this being the earliest known reference to a process of reclamation which has continued locally down to the present day. Other entries listed include the 3s.0½d. (15p) revenue from port tolls, and 2s.6d. (12½p) from the sale of the skins of two oxen.

Amongst the fines levied are included no less than twenty-four cases of 'breaking the assize of ale', the regulations linking the cost of ale to the current price of barley. The interests of the consumer were protected to ensure he got his correct measure. In addition the brewing and sale of ale could only be carried on with permission, and 'breaking the assize of ale' meant failure to comply with any or all of these regulations. One is left with the feeling that the main offence was a little bit of private brewing on the side!

Robert Budda was fined 6d. (2½p) for ploughing on a road, and he clearly had territorial ambitions for on another date he was fined the same amount for infringement of pasture. There appear to have been ways of evading the regulations, for three entries record 6d. (2½p) payment for the 'relaxation of a rule'. Other fines include those for brawling and failure to pay debts.

All Saints Church, Wyke Regis, as painted by J. W. Upham in 1821. The Manor Farm on the corner of Lanehouse Rocks Road still stands today, as does the Old Vicarage adjoining the church. The large building just beyond the Vicarage was 'Wyke House' which ended its days as a hotel and was demolished in 1974.

The account rolls also give some idea as to the wealth of the manor. The livestock remaining at the end of the year amounted to 1 horse, 29 oxen, 1 bull, 11 cows, 4 yearlings, 7 calves, 5 rams and 498 other sheep, 7 pigs and 17 fowls. 351 animals had died during the year, giving a hint of the tragedy that could strike the medieval farmer if the harvest failed or the winter was severe.

Amongst the expenses is a routine entry which reads: '3s.10d. (19p) for the expenses of a servant who went several times to Winchester'. The legitimacy of those expenses is open to question, for alongside in another hand is written 'In future give details of the expenses and of the nature of the business'.

Other entries record the day-to-day life on the manor: the meagre 8s.0d. (40p) from the sale of wine from a wreck because it had been tainted by salt; the £1.18s. (£1.90) spent on entertaining the Prior on a visit, and, more happily, the gift of £3 he left in his wake.

In 1249, the Abbot of Cerne, as Lord of the Manor of Radipole, is recorded as holding one carucate of land with its appurtenances in the vill of Melcomb. As the Norman carucate was the same as the Saxon hide, i.e. about 60 acres or as much arable land as could be tilled by one plough in one year, this could not have been on the Melcombe sandspit and must have been on the 'mainland', i.e. between modern Greenhill and Radipole. Five years later the Abbot gave Melcombe as a marriage gift to the bride of Prince Edward (later Edward I), Eleanor of Castile. The Abbot's generosity meant that the townspeople had to pay an annual sum of eight marks to the treasury. Half of the port was granted to Melcombe, and it is from this time that the rivalry between the ports of Weymouth and Melcombe begins, probably having its roots in the arguments between the Prior of St Swithuns and the Abbot of Cerne over the ownership of Melcombe.

The earliest charter now in the possession of the Borough of Weymouth and Portland is one dated 1252, granted by William of Taunton, Prior of St. Swithuns. It relates to Weymouth only, granting immunities similar to those of Southampton and Portsmouth, and describing the boundaries of the town. Six years later, in 1258, Richard de Clare, Earl of Gloucester and Hertford, was appointed to keep Weymouth and Wyke.

The boundaries of Weymouth as set out in 1252 cannot be identified today, as in several cases they refer to houses owned by individuals, of which no modern record exists. One point on the boundary which is mentioned is 'The Cross', possibly the fair cross, whilst another reference is to the spring which is called 'Tunne'.

The oldest surviving seal of the Borough of Melcombe, dating from about 1285. The arms on the shields are those of Queen Eleanor (Castile and Leon) and at each end of the ship is a sprig of planta genista *– the badge of the Plantaganets.*

In 1280, Edward I granted a Charter of Incorporation to Melcombe, making it a Borough. The Charter has long since disappeared but it granted to the new Burgesses of Melcombe several liberties claimed by the citizens of London. At this time Melcombe must only have been a very small township, perched on the sandbank opposite the older community of Weymouth. The suffix 'Regis' indicating its royal connection first appears in 1336, and about this period funds were made available for building fortifications at Melcombe, but nothing appears to have been done.

Four years after it was created a Borough, Melcombe was in dispute with Weymouth over harbour rights. The Queen, as Lady of the Manor, took legal action against Hugh de Cole and others, regarding the free use of the Harbour. This was the first record of the dispute which was to rage until the union of the two boroughs 300 years later. It included the claim that Melcombe owned half the water of the River Wey and with it the right to load and unload ships, and that prior to 1282, these rights had not been queried. The men of Melcombe were insistent that their Weymouth neighbours were interfering with this trade. They also argued that Melcombe ships had been prevented from bringing in Portland stone to build and repair their homes. So bitter was the quarrel that one Melcombe ship had been sunk and a man drowned.

It is almost certain that the grid-pattern layout of Melcombe dates from this period. Overall planning is obvious in that the main streets are all straight and not influenced by the shape of the shoreline. The Earl of Gloucester, Lord of the Manor of Weymouth, had married Edward I's daughter, and for a period following the death of the earl, his widow was 'Lady of the Manor of Weymouth'. This family connection did nothing to ease the growing animosity between the rival towns.

It was during the 13th century that the ports of Dorset – Weymouth, Melcombe, Poole and Lyme – were first called on to provide ships for the French and Scottish wars. This clearly indicates their growing importance as trading ports. Other rivalries followed. In 1293 Edward I called on Weymouth's sailors to keep the peace at sea with the French port of Bayonne, 'for the discords are numerous'.

With Melcombe now an incorporated borough, it was obvious that its rival Weymouth would seek to obtain the same status, but it was to be thirty-eight years before the town received its charter, finally granted during the reign of Edward II in 1318. The unusual feature of its elevation to a borough was that it was never granted the right to elect a mayor, the principal citizens being two bailiffs. Even after the amalgamation with Melcombe Regis in 1571, the elected officers of the united borough included two bailiffs in addition to a mayor, a combination which endured until the 19th century.

One of the strange features of the history of Weymouth and Melcombe Regis is that neither port had a church of its own until the 17th century (Melcombe Regis) and the 19th century (Weymouth). Melcombe had a chapel, but it must have been small, for in 1426 it was claimed that the town lacked a 'place dedicated to God'. Until the building of St Mary's in 1606, Radipole acted as its mother church, as did Wyke Regis for Weymouth.

St Ann's Church at Radipole, the mother church of Melcombe Regis, drawn by J. W. Upham. Dating from the end of the 13th century, it was originally dedicated to St Mary, but in 1927, after more than 300 years as a Chapel of Ease to St Mary's, Melcombe Regis, it once again became a parish church, and was re-dedicated to St Ann.

During the reign of Edward II Melcombe Regis (1315) and Weymouth (1319) were each granted the right to send two members to Parliament, this privilege continuing (apart from a short break during the Commonwealth) until the Reform Act of 1832. At the time it was granted it was a good indication of the relative importance of the two ports, but for many years before the Reform Act it had become an anachronism, since many towns far larger than Weymouth had no parliamentary representation at all. During the 18th century, when political chicanery was at its worst, the representation of Weymouth and Melcombe Regis was something of a scandal.

Detailed lists exist of all the men who have represented the towns in Parliament, but almost nothing is known about the majority of them, or what they achieved. An odd record dated 1463 states that James Sackville was appointed a Weymouth burgess for the Parliament, his payment to be a 'Cade of Mackerell' (a barrel containing 500 fish). It is not known if this was the usual form of reward!

The growing importance of Weymouth and Melcombe was not only recognised by granting them parliamentary representation, but also by the enhancement of their status as ports when in 1310 Weymouth was created a staple port (i.e. granted a Royal Licence to trade) for French, Gascon and Anjou wine, whilst at the same time Melcombe was created a staple port for wool. Only ten ports in England enjoyed such privileges. As there was far more wool exported than imported, it seems that Melcombe was exporting and Weymouth importing, a logical sharing of trade, but the arguments continued. The value of the cargoes passing through the twin ports was also recognised by French privateers and pirates who made a number of raids on the towns, often choosing a Sunday or Feast Day when they knew that a good proportion of the local residents would be away attending church at Wyke Regis and Radipole.

The Weymouth seamen were not always peaceful traders themselves. In 1322 William de Ekkeworth of Tavistock, complained that his ship, loaded with cloth, linen, iron, wax etc., on passage to 'Sutton' (Plymouth) was attacked by men of Weymouth and Portland, who stole his cargo and scuttled his ship. Two years later Weymouth and Melcombe between them provided 10 ships for war service, as against 4 from Poole and 2 from Lyme.

Edward III landed in Weymouth in 1343, having been blown off course during a gale, and three years later, in 1346, following his victory at Crecy, the two ports supplied him with 20 ships and 264 men for the siege of Calais. This figure compares with 4 ships and 95 men from Poole, 4 ships and 62 men from Lyme, 22 ships and 608 men from Bristol, and 25 ships and 662 men from London. Famine forced Calais to surrender in 1347, and a truce was made with France, but the following year England itself was to suffer a far more deadly invasion.

In a little over six months an outbreak of the dreaded bubonic plague had spread from the Middle East, right across Europe. Known to history as the Black Death, this terrible epidemic arrived in England during July 1348. A monk, William of Malmesbury, later described its arrival: In the year of our Lord 1348, about the feast of the Translation of St Thomas (July 7th), the cruel pestilence, terrible to all future ages, came from parts over the sea to the south coast of England, into a port called Melcombe, in Dorsetshire.

During the next two years the plague spread throughout the whole of the British Isles, and estimates of the death toll range between 30% and 50% of the population. The effects on everyday life were terrible. Entire villages and hamlets disappeared because there were too few survivors to work the land or continue trade. The death rate among the clergy was the highest, and within two months of the plague's arrival the incumbent at West Chickerell was dead. His successor survived until the following March. Bincombe changed its incumbent in November and again in March, whilst both Osmington and Radipole record the death of two successive priests.

Gradually trade recovered from the effects of the Black Death. Weymouth ships were now trading with France, Spain, Portugal and the Mediterranean, but the resumption of war brought fresh raids. In 1377 the Bishop of Salisbury granted permission to the people of Weymouth to build a chapel, dedicated to St Nicholas, because until then they had been obliged to use Wyke Regis Church and risk the destruction of the town whilst at mass – as had happened in the previous spring. The chapel was built on the heights above Weymouth, giving the popular name of 'Chapelhay' to this part of the town.

The threat of pillage was constant, leading to merchants leaving and a reduction in Melcombe Regis's taxes. A contemporary record chronicles one such disaster that took place whilst the townsfolk were at mass: '. . . and the Normans, Genoese, Bretons, Picardes and Spaniards entered into the town and robbed and pillaged the town, and slew divers, and defouled maidens, and enforced wives, and charged their vessels with that pillage, and so entered again into their ships, and when the tide came, they disanchored and sailed to Normandy, and came to Dieppe, and there departed and divided their booty and pillages.'

Records of individual residents of Melcombe Regis date from the end of the 14th century, and as so often happens, it was the wrongdoers who made the news. Minutes have survived of Law Courts held here between 1396 and 1400, the crimes coming before the court being quite familiar to us today, although the punishments were severe. Assaults account for a number of cases, weapons ranging from a sword to a rake. Others include the dumping of refuse in the streets and illicit brewing. One offender was fined for giving short measure when selling beer; another for stealing a barrel of pitch which had been left standing in the street.

Another indication of conditions at Melcombe at the end of the 14th century comes in a petition pleading a reduction in taxes, submitted to Henry IV in 1399. This stated the town possessed 79 tenements belonging to wealthy merchants, who had 18 large ships and 6 barges fit for merchandise, and 40 fishing boats. According to the petition, which was successful, storms and the French had led to the destruction of the boats and the death of many of the merchants. In spite of such setbacks and the decline in trade, it does seem that there were some ships operating from the port. In 1413 Richard Hill of Weymouth was granted a licence to carry 40 pilgrims in his ship the *St Leonard*.

Further such licences were granted in 1428 to a number of ports, where ships were authorised to carry pilgrims to the shrine of St James the Apostle in the city of Santiago de Compostella in north-west Spain. Pilgrims were required to swear 'not to take anything prejudicial to England, nor to reveal any of its secrets, nor carry out with them any more gold or silver than would be sufficient for their reasonable expense'. Weymouth, including Melcombe Regis, was one of the ports granted a licence, and embarked 122 pilgrims that year, this comparing very favourably with 280 from London and 200 from Bristol.

Pilgrims passing through the port undoubtedly benefited from the existence

The old doorway in Governor's Lane which is believed to be the last fragment of the Melcombe Friary to remain standing. It disappeared when the area was cleared to form a car park during the 1960s.

of a Dominican Friary. Melcombe Regis Friary, the last Dominican House to be established in England, was founded in 1418. It was never a wealthy establishment but it did provide a place of worship for a community which still lacked a church of its own. It occupied a site approximating to the area enclosed by modern Maiden Street, St Alban Street, the Esplanade and the harbourside, and it is believed that the last fragment of the old Friary to remain above ground was a doorway which stood in Governor's Lane until the 1960s when a car park replaced the old dilapidated houses which had been built on the site of the Friary.

The friars played an important role in the life of the town, helping with defence works and building a jetty for the port. In 1446 they erected a tower for the protection of their own house as well as the town and port, for which they received financial assistance from Henry VI, plus a considerable grant of land. Shortly afterwards Parliament declared void all the grants made by King Henry, but his grant to the Melcombe Friary was given special exemption, 'in consideration of the great charge and cost they have had and must have, in making and repairing the jetty in defending the Town of Melcombe against the flowing of the sea.' It is obvious from contemporary descriptions that the sea washed the Friary lands on the east side.

By the middle of the 15th century the fortunes of the ports of Weymouth and Melcombe Regis had begun to improve, in spite of the fact that in 1433 Poole managed to get the Customs House transferred from Melcombe Regis, thus becoming the premier port in Dorset and the staple port for wool and wine. By 1450 the twin ports were exporting some wool, corn, draperies, pilchards and salt to France, Spain, Holland and Ireland, whilst importing wine and fruit from Spain and France – although recovery was very slow.

Wyke Regis Church, the mother church of Weymouth, has Saxon origins. Some two or three churches have stood on the site, but the Wyke Church which stands today dates from 1455, when it was dedicated to 'All Saints' and equipped with three altars and four bells. The small Chapel of St Nicholas on the high land above Weymouth, built in 1377, was attached to it, and it was here that the first guild was formed in 1442. Little is known of this guild, other than it held lands at Weymouth, Knighton, Wooton Glanville, Portland and Wyke Regis, and on at least one occasion is referred to as the Guild of St George. The licence authorizing the guild included the following order: 'None shall fail at the setting forth of the procession on Corpus Christi Day, on pain of forfeiting one pound of wax, and each brother shall pay six pennies to the procession, and pay yearly.'

Converted into a fort during the Civil War the building was then so badly damaged that it was never used again. From the mid-19th century the site was occupied by Holy Trinity Schools, which were in turn damaged during the 1939-45 war, and today a block of houses stands on the site of Weymouth's first chapel.

THREE

Union

One morning in January 1506, following a gale in the Channel, the local inhabitants awoke to find a number of foreign ships in the bay, with landing parties coming ashore. They sent to Dorchester for the Sheriff, Sir Thomas Trenchard, who arrived with troops, only to find that for once they were safe from attack, and that their visitors were Queen Joana of Castile and her husband, the Archduke Philip of Austria, the victims of seasickness whilst on passage from the Spanish Netherlands to their home in Spain.

As there was nowhere suitable in Weymouth or Melcombe Regis to entertain them, Sir Thomas Trenchard insisted that they accompany him to his home at Wolfeton House near Dorchester. Word was sent to the King, who in turn insisted that Philip and Joana join him at Windsor. One relic of their stay at Wolfeton is an old chest which they left behind and is now in Weymouth Museum.

The interpreter to the royal visitors during their stay at Dorchester was John Russell of Swyre, near Bridport, who had travelled in Spain and could speak Spanish well. He accompanied the party to Windsor, stayed on in the service of Henry VII, rose in power and wealth, and was finally created Earl of Bedford by Edward VI. From John Russell descends the present Duke of Bedford, owner of Woburn Abbey.

Philip and Joana, unwilling visitors to Weymouth in 1506.

There is little evidence of any major improvement in local prosperity and in 1512, the new king, Henry VIII, confirmed his father's reduction of Melcombe Regis's taxes. Whilst the arguments between Weymouth and Melcombe Regis continued, there is no evidence that either town prospered whilst the other declined. The general depression in trade must have applied equally to both, but only documents relating to Melcombe Regis have survived.

A description of Tudor Weymouth has come down to us in the writings of John Leland, who in 1538 recorded his impressions of the town. Approaching from Upwey he wrote:

> There is a townlet on the other side of the haven of Waymouth called Miltoun (Melcombe Regis), being privileged and having a Mayor. This town as it is evidently seen has been far bigger than it is now, the cause of this is laid on the Frenchmen, that in time of war razed this town for lack of defence. For so many houses as be in the town, they be well and strongly builded of stone. There is a Chapel of Ease in Milton.
>
> The parish church is a mile off, a manifest token that Milton is no very old town. There is a fair house of Friars in the east part of the town, and the Chief of the house of Rogers in Dorsetshire was founder and patron of it. Milton standeth as a peninsula, by reason of the haven, that a little above the town spreadeth abroad and maketh a bay, and by the bay of the main sea, that gulfith in on the other side.
>
> The Townlet of Waymouth lieth straight against Milton on the other side of the haven, and at this place the water of the haven is but of small breadth, and the trajectus (crossing) is by a boat and a rope, bent over the haven, so that in the ferry-boat they use no oars. Weymouth has certain liberties and privileges, but there is no Mayor in it. There is a quay and wharf for ships. By this town, on a hill, is a Chapel of Ease. The parish church is a mile off.

A map, drawn by Eric Ricketts, showing the town in the early 16th century, before any land was reclaimed from either the sea or the Backwater.

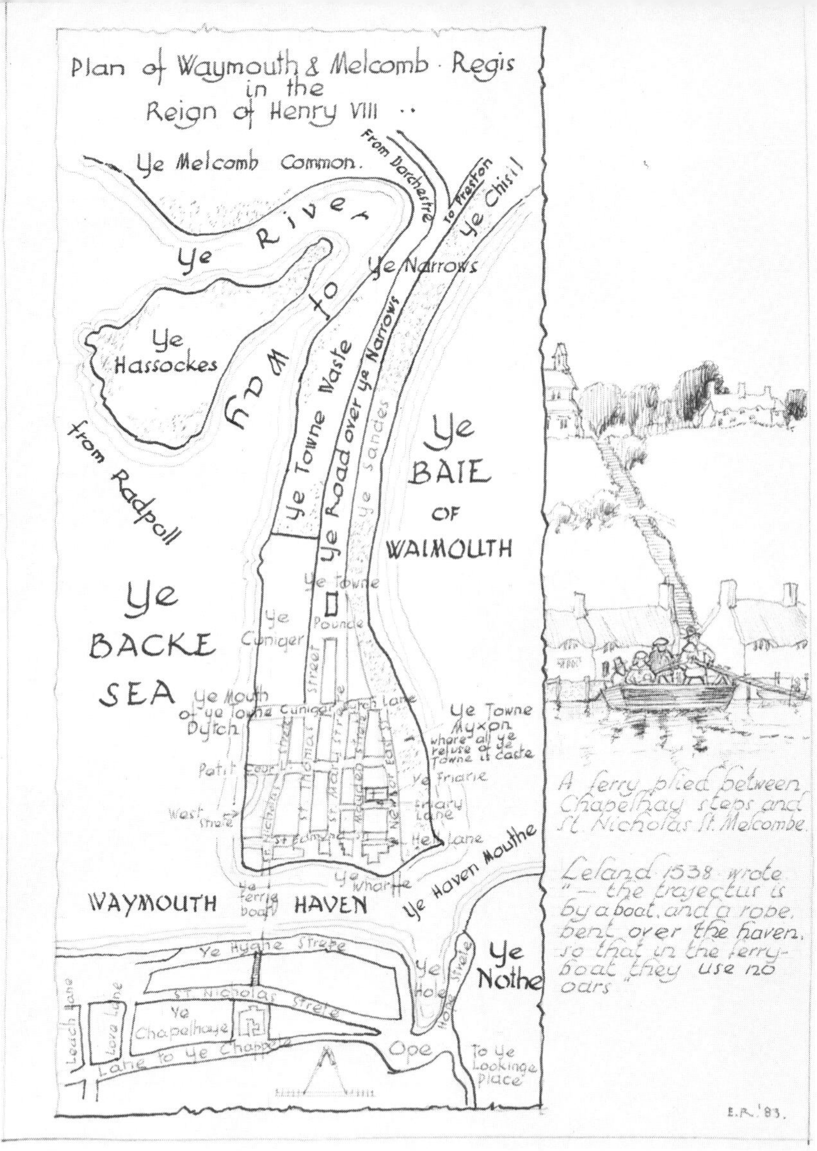

The sea ebbeth and floweth up about a two miles beyond Weymouth. There is a little bar of sand at the haven mouth. There runneth up by the right hand of the haven a great arm of the sea, and scant a mile above the haven mouth, on the shore of this arm, is a right goodly warlike castle made, having one open barbican. This arm runneth up farther a mile as in a bay to a point of land where a trajectus is into Portland by a long causeway of pebble and sand.

The use by Leland of the place-name 'Milto(u)n' for Melcombe Regis is unique, no other record ever having employed this variant. Otherwise his description can easily be followed almost 450 years after it was first written.

The 'Fair House of Friars' at Melcombe Regis did not long survive the visit of John Leland. The Church appears to have been on the south side (on the site later occupied by Stewards Court) whilst the cemetery was on the north. There must have been a strong link between the Friary and Radipole Church, as in 1533, Owen Watson, Rector of Radipole and Portland, willed that his body be buried in the Friary where he had built a tomb for himself. In 1538, following the Dissolution of the Monasteries, the reign of the Black Friars of Melcombe came to an end. The Friary was never wealthy, and all that could be taken from it of value was an 11½ oz chalice. A detailed inventory mentioned even a broken saucer and the fact that the timber available was barely sufficient to keep the fences in repair.

One traditional link with the Melcombe Friary is the Prior's Chair. Legend suggests that this was given to the Friary by a visiting cardinal, and certain symbols of his office are carved in the back of the chair – a cardinal's hat, the flails and keys of office. It was claimed that anyone who died whilst sitting in this chair was welcomed by St Peter at the Gates of Heaven with the assurance that all his sins were forgiven and a place in Heaven guaranteed. The monks are supposed to have made good use of this tradition, helping the dying to spend their last minutes in the holy chair. For many years it was lost, but after being found and restored it was used to 'chair' the successful candidate in Parliamentary Elections as he processed around the town. It is now preserved in Weymouth Museum.

With the closing of the monasteries came the redistribution of their assets. The Friary lands at Melcombe were granted to Sir John Rogers for £738.18s.5d. (£738.93), whilst in 1540, the Manor of Radipole, lately held by Cerne Abbey, was granted to Humphrey Watkins. His son, Richard Watkins is credited with building what is now known as 'The Old Manor House' at Radipole, his initials R.W. being carved above the entrance.

The manors of Wyke Regis and Weymouth, which had reverted to Royal ownership during the Wars of the Roses, were granted in turn to three of the Queens of Henry VIII; Katharine of Aragon, Anne of Cleves and Catherine Howard.

In 1539, the year following the closure of the Melcombe Friary, Henry VIII completed the construction of the 'right goodly and warlike castle' mentioned by Leland. War with France had become almost commonplace during the Middle Ages and Henry's break with the Church of Rome caused further deterioration in relations with Catholic Europe. The threat of war resulted in the King building a chain of fortifications along the south coast of England, and on the edge of the cliff, about one mile south of Weymouth Harbour, stand the ruins of Sandsfoot Castle, one of the two local castles built to protect Portland Roads.

A detail from a map of the Dorset coast made in 1539 when an invasion by the French seemed likely. Note the beacon on the Black Rock.

Long before the breakwaters were built in the 19th century, Portland Roads had been a haven for shipping, and such concentrations of valuable cargoes presented an ideal target for enemy warships or raiders. It would appear that the very existence of the two castles was protection enough, as there is no record of shots being fired in anger. Much of the stone used in the construction of Sandsfoot Castle is believed to have been brought across the bay from Bindon Abbey, near Wool, and examples of both Norman and Early English carving have been discovered built into some of the castle walls.

The castle cost £3887.4s.1d. (£3887.21), yet it had a comparatively short life, and the Governor appointed in 1685 at the time of the Monmouth Rebellion was almost certainly the last 'active' commander. It was of a different design from that of Portland, and had a large open gun-platform surrounding the southern part of the main building. All traces of this and of the main gun room have now vanished as coastal erosion has slowly undermined the castle. The last major fall was during the 1950s, and unless erosion is halted more of the old ruin is bound to go.

A glimpse of one of the hazards of life in Tudor England comes in 1562 when the Buckler family of Causeway Farm, Radipole, gave shelter to a stranger who had landed from France, and who was clearly ill. He died of the plague and by the following year, the Buckler's hospitality had caused the death of no less than eight members of the family.

The ruins of Sandsfoot Castle, being slowly undermined by the sea.

The Weymouth Harbour where this unfortunate traveller had landed was somewhat wider than the one of today. Successive improvements to the quay walls and the building of landing stages have tended to encroach on to the river, and nowhere is this more obvious than west of the town bridge. The old shoreline ran approximately along the front of the modern Municipal Offices and houses in old High Street actually backed on to the water. One particularly fine example of Tudor domestic architecture survived on this site until 1961 when, sadly, it was demolished as part of the general clearance of the North Quay area.

A Lay Subsidy Roll of 1524-5 is of interest in that it reveals the emergence of a few reasonably affluent men, whose property (and consequent taxation) was far in excess of their fellow residents. In Weymouth, Robert Samways owned some 22%, whilst in Melcombe Regis, John Raynolds paid 75% of the total taxes levied. The families of Samways and Raynolds were to play a major role in the final stages of the long dispute between Weymouth and Melcombe Regis, a dispute which was now approaching its climax. The early years of the reign of Elizabeth I were to see a remarkable recovery in the fortunes of Melcombe Regis, and there are indications of definite jealousy on the part of the Weymouth leaders.

The Tudor Town Hall of Weymouth, as drawn by J. W. Upham in 1825.

The local government of the old Borough of Weymouth was administered from its Town Hall at the end of old High Street. The building still stands today, although very much 'restored' in Victorian times: Melcombe Regis had its own Town Hall on the site of the present-day Guildhall. The major problem facing the civic leaders on both sides of the Harbour was the continued dispute over harbour rights. Weymouth had always disputed the rights of Melcombe to the Harbour, although there is ample evidence that both towns were active ports, using the comparatively narrow outlet at the mouth of the Wey. By 1567, Weymouth was said to be 'thrice as populous' as Melcombe, but no details of actual population are available.

The years following the accession of Queen Elizabeth were to see a concerted attempt made to end the long dispute between the two towns, and

This group of Tudor houses on the Weymouth side of the harbour is believed to have stood between the Town Bridge and modern Trinity Street. The original sketch on which this drawing is based was made in 1790.

one of the first steps was the issue of the following decree on 28th October 1564.

1. That the Port of Weymouth shall be common to the freemen of both sides to intermedle in merchandize.
2. The Freemen of Melcombe shall have half the Petty Customs on Weymouth side and the Freemen of Weymouth shall have full liberty to buy and sell on Melcombe side.
3. The Freemen of Weymouth shall have half the cartage and rents of a 'Watter Mill' and of the Cuniger in Melcombe Regis.
4. That the Bushellage and Head of Fee Fishes are to remain in the possession of the Bailiffs of Weymouth.

A letter from the Weymouth bailiffs dated 1568 asserted that they were ready to pay and receive all profits according to the agreement, but 'nevertheless we think all these things may be done between us, being so near neighbours, without any letteral messages', signing the letter 'your poor neighbours and loving friends'. The following year Weymouth sought help from the Earl of Pembroke (Steward of Weymouth, Wyke Regis and other Royal Manors), who in turn wrote to the Mayor of Melcombe Regis, recommending the people of the town to refer the dispute to a lawyer. If this was not done, he threatened 'some sharper order of way to be taken both to repress your obstinence . . . and to preserve . . . the . . . liberties . . . of Weymouth'.

And so it went on, accusation and counter-accusation followed. The citizens of Melcombe Regis accused their neighbours of being 'obstinate offenders' and of 'disobedient doings', one document haranguing Weymouth ending:

It is more than marvellous unto us what your cause of grief should be or wherefore you thus disorderly storm with us, for against right, ye possess all, against conscience ye take all, against reason ye keep all, and some think that against law ye abuse all. . . . Beseeching Almighty God to mollify your hearts and so to open your eyes that ye may see and reform your malicious injurious doings towards us.

The document is signed 'Your poor oppressed neighbours of Melcombe Regis'.

Commissioners were appointed to enquire into the disputes, and in 1570 they advised the union of the two boroughs. In June a treaty between

The Arms of the Borough of Weymouth and Melcombe Regis granted in 1592. The arms on the banner flying from the foremast are those of Edward I, who granted Melcombe Regis its first charter, whilst those on the second banner belong to Eleanor of Castile (Castile and Leon), who was Lady of the Manor. The chevrons on the shield are those of Gilbert-de-Clare, Lord of the Manor of Weymouth in the 13th century.

Weymouth and Melcombe Regis was issued, carrying nearly sixty signatures. Amongst other things they agreed that the weekly court was to be held in each town on alternate Mondays, and that each town appoint a Chamberlain to collect all taxes and fines.

On 1st June 1571, Elizabeth I granted what is now known as the Charter of Union. The Charter ordered the appointment of a Corporation headed by a Mayor, responsible for the joint administration of the two towns. It had a seal of office, could purchase land, pass bye-laws and fix fairs and markets.

The act of union was not an unqualified success. Although supported by Melcombe Regis, Weymouth remained strongly opposed to it. Feuding continued long after the official union, and the town minute books record many incidents when the Weymouth leaders showed their dissatisfaction with the situation. In 1579 men from Weymouth pulled down a quay which had been erected on the Melcombe side, claiming it was an encroachment since all the water belonged to Weymouth. Henry Michell of Melcombe, tax collector for the united borough, was seized and illegally imprisoned while carrying out his official duties on the Weymouth side. Even murder was threatened. John Brooke of Weymouth, under arrest for various misdemeanours, drew a knife and swore he would kill the mayor. The first mayors of the new Borough were all Melcombe men; clearly Weymouth wanted nothing to do with the joint administration. By 1584 some measure of law and order must have been restored, as Hugh Randall, leader of the obstinate Weymouthians was elected mayor of the combined borough, but in October 1586, fifteen years after the official 'union', the mayor and several others were summoned to appear before the Exchequer to give evidence against Weymouth men who were still refusing to accept the authority of the new borough. John Brooke was in trouble again, and together with Thomas Samways had resisted arrest. Another Weymouth man, William Ledoze, had seized a sail as payment of harbour dues he claimed, and had prevented the mayor from entering Weymouth Town Hall.

Viewed from a distance of four hundred years, it does seem remarkable that the Privy Council, having ordered the union, then tended to give way to the demands of the Weymouth men and to make special provision for them. Its decision of 1576 that the Royal Manor of Weymouth should retain its freedom from outside jurisdication, including matters of Admiralty, can only have confused matters. The arguments continued off and on for almost half a century until the Charter of James I in 1606 finally made the union a working success.

It is all too easy when studying surviving documents to get the impression that the men of Weymouth were the 'offenders' in the long dispute between the two towns. The fact is that the leading figures of the Tudor period were a tough rugged lot, shipowners and sailors, some of whom were deeply involved with the local pirates. There may have been arguments over harbour rights, but mutual self-interest often encouraged co-operation and merchants from both sides of the Harbour equipped and victualled ships for piracy.

Robert Gregory, Mayor of Melcombe Regis in 1570, was a typical example of a wealthy merchant who had close links with the local pirates. He is known to have bought pirate prizes and then sold them back to their rightful owners and to have equipped at least two ships for raiding, the *Elizabeth* and the *Daniel*. He worked very closely with Bartholomew Belpitt, another pirate-merchant of Weymouth and Melcombe Regis and yet at the same time held the offices of deputy Searcher and deputy to the Vice-Admiral of Dorset. In 1577 he was called on to sit as a member of a Commission to enquire into local piracy, but managed to avoid incriminating himself.

One of Gregory's rivals was Hugh Randall, a belligerent Weymouth bailiff, later to become the first Weymouth man to take office as mayor of the combined borough. He was accused of a number of offences at the Commission of 1577 and is known to have had regular dealings with a Welsh pirate named Callice who often brought his ship into Portland Roads. Even thieves and pirates fall out amongst themselves; in 1583 Thomas Purser, a notorious Dorset pirate, threatened the town with 'spoile and fire' because it had prevented him from boarding a French ship near Weymouth.

Tudor Weymouth, based on a drawing by Samuel Grimm made in 1790. On the right of the picture is part of Weymouth Town Hall.

A much greater threat to the inhabitants was the increasing fear of war with Spain. Ships trading into the port brought news of preparations in Spain, and there was considerable checking and strengthening of local defences. A Law Court minute of 1586 records that two men, Nicholas Abraham and J. Lambert, had been in prison for twelve months in Bilbao, where they heard of '700 sailles of Shippes, Gallis, Galiasses, Pynesses and Pattasses' and two-hundred-and-eighty-thousand men, said to be bound for England. In August, a Portuguese sailor reported hearing rumours that a Spanish fleet of 80 ships had gathered at Lisbon. By 1588 rumour had become reality. That April a report was prepared into the state of the coastal defences.

It was found that between Portland and Lyme, are many places commodious for landing, viz., the entry to Charmouth and Bridport, and the whole coast from two miles beyond Bridport to the Isle of Portland. The whole force of the County amounts to 3000 armed foot, and some light horse. The coast is 35 miles in extent, nor are the landing-places to be strengthened with new bulwarks, and even those made are of no service. The whole force at the approach of the enemy should assemble at Weymouth, except such as are appointed for the guard of particular places, as at Lyme, 60 foot, at Bridport 20 horse, 100 foot at Portland, 50 foot at Sandsfoot Castle, and for the Isle of Purbeck, 200 foot.

These forces being assembled are sufficient for a time to prevent any landing in the Bay of Portland, the aptest and most dangerous place, for though the Bay between the west side of Portland, and Lyme, contains many landing places, it is large and deep, so that a Fleet there in any south wind, is neither able to ride or to land. The enemy is more likely to land in the Bay of Portland, not subject to these discommodities.

If he attempts that Bay, or any place between Weymouth or Poole, the forces assembled at Weymouth must march thither . . .

Weymouth, though surrounded by hills about it, yet the forces of the county arriving before the enemy, it might be defended, and then it would be necessary to make a bridge of boats between the two towns on the east side of the Bay of Portland . . .

A separation of forces would be dangerous, for if the enemy should attempt to land at Portland Bay, which all think the fittest place, and not to be defended by a few, the forces would not be able to join nor recover Dorchester. Therefore the greatest body should be at Weymouth, but if the forces out of the other counties should arrive before the enemy land, 1000 men should be lodged at or near Abbotsbury, and 1000 at Lulworth, to oppose the enemy till more arrive. The horse should be drawn to Weymouth, the general repair for the foot, except such as are appointed to watch along the sea coast.

Two ships, the *John* (90 tons) and the *Reprisal* (60 tons) in company with a pinnace sailed from Weymouth to report to Sir Francis Drake at Plymouth, having been fitted out partly at the cost of Dorchester as well as Weymouth. In July 1588 the great Spanish Armada was sighted off the Lizard and the warning passed along the south coast. Beacons were lit at Blackdown (the site of Hardy's monument), Ridgeway Hill, Sutton Poyntz, and at 'The Beacon' on Wyke Road, Weymouth.

Six ships were fitted out at Weymouth to serve as coasters, two of which were equipped by the county at its own expense, *The Gallion* (100 tons, 50 men) and the *Catherine* (60 tons, 30 men). The four other ships were the *Heath Hen* (60 tons, 30 men, Captain Richard Millard), the *Golden Ryal* (120 tons, 50 men, owned by Thomas Middleton), the *Sutton* (70 tons, 40 men) and the

The old Tudor House which at one time faced up St Thomas Street and had its back to the harbour. The gentleman with the umbrella is crossing the road leading to the Town Bridge.

Bond (150 tons, belonging to the Lord Mayor of London, Sir George Bond). Another ship believed to have sailed from Weymouth was the *Expedition* with 50 mariners.

Sea battles were fought off Portland and Purbeck as the Armada sailed up the Channel to eventual defeat. One of the ships, a Portuguese carrack, the *San Salvador* was captured and brought into Weymouth Bay, being far too large to be brought up harbour. The *San Salvador* was a squadron flagship, and prior to capture had been seriously damaged by fire and internal explosion. It is known from inventories compiled at the time of her capture that the vessel was not seriously damaged, and that the guns, equipment and provisions were salvaged. Just how much of this salvaging was official is difficult to say, but there is a strong local tradition that whilst the mayor, in whose care the ship had been placed, sent to London for detailed instructions as to what he should do with it, the residents of the town and surrounding countryside boarded the captured ship and then looted it. Eventually the *San Salvador* was stripped of everything of value and was so light in the water that it capsized whilst *en route* for Portsmouth and sank in Studland Bay.

There were rumours of a great treasure which vanished from the ship, but nothing was ever discovered. The one traditional link with the *San Salvador* is the great iron treasure chest which now stands in Weymouth Museum. It is said to have been brought ashore from the Portuguese prize, but no records exist to show what it contained.

The only prisoners noted, most of whom had been badly burned in the fire, were Don Melchior da Pareda, nine Spaniards, two Frenchmen, four

'Allemaines', and one 'Allemain' Woman. They were placed in prison at Weymouth, and remained there for several months. Apart from six who were drowned when the ship eventually sank off Purbeck, what became of them remains a mystery. In 1590 there was a charge of 1/- (5p) entered in the Corporation accounts for taking a Frenchman to Radipole for burial, as well as another 1/- (5p) for escorting three Spaniards to Dartmouth – were these survivors of the *San Salvador*? The existence of a woman is also something of a mystery as no women were supposed to have sailed on board any ship of the Armada – to the Spanish it was a Holy Crusade.

In May 1592 a coat of arms was granted to the Borough, and the original illustrated 'grant' is one of the prized items in the town's archives. The design had many links with the earlier history of the two towns, and incorporated part of the arms of the Clares and Queen Eleanor of Castile, past Lords of the Manor.

A year later, an attempt was made to pipe supplies of fresh water from two springs at Southdown Common, the existing sources being wells, with water described as being 'something brackish'. In his letter to the mayor agreeing to the supply of water, Thomas Howard of Lulworth, owner of Southdown wrote, 'The going forward of your bridge liketh me well, hoping Christian love will increase thereby'.

It is clear from the last quotation that work on the construction of a bridge across Weymouth Harbour was under way in 1593. A bridge to link the two halves of the town seems such an obvious need that it can only have been delayed by the bitter animosity between the opposing sides. A bridge of boats had been suggested by the pre-Armada survey of defences, but the first permanent bridge was of timber, with seventeen arches and a drawbridge, having been built by London merchants whose business interests required it. A record dated October 1597 reads '. . . there is a bridge made over the haven of this town, which will shortly decay if special care is not taken for its maintenance, a great cause of such decay being the drawing up of the drawbridge and the passing over of carts.' The accounts for 1596-7 shows an item 'For carts, and drawing up the bridge for the whole year, £1.10s.2d. (£1.51) which would seem to indicate that either traffic was small, or funds were being diverted! At this time Weymouth Harbour had a considerable colonial trade with the Virginian States, Newfoundland and the West Indies.

The new bridge replaced the ancient ferry, (the 'trajectus' mentioned by Leland in 1538) which had been the only link between the two halves of the town other than the long road journey by way of Radipole. There is good evidence that this first bridge crossed at a point slightly seaward of the present day site. From the Tudor/Stuart period onwards, a large private house stood facing up St Thomas Street, with its back to the Harbour, and the approach road to the bridge must have been to the east of this building. In 1617 it was owned by Thomas Powlett, and in 1790 when Samuel Grimm drew a picture of this house it was known as 'Mrs Johnson's House'.

The construction of the bridge suggests that the people of Weymouth and Melcombe Regis had begun to forget their differences. James I had granted his new Charter in 1606, from which date the term 'Weymouth' becomes accepted as meaning the town as a whole and not merely the ancient borough south of the river.

GENTLEMEN'S
SALOON
THE LYRIC CONCERT PARTY

FOUR

Trade and Expansion

Victorian Weymouth. The sands in summer.

From the Tudor period onwards there are sufficient surviving records to provide at least a glimpse of the day-to-day life in Weymouth and Melcombe Regis. The arguments between the two halves of the town were undoubtedly the main local issue, but only the wealthier merchants and the civic leaders were directly involved.

The annual accounts of the mayors often shed light on events and customs of the period. In 1589 the Freedom of the Borough cost £2.00, two men paying this amount to trade in the town. Entertainment of distinguished visitors was expensive. One of the mayor's guests was Sir George Trenchard of Wolfeton House, Dorchester, newly knighted for his work in planning defences against the Spanish Armada.

A later mayor (William Waltham, 1596) sold a wreck 'behind the town' (i.e. on the sands) for 10s.0d. (50p), but spent 3d. (1¼p) on 'conveying a madman out of the towne' and 3s.4d. (17p) on 'a shroud for a poor man that died in Johnson's porch and to the woman who shrouded him'. A 'bad fellowe from Langton' was returned from whence he came at a cost of 6d. (2½p).

The accession of James I in 1603 incurred various items of expenditure. The messenger who brought the proclamation from Court was paid 10s.0d. (50p); a gunner for Coronation Day cost 10d. (4p), whilst beer for both Weymouth and Melcombe Regis sides of the Harbour cost £1.10s.0d. (£1.50).

On one occasion £1.10s.0d. (£1.50) was 'given to the queen's players for not playing here, by order of the Aldermen' leaving one wondering if they were so bad they were paid not to perform!

Regular mention is made of the stocks, pillory and cucking stool. The cucking stool has not survived, but the stocks and pillory now on show at Weymouth Museum must be at least two hundred years old, if not more. They were certainly in regular use. In 1620 it was found that Temperantia Stickland, K. Ashe, Gratia Turner, Alicia Godfrye and Thomasina Longe had all been 'quarrelsome . . . to the great offence and disturbance of their neighbours'. K. Ashe was found not guilty, but the others were sentenced to be ducked.

In 1616, J. Luke was condemned to sit in the stocks for six hours for stealing three quarts of 'train oil' (oil obtained from the blubber of a whale). Two years later, three of the town's watchmen, Trewen, Sanger and Bread, were condemned to the stocks for being found asleep on duty. T. Angell, a fiddler of Wyke Regis was fined 9d. (3½p) for playing his fiddle in Widow Wilforde's house, and was put in the stocks and fined 2s.7d. (13p) for a second offence whilst drunk.

A glimpse of Stuart Weymouth was revealed in 1971 when demolitions at the rear of the Black Dog Inn uncovered the gable-end of the building which in earlier days had looked out over the sea. Formerly known as 'The Dove Inn', it is the traditional scene of a brutal murder at the end of the Civil War. The original painting is by Eric Ricketts.

In October 1634, an order was made for a new pillory and cucking stool to be provided, but in 1657 there were complaints that the town was still without a pillory, as well as buckets and crooks in case of fire. On 1st March, 1683, a bill for the pillory amounting to £6.1s.8d. (£6.8½p) was approved.

Special courts were held both in Weymouth and in Melcombe Regis to control daily life in the borough. Water courses had to be cleared, damaged quays repaired, dangerous chimneys made safe and encroachments on public lands discouraged. A favourite occupation seems to have been leaving piles of dung in the street, preferably in front of someone else's house. Other concerns included standing pools of water near the Friary and in St Mary Street, so deep the local inhabitants feared their children might drown in them.

Sanitation was a serious problem. One decree stated 'that no man, woman or childe, *or any other person* above the age of 7 years, should henceforth filth, or do his or her excrement of body, in any of the keys, streets or lanes of the Borough, under the penalty of 6d. (2½p).' Nor were the children under seven excused. They were liable to a 3d. (1.25p) fine, 'and all such filth to be cleared away by every householder before his house by 9 a.m.'

Strict control was kept over the licensing of inns and ale-houses. On 7th October, 1616, Margaret Page was one of seventeen applicants granted licences. Two sureties had to be provided for her good behaviour, and a number of conditions were laid down:

No carding, dicing, tabling or any other unlawful games.

No tippling on Sundays and festival days or during divine service, or at any time after 8.00 p.m. in the winter nor 9 in the summer months, (except as to travellers lodging in the house).

Not to brew in the house, but to take the beer of the brewer, which he was to supply the best at 6/- (30p) and the small at 3/- (15p) per barrel.

The best drink to be sold for a penny the quart, and the second for a penny the pottle (½ gallon) and to be sold 'by the alequartt and not by juggs or cupps'.

The following year several publicans had their licences taken away for three years for breaking the regulations. In 1618 the supervision of ale-houses was further strengthened. The list of unlawful games was extended to include 'Cardds, Dice, Tables, Quaits, Loggetts, and Bowles'. The victualler must not harbour 'masterless men' or other notorious offenders. Strong beer (not above 1d. a quart) and small beer (not above ½d. a quart) must be sold 'by sealed measure'. Finally they 'shall not utter, nor willingly suffer to be uttered, drunck, or taken, any tobacco'. James I is known to have had a hatred of tobacco!

This map shows the location of Clark's Hill where the plague victims were buried. The exact boundary between Radipole and Melcombe was a matter of regular dispute until agreement was reached in 1835, when this map was published.

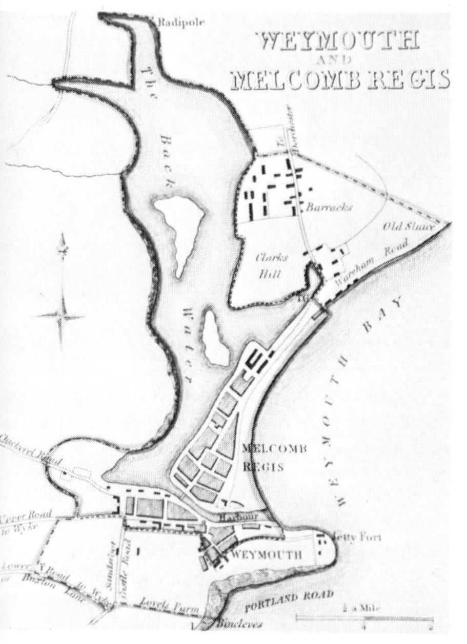

A watchful eye had to be kept on the activities of the local butchers. In 1616 one was prosecuted for operating a slaughterhouse in the middle of a street in the town, whilst two years later Maximilian Loader, one of the 'Searchers of corrupt flesh' reported that a boy employed by Justinian Hingston, another butcher, offered for sale 'oxe flesh which died of itself'. The meat was ordered to be given to the dogs. Later the same year, John Hingston was fined 3s.4d. (17p) for killing a bull unbaited!

In view of such conditions it is hardly surprising that during the early 17th century there was a serious outbreak of plague in the town. It broke out first in 1604 and was at its worst in the summer of 1607, when burials had to be made on Melcombe Common as a precaution. It is believed that the burials were made on a site called 'Clark's Hill' where a Pest House had to be erected. Special watchmen were recruited to deal with the problems arising from this outbreak, and the accounts show that the plague was worse on the Weymouth side. There was a return of the plague in 1624 and 1625, when there was a high mortality amongst children. 12 burials occurred in Melcombe in May 1624, and 36 from March 1624 to March 1625. Typical of the precautions taken was the decision to forbid the landing of the cargo of a coastal barque, the ship having come from London where the plague was rife. All goods had to be 'thoroughly ayred' before landing, and the crew were banned from the town.

In 1603, the people of Melcombe were authorized to build a church on the land where the old chapel stood, the waste ground to the north and south being enclosed to make a churchyard. Radipole Church was to revert to a Chapel of Ease retaining certain parish rights, and an East Street mansion with a garden, bounded on one side by the sea, became the rectory. The new church was consecrated in September 1606. It was to be attended by George III and the Royal Family during their visits to Weymouth, and it survived until 1815, when it was demolished and the present St Mary's church constructed. The altar painting by Sir James Thornhill in the present church was designed to fit the end wall of the old St Mary's, giving a good idea of how small the original parish church must have been.

The first parish church of Melcombe Regis, opened in 1606. Originally known as Christchurch, it was re-dedicated to St Mary, and survived until 1815. The present day St Mary's Church stands on the same site.

Records from the Tudor period show how the town was beginning to expand and develop as individual properties were leased or sold. The Mayor (for Melcombe) and the Bailiffs (for Weymouth) would take bids for vacant sites or properties in the town, these being accepted at the weekly courts; in consequence an auction could go on for several weeks. Bartholomew Belpitt, bidding for a plot of land in 1606 started at 6d. (2½p) for a year's tenancy and later increased it to 12d. (5p) to meet the challenge of his prospective neighbour Robert ffraunch (Robert Frannces, or Knight!). We first met Bartholomew Belpitt when he was an acknowledged merchant-pirate of Melcombe Regis, working in association with Robert Gregory. Later he charged eight pirates of Poole with having attacked his ship and became mayor in 1583.

The old Coneygar Ditch no longer marked the northern development of the town and a number of houses had been erected in extensions of both St Thomas and St Mary Streets. In 1606 a house with a garden or 'cuniger' in St Mary Street was sold for £25. It was burned down in 1689 and the empty site plus the adjoining house was sold for £40. The Wilts and Dorset Bank (now Lloyds) was built on this same site in 1883. Many of the houses in Melcombe Regis had their own water supply from wells, and one is recorded at the back of a house which stood in St Mary Street on the site now occupied by Woolworths.

From the few Tudor/Stuart buildings which have survived in Weymouth until modern times it would seem that they built both large and small town houses of local stone, many with stone roofs although thatch was still a very serious fire risk in the crowded streets. It is more than likely that there was a proportion of half-timbered dwellings, and even some wattle and daub, but none have survived the rebuilding of the last three hundred years.

In 1617 'A Survey of the Rents of the Burgages, Tenements and Lands of Weymouth and also of Melcombe Regis' was prepared. This survey amounts to a virtual 'directory' of the town and provides a detailed description of the period before the Civil War. Today, several shops often occupy the site of what in Tudor/Stuart times was one large house with garden, stables and stores.

John Pitt, an alderman, and a member of one of the most wealthy and influential families in Dorset at that time, lived at 1 St Edmund Street, on the corner of Maiden Street, in the house known to us today as 'The house with the cannon ball' – and one of the three properties listed in 1617 which are still standing today. The plot of land bounded by The Quay, St Thomas Street, St Edmund Street and Lower St Mary Street was not yet built on, whilst the Town Hall of the old Borough of Melcombe Regis still stood on the site of the modern Guildhall.

No. 4 North Quay – the Tudor house which survived until 1961, but which had to be demolished as part of a general clearance prior to the building of the new Municipal Offices.

The home of John Pitt, Mayor of Weymouth and Melcombe Regis in 1609, this old house on the corner of Church Passage and St Mary Street survived until 1883.

The house on the other corner of St Edmund Street and Maiden Street, (No. 23 St Edmund Street) belonged to the heirs of Bartholomew Belpitt, and the land attached to this house reached along as far as St Mary Street. Converted into a shop, this house also survived until the early years of the present century.

William Waltham, Mayor in 1605 and 1616, lived in a house in West Street on the corner of what is today Lower St Alban Street, the property then being described as bounded on the north and west by the sea, a reminder of the extent of the Backwater in those days. This was to be the site of Melcombe Regis Poorhouse during the 18th century, part of the buildings of which still stand – providing yet another link with the Melcombe of Stuart days. Then, as now, St Nicholas Street provided the rear entrance to houses and gardens in St Thomas Street, whilst the area between St Nicholas and West Street was largely gardens and stables.

Sir John Brown occupied a house which has survived until today as 'The White Hart' in Lower Bond Street, the size and importance of this property being indicated by the fact that it paid twice as much ground rent as any other house in the street.

John Pitt, Mayor in 1609, lived in a gabled house in St Mary Street on the corner of Church Passage. Built in 1580, this house survived until 1883, long enough to be photographed, and even today details of the old house can be seen incorporated into the red-brick shop which was erected to take its place.

Giles Green, M.P. in 1604, 1620, 1625 and again in 1647 owned a house called 'Hell' which stood in East Street on the corner of Hell Lane (Now Helen Lane). In 1622 the Corporation made a gift of £1.13s.4d. (£1.67) to Giles Green in consideration of the quay and slip which he had built on Town Ground to the east side of his house in Hell Lane. This must have been an extension or repair of the work done by the friars in the early years of the 16th century. It is known that at the time of the survey (i.e. 1617) the land between Hell Lane and the Harbour had not been built on, and it is more than likely that prior to the additions by Giles Green, the Quay ended at what is now 'The George Inn'. In all 217 properties were listed in Melcombe.

The survey of the Weymouth side of the harbour was nothing like as detailed as that of Melcombe, but does indicate the existence of 241 properties on the following sites: Hope, High Street, West Street, St Nicholas Street, Newbury and Franchis Street. The existence of a West Street and St Nicholas Street on each side of the harbour must have led to some confusion. Eventually West Street, Weymouth, became known as High West Street, but St Nicholas Street, Weymouth, retained its name until 1872, when it was renamed Chapelhay Street. Love Lane in Weymouth is known to have existed in 1617, but any properties there must have been included in either West Street or Franchis Street between which it then, as now, formed a link.

'A very melancholy event happened at Melcombe this day' announced the Corporation records of February 1618. Brian Gates had offered a fowling piece for sale to W. Keynes of Hazelbury, gun-maker. He refused to buy it until he had tried it, so accompanied by several countrymen, they repaired to Melcombe Sands, where they set up a mark, about 40 yards north of the end of the Jetty. A shot was fired at this mark by P. Allin, which went over the Jetty into the Harbour, and immediately a cry was heard 'Hold the man that made the shot, for he hath hurt a man'.

Unfortunately a boat with seven men was crossing the Harbour, from a ship lying in the Hole (i.e. McSaunders Hole) and the bullet struck one of the men, William Pitt, on the right side of the head. 'He cried out "Lord have mercy upon me" and was brought to the quayside, where William Hunt, a Surgeon of the town, immediately leapt into the boat, and found a little breath in him but no hope of life, the skull being broken and the brain oozing out.'

Pitt was brought ashore on a bed, and Allin came and knelt down by his bedside and prayed him to forgive him, to whom poor Pitt answered 'I do with all my heart'. He survived three hours.

This pair of semi-detached cottages in Trinity Street dates from the Stuart period, and has been carefully restored by a local architect, the late E. Wamsley Lewis.

The account of this accident comes as a reminder that the shoreline of Melcombe Regis then ran almost straight with just two houses in East Street backing on to the beach. It is also clear from the description that a small jetty projected beyond the Harbour.

Although St Mary and St Thomas Streets had extended northwards beyond the old town boundary of Coneygar Ditch (Bond Street), there was still much open land to the north of the town, and in 1619 the Corporation granted to H. Russell, a piece of ground 'lying without the Cuniger on the west side of the highway, towards the narrows' for the erection of a windmill. This piece of land was where, 160 years later, the Duke of Gloucester was to build himself a summer residence, to be known as 'Gloucester Lodge' and to become the eventual centre of 'Royal Weymouth'.

The 17th century witnessed the settlement and growth of many of the American colonies, and Weymouth was to play its part, both in colonization and subsequent trade. In 1623 Robert Gorges, the son of Sir Ferdinando Gorges, of Bradpole, near Bridport, led a company of settlers to the village of 'Weymouth' (formerly known as 'Wessagusset') in New England, and in the same year Robert Gorges was appointed Governor of the colony. In June 1628, John Endicott sailed from Weymouth in the *Abigail* with an expedition

The unveiling in 1914 of the Clark and Endicott Memorial on its original site outside the Pavilion Theatre. The ceremony was performed by Mrs Joseph Chamberlain, a descendant of John Endicott.

to found another new colony in North America. They arrived at Naumking (Salem) on 6th September, and from this and similar ventures, many of which originated from Dorset, grew the colony of Massachusetts. Endicott became the first governor of the colony, and a memorial to him and another Dorset seaman, Captain Richard Clark (born in Weymouth), stands in the Alexandra Gardens. Clark had an adventurous life, and in 1583, as Master of the *Delight* he accompanied Sir Humphrey Gilbert on his voyage to Newfoundland, was shipwrecked, but survived.

Ships trading out of Weymouth and other Channel ports were under continuous threat of attack by North African galleys, which cruised in the Western Approaches. The crews of these raiders often included Christian slaves and in 1623 those on one such ship were able to overcome their captors. They, in turn, were attacked and captured by a Dutch ship, which brought the galley into Portland Roads and landed eight former slaves, including four Englishmen and one Scot. There are regular entries in the accounts of refugees such as these being clothed, fed and assisted.

Weymouth ships faced other such threats. Early in the reign of Charles I there was renewed danger of another Spanish invasion, and the preparations made to meet it rivalled those of forty years earlier in the reign of Elizabeth I. Weymouth and Poole were required to provide and equip two ships. Local fortifications were to be rebuilt and strengthened and the trained bands drilled and equipped. All men from 16 to 60 were to be enrolled, exercised and armed, due care being taken to exclude any 'recusants' (Catholics) from being included in these preparations. The beacons were to be repaired, provisioned and watched. The invasion never took place, and the main local problem seems to have been the large number of troops billeted in the town.

About this time, there is evidence of a considerable rift between the merchants of Exeter and those of Weymouth. In about 1625 it was proposed that the merchants of both ports should be mutually exempt from customs payments. The Weymouth merchants, however, considered that those of Exeter would get the best of the bargain and prepared a document listing 'the many and great inconveniences which will befall that town (Weymouth)' if the proposal was successful.

The document went on to claim that the greatest part of the Weymouth revenue was spent repairing and dredging the Harbour. It also argued that £500 needed to be spent on the bridge to prevent it falling down, and that money had been spent on fortifications against invasion, 'whereunto it is very subject'.

The dispute with Exeter hints at the endless expenses that plagued the Corporation over the Harbour. The quays and jetties as well as the new pier at the Nothe point (built in 1621) were regularly repaired and a detailed schedule of port charges was approved. Special charges were levied when a ship tied up in the Harbour with the object of careening and trimming, and if the owners chose one of the special places reserved for this task, where presumably the facilities were better, an additional charge was made if they overstayed their allotted period.

A special lighter was built for the purpose of scouring and cleaning the Harbour at a cost of £45, the boatbuilder being one John Damon, a surname known in Weymouth for centuries. A ballast wharf was built on the Weymouth side of the Harbour 'at the lower end of Hope' and all ships discharging or taking on ballast were required to use this wharf. Prior to this the handling of ballast had been unorganised, and piles of unwanted ballast were often left deposited on the quays or even just tipped into the harbour, leading to silting up. Once again, failure to comply with the new regulations produced heavy fines, but it is obvious that there were difficulties in keeping track of all ships using the Harbour. The local pilots were not above trading illegally and in 1639 a special directive had to be issued ensuring that all pilots bringing in 'strangers' to the Harbour must report to the mayor or an officer of the town. Bridport and other 'foreign' boats were only to be allowed to winter in the Harbour if they were moored above the bridge, thus keeping the quays clear for trading vessels. The firing of ships guns whilst in Harbour was also forbidden, the fine being £1 plus a charge for any damage done to property.

Considerable damage was being caused both to the town bridge and to newly paved streets by carts fitted with wheels banded with iron, or worse still, fitted with iron studs. In 1635 a special order was made prohibiting the use of iron-bound wheels in any streets of the Borough, a decision which must have angered those who were trying to protect their vehicles against excessive wear and tear, and which must have provided good business for the local wheelwrights.

Strict control was kept over trading in the town, so it was restricted to 'freemen' and those granted special licences. Numerous court cases arose over strangers attempting to trade without permission, whilst other regulations penalized farmers from the surrounding countryside attempting to sell their wares before they reached the market-place in St Edmund Street.

Confirmation that Melcombe Regis was the more progressive part of the borough comes in the description of the town written about 1630 by Thomas Gerard, but not published until over a hundred years later, and then under the misleading title of *Coker's Survey of Dorset*. Entering the district by way of Abbotsbury and Portesham, he wrote:

> Weymouth, is but little, consisting chiefly of one street, which for a good space lieth open to the sea, and on the back of it riseth an Hill of such steepness that they are forced to climb to their

Chapel by 60 steps of stone, from whence you have a fair prospect of the town and haven lieing under.

Melcombe on the other side of the River much surpasseth the other for convenience of site, for this standing on a flat, affordeth room for buildings, with a Market Place and convenient streets, and also yards for their wares by means whereof most of the Merchants have chosen this for their habitation, which of late years is fairly newly built.

These towns now united gain well by traffic into Newfoundland, where they have had 80 sail of ships and barques, as also by a nearer cut into France opposite unto them, when they return laden with wines, cloth and diverse other useful commodities with which they furnish the country.

Gerard's account also mentions the danger of shipwrecks and there is a tradition that at least one of the Spanish Armada ships met disaster on the Chesil Beach. One of the first wrecks of which there is any definite account is of a ship called the *Golden Grape*, bound to Dover from Cadiz, when it was wrecked in West Bay in December, 1641.

The *Golden Grape* was driven ashore on the pebble beach at Wyke Regis 'by extremity of fowle weather', and of the twenty men on board, seven were drowned. During the several days it took for the ship to break up, a mob ready to risk the wintry weather and heavy seas looted the vessel's cargo as it came ashore, providing a fine range of necessities and luxury goods for the people of the local villages. In the days following the wreck the illicit removal of her cargo became so well organised that much of the plunder was carefully concealed for later use or sale. It was a useful collection – 2000 barrels of raisins, 400 jars of oil, 12 butts of wine, fruit, silk, silver plate and bullion, and gold and silver coins. A man who earned his living fishing from the Chesil Beach could supplement his income on these occasions by rowing looters from the shore across the Fleet to the beach – as well as collecting his own share of the harvest so bounteously provided by the sea.

An enquiry was later held into the whereabouts of the missing cargo, particularly the gold and silver carried by the *Golden Grape*. But the locals were practised at disposing of their booty and although some 'official' salvage had taken place, it is unlikely that much else of value was ever recovered. There is no record of any harm having come to the survivors of this shipwreck, but later accounts prove that a callous attitude towards wreck victims was commonplace, as were the brawls which broke out between rival gangs of plunderers as they disputed ownership of goods which belonged to none of them. Fights were a frequent occurrence when casks of brandy, gin and rum were washed ashore, much of it being consumed on the beach before it could be carried away!

FIVE

The Civil War

In 1642 the long struggle between Charles I and Parliament flared into Civil War. Fighting broke out in August, ending locally four years later when Portland Castle surrendered to Parliament. Although minor skirmishes characterised Weymouth's part in the war for all but three weeks, it brought business to a standstill and accelerated a decline in its prosperity that lasted much longer than the war itself.

The real fighting was restricted to February 1645, when the twin towns of Weymouth and Melcombe Regis were held by opposing forces. Portland remained Royalist from 1643 to 1646, providing a constant threat to Parliamentary Weymouth.

The town was occupied on the outbreak of war, without fighting, by Parliamentary forces under Sir Walter Erle and Sir Thomas Trenchard. Colonel William Sydenham, son-in-law of John Trenchard of Warmwell, was appointed Governor of Weymouth and Melcombe Regis, and some fortifications were set up. The 14th century Chapel of St Nicholas, on the heights above Weymouth, was converted into a fort, and remained a key position throughout the war. A second fort was erected at the Nothe, (then referred to as the 'north' point), a smaller fort was built at Bincleaves, and earthworks thrown up at the northern entrance to Melcombe Regis and the westward end of Weymouth. Drawbridges and town gates were erected, but the exact positions are not clear.

Portland Castle was occupied by Royalist supporters from the commencement of hostilities. In March 1643 the King wrote from Oxford to the Mayor and Corporation of Weymouth, commanding them to send supplies to his forces and subjects in the Isle of Portland. This brought an immediate response from Parliament, which countered with its own order indemnifying Matthew Allen, the Mayor of Weymouth and all others for failing to give the assistance demanded by the King. Here, as in most parts of the country, these early months of the war marked a period of marshalling forces and testing loyalties, and in May 1643 Portland passed under the control of Parliament.

For a brief three months, the whole of the Weymouth-Portland area was under the control of Parliament, and then, early in August, the Earl of Caernarvon with a strong Royalist Army entered Dorset and obtained the surrender of Dorchester, Weymouth and Melcombe Regis. The towns surrendered on the understanding that the inhabitants should not be plundered or subjected to any ill treatment, but the Royalist troops under the command of the King's nephew Prince Maurice, got out of hand and raided the homes of the inhabitants.

On 3rd August, a ship sent by Parliament to assist their forces at Weymouth, and laden with ammunition, was seized by the Royalists as it arrived in port, just one day after the town had been occupied, and a week

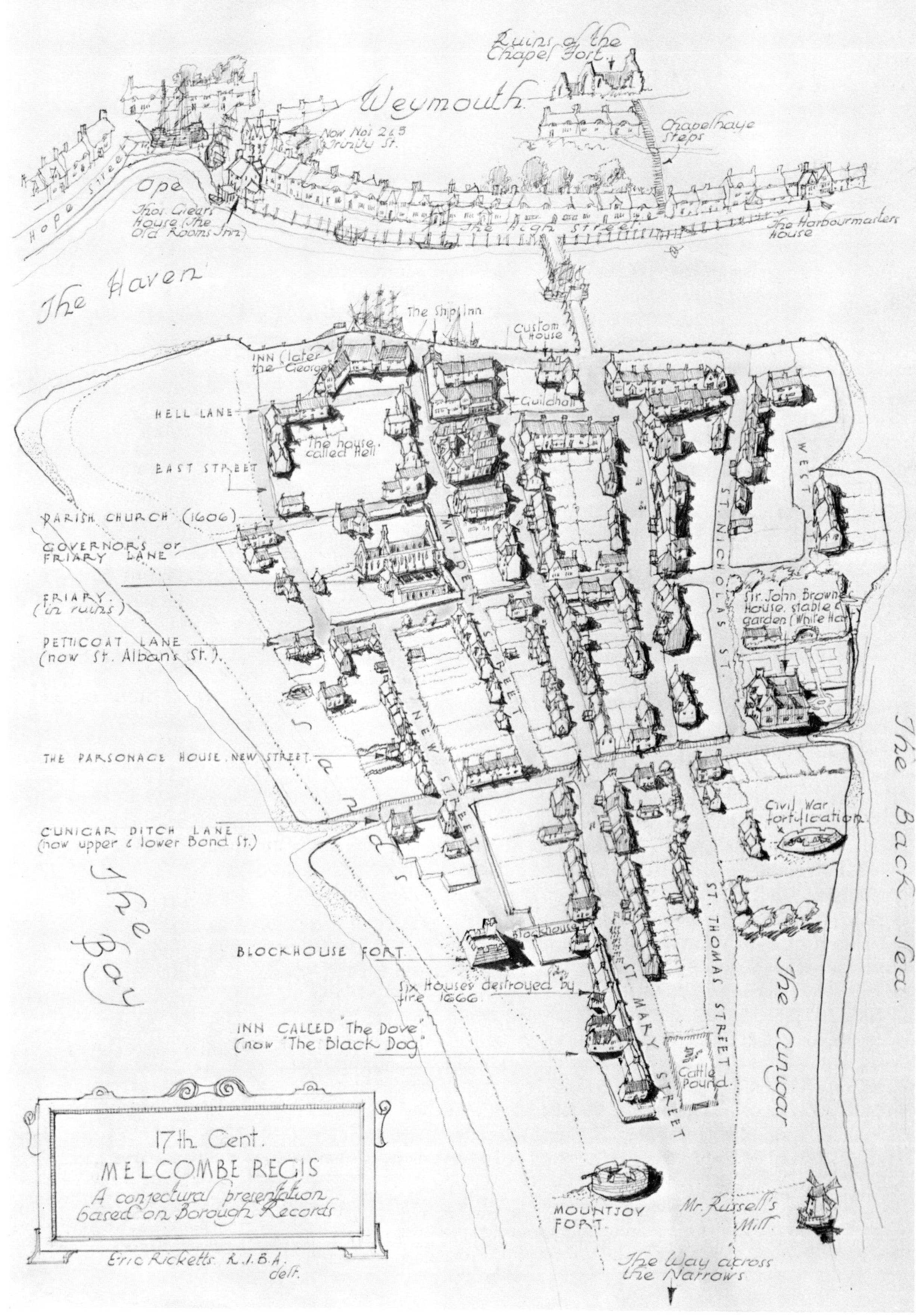
Ruins of the Chapel Fort
Weymouth
Now Nos 2 & 5 Trinity St.
Chapelhaye Steps
Hope Street
Ope
Thos. Giears House (the Old Rooms Inn)
The High Street
The Harbourmasters House
The Haven
The Ship Inn
Custom House
INN (later the George)
Guildhall
HELL LANE
The house called Hell
EAST STREET
PARISH CHURCH (1606)
GOVERNOR'S or FRIARY LANE
FRIARY (in ruins)
PETTICOAT LANE (now St. Alban's St.)
MAIDEN STREET
NEW STREET
ST. NICHOLAS ST.
WEST
Sir John Browne's House, stable & garden (White Hart)
THE PARSONAGE HOUSE, NEW STREET
Sands
CUNIGAR DITCH LANE (now upper & lower Bond St.)
Civil War fortification
The Back Sea
The Bay
BLOCKHOUSE FORT
Blockhouse
Six Houses destroyed by fire 1666
ST. MARY STREET
ST. THOMAS STREET
The Cunigar
INN CALLED "The Dove" (now "The Black Dog"
Cattle Pound
17th. Cent.
MELCOMBE REGIS
A conjectural presentation based on Borough Records
MOUNTJOY FORT
Mr. Russell's Mill
Eric Ricketts. R.I.B.A. delt.
The Way across the Narrows

later, Portland Castle was captured by subterfuge. The Royalist occupation of the area was not a happy period, and matters were made worse when in November some 300 Irish soldiers were landed at Weymouth to strengthen the garrison.

The Royalist occupation lasted for just over ten months, and it was during this period that a Royal Mint was established in the town, almost certainly at Sandsfoot Castle. A large number of half-crowns and shillings were struck, and sixpences, groats, threepences and half groats are known. The coins were of coarse workmanship, and can be identified by a letter 'W' (or 'SA') incorporated in the design. Specimens of these coins do come on the market from time to time and fetch very high prices.

Colonel William Ashburnham was the Royalist Governor of the area, but he failed to improve the local fortifications, which had clearly been inadequate from the start. In June 1644, The Earl of Essex, Commander in Chief for the Parliament, arrived at Blandford with 13,000 troops and later that month occupied Dorchester. Although his main object was to relieve the siege of Lyme Regis, he did divert a party of cavalry under Sir William Balfour, to attack Weymouth. Immediately the Weymouthians offered to surrender, and on 17th June, 400 Royalist troops marched out of the town and Parliamentary forces re-occupied the area. The Earl of Essex spent some days in Weymouth and negotiated the surrender of Sandsfoot Castle, but Portland remained loyal to the Crown and Colonel William Ashburnham made the Island his new headquarters.

From the beginning of the conflict, the Royalist cause had lacked any naval power, the entire fleet having passed into the control of Parliament under the Earl of Warwick. Having helped to relieve the siege of Lyme Regis, he was then able to transfer part of his fleet to support the attack on Weymouth. The defeated Royalist troops were allowed to march from Weymouth to Exeter,

In this specially drawn map, Eric Ricketts has included the various sites associated with the Civil War years.

Portland Castle, built at the same time as Sandsfoot Castle, was held by Royalist forces for the major part of the Civil War, and presented a constant threat to the security of Parliamentary-controlled Weymouth. It was from here that the attack of February 1645 was mounted.

officers retaining their swords and pistols, but the soldiers were permitted staves only. Considerable military supplies fell into the hands of the Parliamentary forces, including 100 pieces of ordnance of various sizes, 2000 muskets, 150 cases of pistols, 200 barrels of powder and 1000 swords. Some 60 ships and 100 guns were captured in the harbour, together with another 180 barrels of powder and 80 pieces of ordnance.

The defence system of Weymouth and Melcombe had now proved inadequate on two occasions and, with the re-appointment of Colonel William Sydenham as Governor of the town, the entire scheme of local fortifications was overhauled and improved. No attempt was made to attack Portland Castle, but the existence of Royalist forces on the Island and the changing fortunes of the opposing armies in the west of England must have affected the everyday life of the community.

Towards the end of November 1644, a Parliamentary officer who was later to play an important part in local affairs, escaped from Portland Castle. Captain James Heane (Haynes) had been captive for a long period, and had refused all offers to transfer to the Royalist cause. He escaped with the assistance of the servant of the Governor, who himself deserted the Castle and the Royalist cause at the same time. Heane, now promoted Lieutenant Colonel was to return to Weymouth in command of a cavalry detachment during the vital days of February 1645.

Little is recorded of the day-by-day life of the townspeople of this time, but the occasional reference has survived. In 1644, Elinor Knott, a married woman, whose husband was abroad, was accused of murdering her newly born child, the father of which was a soldier in the town. The account of any war can never include the thousands of personal tragedies which come as a result of the unnatural conditions in which people find themselves.

Weymouth may have been held by the Parliamentary forces but there were many local supporters of the Royalist cause. Back in October, when the King had been at Maiden Newton and Sherborne Castle, he had directed Sir Lewis Dyve, the new Commander-in-Chief of the Royalist Forces in Dorset, to capture both Weymouth and Melcombe Regis. By Christmas of that year, Dyve was in touch with Royalist plotters within Melcombe (Fabian Hodder, John Cade, John Mills and Philip Ashe), and with Sir William Hastings, the newly appointed Royalist Governor of Portland Castle. Communications were difficult and dangerous, and a Weymouth woman, Elizabeth Wall, acted as courier to avoid suspicion. The Royalist plotters were all important local men. Hodder was a merchant of some standing, Cade was both a local alderman and also a former Captain in the Royalist forces, whilst Mills was one of the Town Constables. The Roundheads had no idea that anything was amiss, and Peter Ince, the local Minister, looking back at the events, wrote 'In the beginning of February (1645) we were in as sweet and quiet security as any Garrison in the Kingdom: no enemy near us but one at Portland and that not very considerable, being about three or four hundred men'.

The Royalist plan of attack was for men from Portland to cross and seize the Nothe and Chapel Forts, whilst Sir Lewis Dyve with his forces from Sherborne would make a simultaneous attack on Melcombe from the north. Some supporters from the outlying villages of Preston, Sutton Poyntz, Upwey and Broadwey would either join in the attack or enter Melcombe in advance to help to open the gates. The attack was scheduled for the night of Sunday, February 9th, 1645, the password was to be 'Crabchurch' and Royalist supporters were to wear a handkerchief tied around the arm.

Smallmouth Ferry, across which the raiding force from Portland was ferried on the night of 9th February, 1645. The Ferry remained the only link with the Island until the first Ferry Bridge was built in 1839.

Sufficient men had assembled at Portland to form two companies, the whole operation being under the command of Sir William Hastings, the Governor. One company made its way along the causeway to Smallmouth, where it was met by John Dry, a Weymouth tanner, who had arranged for the ferryman to transport the force across the water. He then led them by little used tracks to the vicinity of the Chapel Fort, where they arrived about midnight.

At the same time, the second Portland party was crossing by water, landing beneath the Nothe headland, where it was met by Walter Bond, a Weymouth fisherman, who led them the short distance to the Fort. It is unlikely that the total force from Portland exceeded 120 men, but the surprise was complete and after a brief but active attack, the two forts were in Royalist hands. The Roundhead troops rallied, and within an hour made a counter attack, but the Royalists were by now well entrenched and they had to fall back to the shelter of the Weymouth houses. They held out against their attackers until the evening of the next day, but realising that they could do nothing with their existing forces, they retreated across the river to Melcombe, and raising the drawbridge left Weymouth in the hands of the victorious Cavaliers.

However, Sir Lewis Dyve had failed to keep his part of the bargain. The Royalist sympathisers from Preston and the other villages had waited in vain on Radipole Common for the arrival of the King's forces and it was not until noon on Monday 10th that the horse and foot soldiers arrived. To understand the troop movements and general tactics of the next few days, we must realize that the road system of the mid-17th century was quite different from that which we know today. Weymouth, on the southern side of the harbour could only be reached by road by leaving the main Dorchester road some two miles north of Melcombe Regis and passing through old Radipole village, and then by way of what we know today as Radipole Lane, and into Weymouth by way of Chickerell Road (all modern road names, not in use in Stuart times). The existence of the Weymouth Marsh, and further north, Chafey's Lake, meant that there was no possible way of reaching Weymouth without going westwards at least as far as present-day Westham Cross Roads.

Sir Lewis Dyve and his forces must have turned away from the road to Melcombe to help in the final stages of the attack on Weymouth, for it is known that their arrival later on Monday was the final factor which forced the Parliament troops to retreat into Melcombe and cut themselves off. To the north of the town, other Royalist troops now faced their defences, probably on the Cuniger, the area of open land between the town and the narrow spit of land which was the only link with Melcombe Common (today the Greenhill, Westerhall and Carlton Road area).

These old buildings at the junction of St Edmund Street and Maiden Street witnessed the fighting of the Civil War, and one, 'The House with the Cannon Ball' still stands today, carrying its scar of battle. Facing it across the road stood the ancient shop, known for many years as 'Hurdle's Corner' and not demolished until earlier this century. A drawing by Will Pye dated 1899.

Although it is clear from contemporary descriptions that the Royalist forces were operating as far south as Melcombe Common, it is also evident that they preferred to keep north of the narrow spit of land as much as possible. Many of the Royalist troops and their local supporters gathered at a part of Radipole called Causeway, returning home 'distempered with beare'. The presence of Royalist troops in the village was still being talked about in the mid 19th century!

Melcombe now became the target for an intense bombardment by the Royalists. From Chapel Fort and the Nothe Fort, a constant barrage was maintained, doing great damage to Melcombe, and setting fire to many of the houses. This is almost certainly the time when the cannon ball became lodged in the gable in Maiden Street, the visual link with the Civil War which has survived until the 20th century. It must have been fired from the Nothe Fort as there were no Royalist ships involved in the fighting. The Royalist forces engaged are known to have numbered at least 4000, whilst there were only some 900 Parliament troops within Melcombe. The use of heated shot had resulted in fires on both sides of the Harbour, and an appeal by the Roundheads to cease this pointless destruction was rejected out of hand by the Cavaliers. Colonel Sydenham the Governor, then resorted to the use of fire ships, setting light to a number of Royalist vessels on the Weymouth side and spreading the fire to the neighbouring houses. This had the required result, and the use of fire as a weapon was discontinued by both sides for the remainder of the siege.

Help was now at hand for the besieged men of Melcombe. William Batten, Vice-Admiral of the Parliamentary Navy, in the *James*, with another ship anchored in the Bay, landed reinforcements and supplies, including two hundred seamen to help in the fight. A similar number of Royalist prisoners were taken onboard, thus relieving the garrison of the need to feed and guard them. In spite of the existence of Royalist forces to the north of the town, Lieutenant Colonel James Heane arrived by land with a detachment of 100 cavalry to help in the defence. Old memories must have returned to him, for it was Heane who had escaped from Portland Castle.

With these additional forces available, the Parliamentarians made a number of sorties from Melcombe. On Sunday 16th February, one week after the original attack, they routed a troop of Royalist cavalry near Radipole, slaying many and capturing 45 prisoners and 80 horses. They then chased the remainder across the open land to the west of Radipole Lake and up to the gates of Weymouth. One wonders just how much control Sir Lewis Dyve was able to maintain over the approaches to Melcombe, as on another sortie the Parliamentarians returned to Melcombe with 900 sheep and one Royalist captain who had mistaken their raiding party for his own troops!

On the third Sunday of the fighting, the 23rd February, major Royalist reinforcements arrived under George, Lord Goring, to face Sydenham and his defenders across the open land north of Melcombe. In spite of much beating of drums and blowing of trumpets, no call for surrender was made and later in the day the Royalists withdrew, leaving a small force in occupation of a new earthwork which they had thrown up about 200 yards north of the Melcombe defences. Even whilst Colonel Sydenham was planning an attack on this fresh threat to his security, a well-aimed shot from the Roundhead cannon in Melcombe landed in the new earthwork, killing many of the Royalist troops and causing the remainder to beat a hasty retreat, leaving their working tools and several horses to be captured by the Parliamentary troops. A large troop of Royalist cavalry watched all this happening from a position on rising ground, not far off.

The additional Royalist reinforcements were still insufficient to bottle up the Roundheads within Melcombe, and on Tuesday 25th February, they made another sortie with horse and foot, capturing a Royalist column taking provisions and stores to Weymouth. They also burned down a house at Radipole which they feared would be used by Royalist musketeers in some future engagement. Some of the Royalist cavalry was chased towards Weymouth, their retreat being observed by their comrades in the Chapel Fort. In an effort to give them assistance and possibly regain the lost stores, a column of 100 foot soldiers was sent out from Weymouth, leaving the fort undermanned. Realising what was happening, Colonel Sydenham quickly gathered a force of some 150 musketeers, then lowered the drawbridge, crossed the bridge into Weymouth, and in less than an hour stormed and captured the Chapel Fort and the major part of the town.

The ease with which the Chapel Fort was captured would seem to indicate that the defenders overestimated the size of the raiding force, and surrendered without putting up any organised resistance. Some five or six Royalists died in the fighting, including Philip Ashe, one of the group of conspirators who had helped to plan the Royalist attack earlier in the month. The Roundheads captured a large number of prisoners, and some stores and provisions which had been brought in by the Royalists only two days before. Supplies in the besieged town of Melcombe had been running low and these replenishments were invaluable.

Among the prisoners taken when the Chapel Fort was captured was Captain Alexander Keynes, the owner of Radipole Farm and a known Catholic. Among his papers was a Commission to employ a ship then at Dunkirk as a Pirate, operating on behalf of the Royalist cause. The loss of the Chapel Fort was a severe blow to the Royalists, and both the Nothe and Bincleaves Forts were completely cut off. Some part of the town of Weymouth must have remained in Royalist hands as it is known that for the next two days the two neighbouring towns battered one another 'both with great and small shott'.

Sir Lewis Dyve was loath to admit defeat, describing the loss of the fort as a 'strange misfortune'. He persuaded Lord Goring to make another attempt to capture the twin towns, and in the early hours of 28th February, the King's forces launched their most severe onslaught of the campaign. The besieged garrison of Roundheads was prepared, having been given warning by an escaping prisoner. With the aid of the seamen landed from the *James* and other Parliamentary ships, and led by Colonel Sydenham and Admiral Batten, they fought off the attack. The most bitter fighting was in the town of Weymouth, where the Royalists forced their way into the streets and alleys of the old town. Irish troops and other Royalists sallied out from the Nothe Fort and attacked Sydenham's men in the rear, capturing a small strongpoint near the town bridge. Colonel Sydenham had his horse shot from beneath him, but rallied his men and once again the Royalists were forced back, many being drowned in the Harbour.

The attack on Melcombe from the north was nothing like as fierce. The Royalists remained behind a protective bank and fired into the town from a distance. When daylight came, all Weymouth, except a small part near the Nothe, was in the hands of the Parliamentarians, and Melcombe was intact. The Royalists with some eighty dead and wounded retreated to Wyke Regis and by ten o'clock in the morning had abandoned both the Nothe and

Bincleaves Forts, leaving their colours, guns and stores almost intact. The final withdrawal was confused and badly organised and after a brief respite at Wyke to deal with the wounded, the entire Royalist force marched to Dorchester and then towards Taunton. The siege of Melcombe had lasted for 18 days and the entire enterprise had proved a costly blow to the Royalist cause. Dyve and Goring had been in command of forces vastly superior in numbers to their opponents, but had failed to capture and hold two important coastal towns. Goring is said to have been a distinguished and courageous soldier, but his achievements in this brief campaign can have added nothing to his reputation. On the other hand, the Parliamentarians had fought with zeal and courage, and were completely exhausted when the siege was raised.

In his report Colonel Sydenham wrote: 'My soldiers, horse and foot, have all had a very hard service of it day and night. I shall entreat you to write to the Parliament for something for their encouragement; they have neither money nor clothes, and yet unwearied in this business'. On March 5th, an Order of Parliament was passed for £2000 to be paid to the officers, soldiers and seamen of Weymouth for their services.

Three days later a ship of 26 guns, with arms and ammunition from Rouen, entered the port and was captured, the crew believing that it was still in Royalist hands. The crew of a Weymouth ship, the *Endeavour*, laden with salt, brought it into Weymouth, in spite of being fired on by Portland Castle.

Immediate punishment was meted out to the men of Melcombe who had conspired to assist the Royalists. Captain John Cade, Constable John Mills, Thomas Samways the Melcombe tailor, Walter Bond the fisherman who had met the party which came by sea from Portland, as well as some others, were tried, and for the most part confessed in full to their part in the conspiracy. On Monday 3rd March, Cade and Mills were both hung on the Nothe headland. A contemporary account records that Mills, 'when he was upon the ladder, he most desperately threw himself off, not shewing any signs of humiliation, or calling upon God for mercie on his soule, but, carelessly, in a most desperate manner, died, not so much as praying to God to receive his soul'. Another plotter, an Irish Catholic, who is not named in the report, put the rope about his own neck and hanged himself.

Samways and Bond expressed regret for their part in the affair and were reprieved and taken back to prison 'to make further discovery of their partners'. Another of the plotters, Fabian Hodder, was held in prison at Poole, but managed to escape punishment and after the Restoration in 1660 returned to take office as a member of the Corporation. Four years after the executions, Mrs Cade, widow of John Cade, was granted an allowance of 40s.0d. (£2.00) a year for three years to clothe her children. The fatherless family had fallen on hard times, but examples of such compassion by the authorities were undoubtedly few.

The recapture of Weymouth was considered to be of such national importance to the Parliamentary cause, that together with a similar victory at Shrewsbury, it was marked by a special Service of Thanksgiving in London on 12th March, attended by the Lord Mayor, the City Aldermen and representatives of both Houses of Parliament.

The use by the Royalists of Irish troops, whose discipline was poor and whose reputation for pillage and looting was notorious, did much to increase the general antagonism to Catholicism, and the mood of the period is shown in the following small pamphlet, published in 1645. The intriguing title is: *A great Miracle at Sea, a perfect Relation of a Mighty Whale which was pursued*

St Nicholas Street, Weymouth, and the rear of the Old Town Hall. St Nicholas Street (sometimes shown as Francis Street on very old maps) was renamed Chapelhay Street in 1872, to avoid confusion with the similarly named street in Melcombe Regis. The drawing made by John W. Upham is dated 1818.

in the Sea, and encountered by a Multitude of other Fishes, as it was certified by divers Mariners of Weymouth, sailing from France in ship called the 'BONAVENTURE', did shoot the Whale, which making to land was found dead upon the shore within three miles of Weymouth, where the Country people (after many days labour upon the mighty fish) having opened its belly, found a Romish Priest, with a Black Box of Pardons, from the Pope, for many Papists in England and Ireland, whose names are here printed.

The fighting over, there was much clearing up to be done. Lighters were used to carry away the town refuse which had accumulated during the siege, and many of the temporary earthworks were removed. By July, they were considering what should be done with the damaged Chapel at Weymouth, as it was no longer required for use as a fort. The Corporation wished to repair and retain it as a chapel, but eventually it was demolished and the materials sold.

Fabian Hodder (the Royalist plotter) and several others were removed from their positions on the Corporation and others, presumably Parliamentarians, elected. The clearing of the damage at Weymouth and Melcombe must have taken several months, as in August men arrived from Sherborne with 'spards and showells, pickaxes and wheale barrows', remaining for some twelve weeks. In October, the Corporation agreed that three persons from Weymouth and three from Melcombe should be appointed to view all damages to the town 'by fire, or pulling down of houses to prevent firing, and of all grounds, pales and walls, which have been converted or employed for fortifications'.

In the following month, three of the four Members of Parliament were declared incapable of sitting, doubtless because they were Royalists, and two days later, Colonel William Sydenham, Governor of the Garrison, John Bond, Recorder of the Borough, and Alderman Matthew Allen were elected as their replacements. Commenting on this election, John Ashe, M.P., writing to the Speaker from Ottery St Mary, wrote: 'Touching elections . . . at . . . Weymouth; where for three vacant places there stood seven men; and so many speeches made against strangers and unknown persons that if three townsmen had stood they had carried it against all that interposed; for they rejected four able men, and chose a poor simple townsman.'

Part of a pillar from the old St Nicholas Chapel at Weymouth. Converted into a fort during the Civil War, the building was demolished at the end of hostilities. The pillar now stands in Weymouth Museum.

On 7th November 1645, the following petition was presented to 'The Honourable the Committee of the County of Dorset'.

The humble petition of the Mayor, Aldermen, Bailiffs, Burgesses and Commonalty of Waymouth and Melcombe Regis.

Herewith That your petitioners have sustained great losses in their estate to the value of many thousand pounds; by occasion of the war and the late siege against this town, in which divers of their houses were burnt and destroyed and the inhabitants of Waymouth plundered of their goods, and before that much of your petitioners lands wasted, and their houses and buildings pulled down and their goods employed for the better fortifying of the Garrison, and have expended much in free quartering of soldiers and cleansing the town after the siege. And your petitioners hitherto at great charge and trouble for the maintenance of the Garrison by quartering, lights for the Guard, watching and bearing arms at their own proper costs and charges, performing that duty of watching in their turns, as often as the soldiers, in which your petitioners shall, and with all readiness and cheerfulness continue as long as God shall enable them. And now your petitioners are informed by the Constables, that a Warrant is granted by you for the raising of four pounds weekly upon them, which (by reason of the war and their extreme poverty for want of trade as in former times), your petitioners are not only unable to pay, but are put to hard shifts for the maintenance of their own families and poor amongst them, And therefore your petitioners are necessitated to present their condition unto your serious consideration.

This rate was for the maintenance of the soldiers and was to have continued for six months. The Corporation was told to make a fortnight's payment and appear at Dorchester to receive an answer, but it is not clear whether or not the assessment was discharged. A regular guard appears to have been maintained by both the soldiers and others in the town, but the soldiers quartered in it were poorly disciplined, and one night a group stole and killed four sheep out of Nottington Mead.

A reference to the events of 1645 came in 1647, when John Hodder was the complainant in a legal dispute with John Vincent. Hodder, a merchant, alleged that in November 1644 'in the tyme of the late Warr when the West Countrie was oppressed with the soulderie' he deposited with John Vincent of Broadwey, potter, for safe custody, £175 in money, two silver beer bowls worth £9, one great silver beaker worth £5, four dozen silver spoons worth £16, a sugar dish of plate worth 20/-, a gilt silver bowl worth 35/- and fourteen gold rings worth £25, together with two silver dishes, five silver spoons, a wine bowl, a silver whistle and chain, and other articles. Vincent claimed that he had buried the goods in a number of different places in his house, but that in February 1645 a party of retreating soldiers had plundered his house, digging up the floors and taking away all Hodder's property, except 22s.6d. which Vincent found the following morning.

John Hodder was the younger brother of Fabian Hodder, an acknowledged Royalist, and must have had some idea of the events to come, when he made these special arrangements for the security (?) of his property, over two months before the Royalist attack on Weymouth.

Following the surrender of the Royalist forces on Portland in 1646, the garrison of Weymouth was reduced, and Colonel Sydenham was directed to place five companies of private soldiers under the command of Captain Wase for general service with the army. All wheat held by the garrison of Weymouth was to be disposed of, other than that which belonged to Colonel Sydenham as arrears of payment. Sydenham was granted for one year, the farm of Radipole, now sequestered, together with its rents, oxen, ploughs and corn, all as part of his arrears.

By March 1647, there were only two companies of foot soldiers in Dorset, one acting as garrison of Weymouth and Melcombe Regis under Sydenham and the other under Robert Coker, the new Governor of the town. Sydenham's company was to be placed under the command of James Heane, and a special watch was ordered to be kept in the Isle of Purbeck and along the coast from Fleet to Burton Bradstock 'for preventing the hurt which may be committed by rogues and pirates'. Heane's loyalty was finally rewarded when he was promoted to colonel and appointed Governor of Weymouth and Melcombe Regis in September 1647, with a garrison of 300 men.

Local records are very sparse for the period of the Civil War. Few Corporation minutes were recorded and there are long breaks in the Melcombe Regis Registers. A small volume of Law Minutes has survived from the period at the end of the war and many of the cases reflect the bad feeling which continued on long after the fighting. Typical is the case of John Waltham, a merchant of the town, who was imprisoned 'for his lewd carriage' and for having abused and threatened to kill a member of the Parliamentary Committee. The report added, 'The said John Waltham carried himself very saucily before the Mayor' and took one of the witnesses by the arm and then took away the Town Clerk's book from him.

In June 1648, Waltham was in court again, but this time giving evidence in a very different type of case. He stated 'having seen Elizabeth Ranger, Widow, and Patience Duggles, wife of Henry Duggles, in Wyke Field, the next close to the Beacon, in the company of a Dutchman; and sayeth that the said Dutchman and the said Patience were in the corn together in a suspicious manner, and the said Elizabeth, perceiving Waltham and other company coming towards them, called unto the said Dutchman and the said Patience, saying "here be people coming, leave off until you come home".' And shortly afterwards Waltham saw the Dutchman and Patience 'down together in one other field of corn, in a very uncivil manner'.

SIX

A Period of Decline

Undoubtedly the most important effect of the Civil War was Weymouth's decline as a port. The Harbour could not compare with that of its nearest rival, Poole, and it had already begun to lose trade as the size of ships grew beyond its capacity. Whilst the war had left Poole unscathed, Weymouth was faced with damaged buildings, a harbour that had silted up and quays in need of repair. The bills totalled £20,000, but Parliament would grant only £2000 towards the cost. Faced with such problems, Weymouth set about trying to put its house in order, and domestic matters were not ignored. 'On Saturday afternoons' demanded one edict, 'at the tolling of the Hall bell, everyone is to clean the street and gutter before his door, by raking them with colerakes and washing them with water and carrying the refuse away to appointed places'.

Weymouth Esplanade in 1789 as seen by the artist J. Crane. Note how the Backwater almost met the Bay at a point north of the Royal Hotel, and how at the southern end of the Esplanade, the shore-line was almost straight.

The presence of a permanent garrison added to the strain on the economy, and there was considerable resentment against the charges made to pay for the soldiers. One of the most important matters to be settled was the appointment of ministers for the local churches. Richard Marwell, Rector of Radipole and Minister of St Mary's, had been removed from office by the Parliamentary authorities. Dr Henchman, Rector of Wyke Regis and Portland, had also been removed and the Chapel of St Nicholas, the only church on the Weymouth side of the Harbour, had been converted to a fort and badly damaged during the fighting.

In 1648, Rev George Thorne accepted an invitation to fill the vacancy at St Mary's. He received a house, plus £13.6s.8d. (£13.33) per annum, free gifts, the Radipole tithes, and four dinners per week at the town's expense. The real history of Nonconformity in Weymouth dates from Thorne's expulsion on the passing of the Act of Uniformity in 1662. He was just one of some two thousand ministers in England ejected from their livings for their refusal to use the Book of Common Prayer, as ordered by the Act.

The Rev. George Thorne, pioneer of Nonconformity in Weymouth. The original portrait is now in the United Reformed Church in Trinity Street, Weymouth.

Ten years later he was granted a licence to preach in a private house, but the persecution continued, forcing him to conduct his meetings in secret. The original Meeting House was in St Nicholas Street, on or near the site of the first Congregational Church, built in 1803. Later converted into Weymouth's second 'Theatre Royal', it was demolished in 1968 and only the entrance still stands.

It was during the Commonwealth that first consideration was given to reclaiming land from the Backwater and Radipole Lake, as well as from the sea itself. The notion that the marsh to the west of Weymouth should lie open to permit the free flow of harbour tides had been abandoned long before the war, and a wall constructed across the outlet. This had been destroyed during the siege, but in 1651 it was rebuilt four feet high, backed with blue clay to keep out the water. Two years later men were appointed '. . . to view the ground overflown by the sea betwixt Melcombe and Radipole, whether the taking of it will not be a damage to the harbour'. The town's merchants and sailing fraternity argued that the free movement of the tides in the Harbour was vital, and should not be obstructed.

The whole question was again considered in February 1663, when a Royal Commission was considering the reclamation of sea marshes. At a public meeting, it was agreed that to embank any of the flats between the bridge and Radipole would hinder the 'indraught which scowreth the harbor . . . and soe destroy itt'.

Although at the time the Corporation appeared to take no action to dispute a claim by the Crown to own all such marsh lands, in 1672 they authorized the payment of £2 to Mr Swaine of Blandford 'for the defence of the Title of the Towne for the drowned lands belonging to the said Towne when Captain Yardley was Mayor' (i.e. 1663).

If there was some hesitation regarding reclaiming land from the Backwater, there was no such reluctance in extending the quays on the Melcombe side in a seaward direction. Much time had been taken up in repairs to the harbour works and to the financing of the operation, the only external help being the authorization of £1000 from the Customs towards the costs. It is during this period that we get the first mention of a town refuse heap 'at the newly enclosed ground at the jetty', and this must have been the first reclamation from the sea. This process has continued spasmodically until the present day, resulting in the large extension seawards of the quay and pier on the northern side of the Harbour. It is difficult to be exact as to the natural shoreline of the Tudor/Stuart period, but it must have been somewhere at the rear of properties on the eastern side of modern East Street.

Extensive Corporation records have survived from this period, but are largely concerned with small detailed domestic items. The burial ground alongside St Mary's Church was so small that special precautions were taken regarding its use. A Minute of 1654 reads:

> . . . because the burying place is so little and burials may prove noisome and dangerous to the Town in general, if the same be not carefully looked into, that the Bedman shall not dig any grave but by the appointment of the Churchwarden or Sidesman, or one of them, unless such as shall be buried near the Widow Gibson's wall; And that the Bedman shall always dig the graves four feet deep, in case he can conveniently do it without digging up the bodies of such have been newly interred, upon pain for every default herein by the Bedman, 2s.6d. (12½p). And that the Bedman keep the Churchyard clean and take care none do annoy the Churchyard by filthing in it. And that he likewise walk up and down every sabbath day in the Church and Churchyard for keeping of the boys in order, and to give the Justices information of those from time to time that do offend.

The boys mentioned in the minute may well have attended the school run by John Knight in part of the old Friary. Knight was given £4. per year for his work, but in 1661 the annuity was stopped following his refusal to give free tuition to seven poor children.

A few years earlier much of the stonework of the temporary fortifications erected or improved during the War was sold off, mention being made of Cold Harbour Fort, New Fort, Mountjoy Fort, North Fort and Chapel Fort. The site of the Chapel Fort was eventually completely cleared, and in 1661 the New or Jetty Fort at the end of the old pier was ordered to be demolished. Much argument went on with the authorities regarding the future use of Sandsfoot Castle, and finally in 1665 it was ordered to be demolished as being unserviceable to the King. From this date no attempt was made to preserve the building, although it is mentioned again at the time of the Monmouth Rebellion in 1685, and was in use as a storeroom for arms as late as 1691.

England's experiment in republicanism ended in 1660 with the restoration of Charles II. The oldest items of Weymouth's official regalia date from this period, namely the two small silver maces, no longer in regular use. They are first mentioned, together with other civic items, in 1687, when they were officially handed over by one mayor to his successor. The large silver gilt maces, now carried in front of the mayor on all civic occasions also date from this period, but were not presented to the town until 1824. Their earlier history has never been traced.

The Great Plague broke out in London in 1665. There was an instant exodus from the cities to the country and in the Corporation Minute Book for 23rd June is the following entry:

In regard it hath pleased Almighty God lately to visit several places of this Kingdom with the pestilence. To the end that this Towne through a gracious providence may be preserved from that noisome disease, to prevent those that come from infectious places from entering this Towne, 'tis by general consent of this company agreed upon that a very good watch shall be kept day and night by the townspeople until further order.

Two watchmen were appointed to keep guard at the north end of Melcombe Regis and two others at the west end of Weymouth.

Three months later, in September, Charles II dined with the Corporation of Weymouth and Melcombe Regis, although few details of his visit have survived. It is known that in order to avoid the dangers of contagion from the Plague, the Court had removed first to Hampton Court, and then later again to Salisbury. From here official visits were made to local towns. On Monday 18th the royal travellers arrived at Weymouth, and the cost of the reception is known to have been over £100.

Just what form the local celebrations took is not clear, but it is evident that they must have got out of hand as that same evening saw the worst fire ever recorded at Weymouth. Thirty-seven houses were destroyed in or near the east side of St Mary Street, together with most of their contents. In the following year, the King issued a 'brief', which authorized collections to be made in churches throughout England and Wales for the relief of the residents of Weymouth who had suffered as a result of the fire. No record has been traced showing how much was raised, but the following three entries relating to individual parishes are probably a good indication of the response.

Stratford-sub-Castle. 24th June, 1666(?). 9s.10d. (49p)
Tissington, near Buxton. 24th October, 1666. 2s.6d. (12½p)
Ealing, 30th June, 1667. Then collected for the Inhabitants of the Borough of
Weymouth and Melcombe Regis in the Countie of Dorset, 13s.4d. (66½p)

Fires of this type were all too common at a time when houses were still built largely of wood and thatch, and the calls for assistance were much too regular to result in the raising of large sums of money. It is somewhat ironic that whilst other parishes were collecting to help repair the damage at Weymouth, the Corporation was arranging to mortgage the Marsh to Captain G. Strangways to raise the £100 required to cover the cost of entertaining the King on the night of the fire!

The danger from fire was always present, and in 1668 a local regulation stated that 'The firing of guns and birding pieces in the streets and lanes within the town, and the carrying of fire uncovered was greatly hazardous, (and) it may prove yee utter ruin and undoing of this towne if not prevented'. It was therefore forbidden. Some twenty years later we read another local ordinance, namely 'that ships were not to be careened between the Bridge and the George Stairs on the Melcombe side, and the Stairs opposite Raymond's House on the

Weymouth side, the nearby buildings being 'slight' and of timber and so subject to be fired'. Similarly, pitch was not to be heated onboard ship, or any harbour stairs, or against any wall within the Borough.

The need to tackle the problems of the damaged harbour and bridge had been recognised by the new administration which had taken over after the Restoration. Charles II even granted an annuity of £100, payable out of the Customs dues, to be used for the specific purpose of cleansing the Harbour and repairing the bridge and pier. This grant was to run for ten years and much of the negotiation seems to have been handled by Colonel Bullen Reymes of Waddon, one of the local Members of Parliament. In 1668 he negotiated an Order to the 'Overseers of His Majesties Quares in Portland' for the gift of 300 tons of stone for the bridge. To help meet the cost of repairs to the bridge, piers and quays, new tolls were introduced.

The bridge crossing Weymouth Harbour had been completed in 1597 and was now some seventy years old. It had been badly damaged during the fighting and its repair or rebuilding was becoming urgent. During 1669 the decision was made to build a new bridge of wood and stone, and a surveyor was appointed and materials acquired. Mention is made of '64 trees, 22 to 8 feet long, and 24 to 18 inches square, 100 deals not under 16 feet long, 500 tons of ashlar, 150 tons of 'fillers' and 50 bushels of 'Tarras Sand'.

Progress must have been slow, as it was 1672 before a decision was made to ask Sir Winston Churchill for the £50 which he had promised for the bridge. Later this same year negotiations were in hand with the 'Islanders of Portland' about the bridge and stone for it. In the end, all the evidence seems to point to major repairs to the old bridge rather than the construction of a new one. In May 1673, repairs were ordered because the structure had been 'dampnified' by ships, and in July the middle of the bridge was reported as being 'cleane broken downe'. In order to effect these repairs, further tolls were introduced.

The Weymouth trade token issued by James Budd in 1666.

The endless repairs to the bridge and Harbour made it necessary to define the exact boundaries of the port. This was done in 1679, when a detailed statement described it as extending 'from the Neck or Point of Land called St Aldham's Head, and so in a supposed direct Line West-South-West to one other Neck of Land called The Beel of Portland, and so from the said Necks or Points of Land West and by North up the River or Stream called Weymouth Stream to Weymouth Bridge'.

These boundaries are surprisingly large, but the wharf itself, known then as 'Melcombe Key', was about 392 feet long and between 22 and 15 feet wide. Because this document was designed to specify the extent of the Customs Quay at Melcombe Regis, no mention was made of the Quay on the Weymouth side of the Harbour, where the ballast wharf was situated.

In the years following the Civil War there was a considerable shortage of small coinage. Traders in many towns issued their own tokens or farthings to meet this shortage, also using them as a form of advertising. Several Weymouth and Melcombe Regis tradesmen issued tokens, and in 1669 the Corporation laid out £10 in farthings which bore the legend 'A Weymouth Farthing for the Poor, 1669' on one side and the Coat of Arms on the other. The following tradesmen are known to have issued such tokens, at dates between 1658 and 1669: Bartholomew Beer, grocer; Sarah Beer, grocer; John Beere, grocer; James Budd, grocer; Thomas Hide, general dealer; John Hodder, general dealer; George Pley, grocer; William Pooke, grocer; Francis Reed, grocer; John Senior, mercer; James Studley, baker; John Swetnam, draper; and Thomas Tunstall, general dealer.

The White Hart Hotel, birthplace of James Thornhill in 1675, and still very much part of modern Weymouth.

The original St Paul's Cathedral in London had been destroyed during the Great Fire of 1665, and the architect of the new Cathedral, Sir Christopher Wren, had control of the Portland quarries during the years 1675 to 1717. Weymouth took advantage of his regular visits to the area by electing him as one of its Members of Parliament for 1702. He is only recorded as serving for this one year.

Another local link with the building of the new Cathedral was the artist Sir James Thornhill, born in Weymouth in the building known as the 'White Hart' in Lower Bond Street, in 1675. His huge painting on the interior of the dome of St Paul's is one of its glories. Weymouth contains two examples of his work, the Altar Piece in St Mary's Church and the Coat of Arms of George I in the Museum. He presented these to the town in 1721 and the following year was elected a Freeman. Knighted in 1720, he was appointed serjeant-painter, and in 1728, history painter to George II. From 1722 onwards he was one of the two Members of Parliament for Melcombe Regis.

In June 1685, when Thornhill was still only a boy, the Duke of Monmouth landed at Lyme Regis in a doomed attempt to dethrone his uncle James II. The Monmouth Rebellion had begun. Six weeks later Monmouth was executed and the prisons at Exeter, Taunton and Dorchester were crowded with rebels awaiting trial. Of the 312 prisoners brought before Judge Jeffreys at Dorchester in September, at what has become known to history as the Bloody Assizes, 74 were executed and the remainder transported to the West Indies.

Weymouth did not escape having to witness their fate. Jeffreys ordered the erection, on or near Greenhill, of a 'sufficient gallows for the executing the several persons sentenced and appointed to be executed on Tuesday next within your said Borough'. Twelve men were hung, and their heads and limbs or quarters were then displayed in Weymouth and the surrounding villages. Those in the town were placed as follows:

Grand Piere	6 quarters	1 head
Townend	2	
Neare the Windmill	4	1
Waymouth Townhall	2	
The Bridge	1	2
Melcombe Townehall	1	2

The final bills included 1s.6d. (7½p) 'for setting up a post with the quarters of the rebells at Weymouth towne end', and the £15.4s.4d. (£15.21) spent on 'ye Gallows, Burning & Boyling ye Rebells executed p ordr att this Towne'.

How many of the twelve were men of Weymouth is uncertain, but we do know that William Wiseman, a barber's apprentice in the town, was ordered to be whipped through all the market towns in Dorset for having publicly read Monmouth's Proclamation at Weymouth. The boy (aged 14) was first whipped at Dorchester, but when a clergyman named Blanchard complained that the gaoler was not severe enough, Jeffreys ordered that the boy be whipped again on the following day, leading to fears that he would die. After Jeffreys had departed, the boy was whipped through the town of Melcombe Regis, and here the sentence ended. Later a Dr William Wiseman is known at Weymouth, possibly the same person.

Many of the rebels whose death sentences were reduced to transportation sailed from Weymouth. In addition to the Dorchester prisoners, 200 were marched from Wells ready for shipment, but 30 escaped on the way. The *Betty* and *The Happy Return* are listed as Weymouth ships transporting convicts at this time. The *Betty* sailed with eighty convicts and 'one serving maid', arriving at Barbados in 1686. Eight rebels from this ship had been buried at sea. *The Happy Return* took all her 91 rebels to Barbados without the death of one.

Although trade through the port had declined when compared with the pre-Civil War era, there are numerous records which indicate a steady flow of traffic in and out of the Harbour. In 1701 it was ordered that goods should not be carried from ships into the town, except by the 'Bearers or Day Attenders on the Quay', charges to be varied according to the distance goods were carried. There is evidence of the import of fuel, and 'Meters' were appointed to measure the large quantities of 'coles, culm or stone coles' arriving from Newcastle etc. There were times when unloading the colliers was a leisurely process, and in 1729 measures had to be taken to reduce the inconvenience to 'Grocery Ships' caused by colliers occupying the quay for two or three months at a time.

Local records of individual ships are few and records of their cargoes even rarer. One odd account which has survived shows that on 20th May, 1709, the *Cerne Galas*, Captain Jacob Wyman, sailed from Weymouth for Cadiz, arriving on 25th June. Her cargo is listed as 4 barrels and 7 boxes of flour, 82 sacks of broad beans and 10 sacks of biscuits: not a large cargo, but perhaps the ship was not fully loaded.

A further extension seaward of the land on the Melcombe side of the Harbour took place in 1723. Instructions were given for piles to be driven from the jetty towards the Harbour mouth, to check the 'outsette of the tide on the north side' and to keep the channel 'in a more direct course'. At the same time the lower part of the jetty, which until then was covered by high tides, was to be raised so as to 'answer 10ft on . . . the Bar'.

Shipbuilding continued, and in 1721, W. Gleade is recorded as building two ships on the 'new Key'. In 1724 a new warehouse was built adjoining the George Inn and in 1732 it is known that eight ships were trading from Weymouth with Newfoundland. Foreign ships continued to use the port, and in 1736 there is a record of a dispute with the master of the *St Peter* of Frederickshall. He had refused to pay 2s.6d. (12½p) per ton for ballast, but after his anchor was seized, he agreed to negotiate!

Damage to the harbour and quays by storm and accidents was a constant cause of expense. In 1691, the Marsh Wall had been destroyed in a gale and repairs cost the tenant of the marsh £57. He was excused a year and a half's rent, so the Corporation were the losers.

Local inns feature regularly in the minutes of the Courts during the early years of the 18th century. Weymouth inns included 'The Bay Tree' (c1703), 'The Fox' (c1705), 'The Compass' (c1720) and 'The Boot' (1723); Melcombe Regis had 'The Bear' (1700), 'The Crown and Sceptre' (c1710) and 'The Golden Lion' (1721), whilst in 1726 we read of 'The Queen's Head' and the 'Thistle and Crown' with no clear indication as to which side of the Harbour they dispensed their beers. They were all obviously popular, for when the constables found a captain and alderman 'gaming and wrangling' in 'The Bear' in 1700, they refused to leave the house. On one occasion, the watchman, hearing a noise in 'The Bay Tree', investigated, but the landlady Mary Jerrat '. . . took him by the shoulders and turned him out'.

The Boot Inn, 1983, a link with 17th century Weymouth.

In 1704 it was the turn of a travelling physician to offend the authorities. Bound, the ostler of the 'Crown and Sceptre', testified that Dr Humfrey Griffin 'who hath a stage in this town', being unreasonably offended at being asked if he could cure the cramp, caught poor Bound by the hair, and with his own head struck Bound's face such a blow 'as amazed him' and covered him with blood. A far more serious incident occurred at the Melcombe Regis beerhouse, 'The Ship Aground', in 1724. Thomas Stuckey, the landlord, was killed in a brawl following the drinking of 'flip' (a mixture of ale, brandy and sugar). He had tried to separate two fighting customers and was killed by John Chick.

The Town Bridge, first built in the 1590s and much repaired in 1673, was finally condemned in 1713, when Thomas Hardy, William Harvey, James Littleton and Reginald Marriott, the four local Members of Parliament, together paid for the building of a completely new structure. Whereas the first bridge had been made to last for 120 years, this second one survived for a mere 28 years, and in 1741 a third wooden bridge was built. As with the others it was fitted with a drawbridge in the centre, but for the first time the suggestion was made that the bridge should be built opposite St Nicholas Street, rather than on the established site at the end of St Thomas Street. The change of site was not made on this occasion, but did take place 29 years later when the fourth (and last) wooden harbour bridge was constructed.

One of the major contributors to the cost of building the 1741 bridge was George Bubb Dodington, of Eastbury House, near Blandford. Later created 1st Baron Melcombe Regis, Dodington was one of the most powerful local men during the first half of the 18th century. He bought and sold votes to protect his own interests and was M.P. for Melcombe Regis between 1727 and 1754. Dodington was a typical product of his era; graft, corruption and a measure of worthy deeds all combined.

George Bubb Dodington, 1st Baron Melcombe Regis, 1691 – 1762.

His interest in Weymouth continued until his death in 1762. In 1747 he was thanked by the Corporation for his good offices in obtaining the Charter of George II, and his diary gives a marvellous insight into the way in which he 'fixed' elections. In an age where the secret ballot, universal franchise and strict control of election expenses are taken for granted, it is difficult to judge what was normal in the political manipulations of the 18th century. It does seem however that electoral irregularities at Weymouth were excessive as in 1710 the House of Commons resolved: That Edward Tizard, Mayor of the said Borough of Weymouth and Melcombe Regis, is guilty of several arbitrary and illegal practices at the late election of Members to serve in Parliament for the said Borough.

Four years later another Committee of the House declared 'that all conveyances to split and divide the interest in any house or lands here (Melcombe Regis) among several persons, in order to multiply votes at the election, were illegal and void'. Anyone, whether an inhabitant or not, who had a freehold in the Borough, even of insignificant value, enjoyed the right to vote. In the space of a few years, by subdividing properties and plots, the number of freeholders had increased from less than 200 to 648.

Violence at elections was almost a norm. In 1727 the Town Clerk had to read the Riot Act 'in the Towne Walk', when an argument arose between Mr Harvey J.P., and John Ward of Hackney, resulting in the mob getting somewhat out of hand. John Ward had been M.P. for Weymouth from 1721-1726, in which year he was expelled from the House for forgery. The following year he stood in the pillory. At the same time as all this active electioneering took place, the Corporation itself grew increasingly lazy. Meetings were infrequent, and between 1724 and 1729 it met on five occasions.

As a port, albeit of limited size, Weymouth often found itself involved in the various continental wars of the 17th and 18th centuries. In 1691 between 200 and 300 English prisoners from France were landed at Weymouth, most of them 'sick in ye flux'. The disease was probably typhoid, and many of the townspeople became victims of the epidemic. The parish registers of Melcombe Regis show that in 1690 there were 22 burials, whereas in 1691 the total was 82, only 13 of which were marked as strangers.

Another wartime hazard was the occasional visit by the Press Gang. In 1706, a riot broke out when a Gang from the galley *Pembroke* landed. At least two of the sailors from the *Pembroke* were wounded as well as two of their intended victims. The commander of the landing party was fined 9s.0d. (45p) for the poor, on a charge of drunkenness and swearing. The Navy was absent

The old Melcombe Regis Town Hall in 1790.

The present day Guildhall on the same site as earlier Town Halls, opened in 1838. Maiden Street Methodist Church of the 1860s replaced the King's Head Inn. The drawing is by Robert Smart, a former art master at Weymouth Grammar School.

however in June 1708 when a French ship chased a Weymouth mackerel fishing boat into Portland Roads, and claimed that the owner, J. Bartlett, must pay a ransom or have his boat destroyed. Bartlett pleaded that England and France had agreed not to molest fishing boats, but in the end he paid a ransom of £10 in 'drapery and hatts'.

In January 1716, Jonathan and Rebecca Edwards willed some land, the income from which was to be used to assist four poor widows dwelling on the Weymouth side of the harbour. In 1829 funds from this charity were used to erect four almshouses at Gulleshayes on the corner of Gypsy Lane and Wyke Road. They survived until 1957, when they were replaced by four homes in Rodwell Avenue.

In 1727 Sir James Thornhill erected a group of almshouses on a site at the northern end of St Thomas Street. He intended these to be used by 'decayed mariners' but having built them he failed to endow them, and although used as a charitable institution for many years, they eventually had to be demolished in the early 19th century. The land had been granted to Sir James in 1722 for 1000 years at 1s.0d. (5p) a year, and was at that time the site of the Town Pound.

The site of Thornhill's almshouses (and of the original Pound) was well outside the old town boundary of Cuniger Ditch (now Lower Bond Street). In 1724 the ditch was still open and the Corporation was accused of failing in its duty in that the Ditch was not being emptied regularly and was 'very much offensive'. Thornhill's birthplace stood adjacent to Cuniger Ditch, and the then owner must have been one of those who suffered from the smells.

Smuggling along the Dorset coast was extensive, although our knowledge of it is only based on the small proportion of 'runs' which were intercepted. In 1724, W. Painter assisted Warren Lisle 'patent searcher of the Customs' to seize a boat-load of wine and brandy which was due to be run ashore near Smallmouth. The smugglers did not appreciate the help which Painter had given the authorities, and he was later assaulted in the 'Queens Head' Inn at Weymouth. Another man. J. Loader, sent by the local Collector of Customs to seize a barrel of 'runned brandy', had his arm broken for his trouble. Four years later, in July 1728, Customs Officer Parker was assaulted in the 'Boot Inn' whilst searching for 'runned goods'.

Quite apart from smuggling and fishing, there were other profits to be made from the sea. A letter sent from Weymouth in 1752 records the fate of a whale:

On the sands near this place has lately been caught a monstrous large fish upwards of fifty feet long and twelve feet thick. Its jaws were nine or ten feet when extended. Its tongue in size may be compared to a large feather bed, and the passage down its throat large enough to receive a coach horse. Its teeth which consist of two rows on the under jaw are about five inches long which sheath themselves in holes in the upper jaw when the mouth is shut. Its body (although one part in three was buried in the sands) was higher than the head of a tall man on horseback.

When it was cut open, numbers – at least thirty thousand fish of various sizes – leapt out of its belly. The two prongs of the tail are twelve feet assunder. Its eyes very small for so large a bulk, not exceeding the bigness of an ox's eye, yet from the tip of the nose to the eyes is ten feet.

The country for many miles round flock to see this surprising animal and not less than three thousand were present when I saw it. The men who took this monster say that an anchor was thrown into its mouth which it spit out with such force as to break three new cables it was fastened to, and at one stroke it overwhelmed three hundred men with its tail. The fish at high water mark came over our bank, and when the tide ebbed it could not get back again. The proprietors expect to make one-hundred-and-twenty hogsheads of oil from it.

Clearly a fishing story which lost nothing in the telling!

Early in the following year, an order was made to secure and sell the blubber etc. of a large fish then on the sands, with due precautions to be taken against fire when boiling. The spermaceti and oil were put up at £25 per tun, and the blubber at £15.10s.0d. (£15.50). Either Weymouth was playing host to a school of whales, or the original one had been around for four months, by which time it must have been something of a nuisance!

The former Turnpike House at Radipole dated only from the early 19th century. The original Turnpike House stood at Greenhill.

The old Turnpike House on the Preston Beach Road, with its gate still in position. The building was demolished in 1959.

One of the most important social changes in the 18th century was the general improvement in transport which came about as the result of the development of the Turnpike roads, the majority of which were set up between 1750 and 1780. The old road system had long been completely inadequate and the funds for the construction of new roads and the repair and improvement of existing ones were to be provided by raising loans. Local Acts of Parliament gave authority for the establishment of Turnpike Trusts and for tolls to be collected at the turnpike gates.

The turnpikes in the Weymouth area date from 1760. The principal road from the north came via Sherborne, over the Giant's Head to Dorchester, and then via Winterborne Monkton to Upwey and Melcombe Regis. Prior to 1824, this road came down over Ridgeway Hill via the route which we know as the 'Old Roman Road', but in that year the new road with the deep cutting over the crest of the hill and the hairpin bend leading down to Upwey was constructed to ease the gradients. In 1983 much of this stretch of road was widened to handle the increased flow of heavy traffic from the port of Weymouth.

From the east the road came through Osmington and then over Jordan Hill, but in 1812 a new road was authorised via Chalbury Corner, and the Jordan Hill route reverted to a by-road.

From the west the road left the Great Western Turnpike at Winterbourne Abbas and thence to Melcombe via Martinstown, Ashton, Gould's Hill and Stottingway to Broadwey. A fourth road ran from Weymouth to Chickerell and a fifth one via Boot Lane and Castle Lane to the shore near Sandsfoot Castle and then along the sands to the ferry at Smallmouth. In 1811 this road was re-routed via Wyke Church and then southwards to the Portland Ferry.

By 1880 the responsibility for all main and turnpike roads had passed to the County Councils, and very few of the original toll houses have survived. Two such houses did exist in the Weymouth area until quite recently. One was half-way along the Preston Beach Road and the other almost opposite the Spa Hotel at Radipole. Both became victims of road improvements!

SEVEN

Royal Weymouth

It is not easy to put an exact date on Weymouth's return to prosperity. Despite the decline in its fortunes following the Civil War, Daniel Defoe, writing in 1724, found Weymouth 'a sweet, clean, agreeable town' and also noted that ''tis well built, and has a great many good substantial merchants in it, who drive a considerable trade and have a good number of ships belonging to the town'.

Throughout the first half of the 18th century there is solid evidence of the continued use of the harbour, requiring the building of a new warehouse and the replacement of the town bridge; and although overshadowed by busier ports, Weymouth never completely surrendered its maritime links. However, it was not trade which launched Weymouth's revival, but a new national interest in the sea as a 'health-giving' force.

The appalling living conditions in many of the larger towns and cities, and the frequent outbreaks of epidemics, had focused attention on the whole question of health. As a result, the privileged had been 'taking the waters' at the inland spas, enjoying a fashionable social life as they relaxed in Bath, Cheltenham and the other spa towns which promised relief from numerous debilitating ailments. Now, however, medical opinion advocated a new 'cure' – sea water, recommending it for both external and internal use. Bathing in the sea and drinking quantities of the 'fashionable liquor' became the vogue, inspiring the rise of the seaside resort.

Weymouth was by no means the first coastal town to realise the commercial possibilities of its position, but on 30th September 1748, R. Prowse and Jos. Bennet had twenty-one year leases granted to them so that they might erect two wooden bathing houses on the north side of the Harbour. Two years later, on 18th September 1750, Ralph Allen of Bath purchased a property on the Weymouth side of the town for £400. Much rebuilt and altered during the Georgian period, this house is now No. 2 Trinity Road.

Ralph Allen, a Cornishman by birth, had made a fortune out of organising an efficient national postal system: he also owned extensive quarries around Bath, and rose to be its Mayor. From 1750 until his death in 1764, Allen stayed at Weymouth almost every year, spending up to three months each summer at the modest but attractive harbour-side house which was soon crowded with visitors – friends and business associates who were no doubt impressed by their host's enthusiasm for the new resort. Allen's guests in 1758 included Royalty, when he entertained the young Duke of York, brother of the future King George III. Ralph Allen's influence on the development of Weymouth as a health resort was considerable and his interest undoubtedly placed Weymouth on the social map.

By the early 1770s the Weymouth summer season was well established, although the *Sherborne Mercury* of September 1771 found it necessary to report that there was a lack of 'genteel accommodation' for the numerous visitors. This omission was soon to be remedied, for a speculative developer

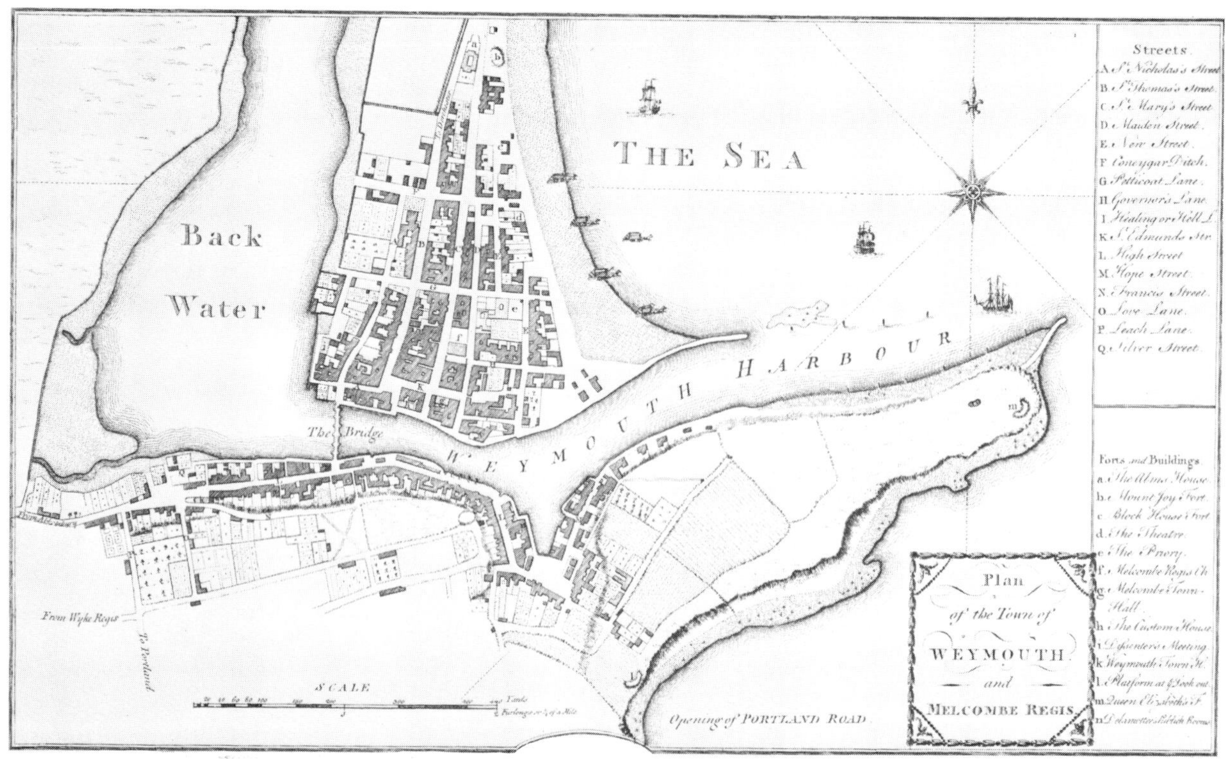

Weymouth in 1774. This plan was first published in John Hutchins' History of Dorset *and is the earliest map of the town which can be considered as accurate.*

The original Royal Hotel, built in 1772 as Stacie's Hotel.

from Bath, Andrew Sproule, had leased waste ground to the north of Melcombe Regis on which he was already constructing a fine hotel and assembly rooms. Sproule's hotel, on the site of the Royal Hotel of today, overlooked Weymouth Bay and stood on open land well beyond the existing town. It heralded a new age of prosperity as Weymouth turned away from the Harbour, its centre and principal source of income for centuries, and looked towards its new assets – the sands and the bay.

An excellent plan of Weymouth during this early period of its development as a resort was included in John Hutchins' *The History and Antiquities of the County of Dorset*, published in 1774. The horse-drawn bathing machines shown on the sands are the most obvious indication of the new seaside industry, but the sea-front has yet to be developed, the buildings shown having back gardens and rear yards leading to what is now the Esplanade. Before the end of the century, fine houses would be built facing the sea.

South of the Harbour, on the Weymouth side of the town, the inlet known as McSaunders Hole was filled in during 1781. Close by were Ralph Allen's house and the resort's first Assembly Rooms. The Duke of Gloucester took tea at these Rooms during a brief visit to Weymouth in 1771 – perhaps this was the first time he visited the town where he was to build his summer home in 1780. When the new Assembly Rooms opened in more fashionable Melcombe, the Weymouth Assembly Rooms gradually declined and were closed by 1785, from which date they were known, as they are today, as the 'Old Rooms'.

In 1772, the new hotel was almost finished and a Mr Stacie became the first proprietor of what was later to become known as the Royal Hotel. During his first season there in 1773, all the apartments were fully booked and some visitors had to seek accommodation elsewhere. With the opening of this hotel, the *Sherborne Mercury* confidently predicted 'there was the greatest probability that Weymouth would be the most frequented bathing place in the Kingdom'. As well as the usual dining rooms, parlours and bedrooms, the bow-windowed hotel and assembly rooms contained a Long Room measuring 70 feet by 40 feet (where a later guidebook claimed one hundred couples could dance with ease), a coffee room, a billiard room, card room and shops for the entertainment of the visitor. To the rear were coach-houses and stabling for sixty horses.

Despite its distance from the major cities, Weymouth was now served by regular mail and passenger coach services. The years since the early visits of Ralph Allen and his friends had seen the establishment of the turnpikes, making travel, if not particularly comfortable, much less hazardous than it had been previously. Weymouth now set about improving the facilities of the town, for wealthy visitors obviously expected certain standards of comfort and safety in the place where they would be spending considerable amounts of time and money during the summer months.

An Act of Parliament which in 1776 made provision for the better upkeep of the streets in the Borough, stated that its streets and alleys were, in general, ill-paved, dirty, badly lighted and often obstructed. To raise funds for improvements, the Act authorised the collection of rates from owners and occupiers of houses and lands. Glass lamps, lamp irons and stands were to be purchased to provide adequate street lighting. Vandalism was anticipated, and a fine of up to forty shillings (£2) awaited anyone should they 'wilfully break, throw down or otherwise damage' these new lamps. The Act laid down the order in which the streets were to be paved, guttered and drained, and authorized the appointment of a sufficient number of able-bodied men to watch and guard the improved thoroughfares of the town.

Some of the other provisions of this Act seem almost to anticipate the 20th century. Parking restrictions were to be enforced. A 5s.0d. (25p) fine awaited any person whose wagon, cart, dray or carriage was left in the street longer than was necessary for loading and unloading, and similar restrictions applied to hire carriages when taking up and setting down passengers.

A glimpse of Weymouth Harbour in 1818, viewed from Barrack Road. It was painted by John W. Upham, and shows the 1770 wooden bridge, as well as the large houses which backed on to the harbour on the Weymouth side.

Numerous rules were to be applied on the town streets. No one was to 'wilfully ride, drive or lead' horses or cattle on the footways. The slaughter of livestock in any open or public place was forbidden. 18th century planning laws did not permit projecting windows, and porches and signs which encroached on to the footway were to be taken down. Thatch was banned from all houses built after the Act, and owners of existing thatched buildings were allowed until 1st January 1784 to replace it with slate, tile or lead. This was an important improvement in crowded streets where fire was a constant hazard, and a better water supply for use in case of fire was also to be introduced.

The Act gave approval for an additional source of income for the town. Toll houses and toll gates were authorized to be erected at the main entrances to the town, where, on Sundays, traffic would be obliged to pay before proceeding into Weymouth:

> For every Horse, Mare, Gelding, or other Beast drawing any Coach, Chariot, Landau, Berlin, Chaise, Chaise-marine, Calash, Vis-a-vis, Curricle or Chair, the Sum of Three-pence. (1¼p)
>
> And for every Horse, Mare, or Gelding, not drawing, the sum of One Penny. (½p)

One payment entitled the ticket-holder to come and go freely on that day. Since the Sunday toll would have penalized the local clergy at their work, all clergymen going to church or chapel were to be exempted from any payment, as were mounted troops, the mails, and animals being taken to and from pasture.

Despite this proposal, there is no evidence that the Sunday tolls were ever levied!

The health benefits and attractions of the growing resort brought Prince William Henry, 1st Duke of Gloucester and Edinburgh, and George III's younger brother, to Weymouth for a longer visit and in 1780 he commissioned a residence for himself. Facing the sea, 'Gloucester Lodge' or 'Royal Lodge' as it was to be known, became the summer palace of King George III during the years 1789-1805.

By 1782 the Corporation was offering to lease all waste lands in the town, and three years later, Weymouth was advertising its attractions in *The Salisbury and Winchester Journal*:

> Weymouth is now, as it has been of late years, the resort of people of the first distinction; and as a Watering Place, it stands unrivalled with any other on the coast. The general Tranquillity of the Bay, the Clearness of the Water, the Softness and almost inperceptible Descent of its Shore, are highly favourable for the purpose of Bathing.

That same year the first edition of De La Motte's *Weymouth Guide* was published, providing interesting glimpses of life at the seaside two hundred years ago. In Weymouth, according to De La Motte, 'Invalids find great refreshment from walking or riding upon the Beach; the Sea Breeze is soft and salubrious; the sands exceedingly firm and pleasant underfoot; and the company are in no wise incommoded by dust'. The bathing machine proprietors thrived as sea bathing grew in popularity. In 1785 'The bathing machines, which are now multiplied to between twenty and thirty, make a formidable arrangement upon the Beach, and are in constant employment for several hours every morning; during which the succession of ladies and gentlemen on this spot greatly enliven the scene'.

Drawn up on the sands ready to take the visitor into the sea for a health giving 'dip', each horse-drawn machine was trundled out to the required depth of water. The horse was then taken back to the shore leaving the bather to enjoy the salt water. If the hirer displayed any reluctance to 'take the plunge' attendants were on hand to assist him down the steps of the machine and into the waves. For the invalid, nervous or cowardly bather, or for those who wished to prepare gradually before entering the sea, there were Hot and Cold Water Baths in a building on the quay.

Another guidebook reprinted part of a famous 18th century treatise on sea bathing, by 'the celebrated Dr. Crane', which recommended that the most proper time for sea bathing was early in the morning, before breakfast. Bathing late in the day would 'occasion great depression of spirits' warned the doctor. His remarks conclude with observations that sea bathing might not suit all temperaments and constitutions in which case it should be discontinued: '. . . sea water being by no means of an indifferent nature; when judiciously managed it does much good; when unadvisedly, and indiscriminately had recourse to, it may do much harm'.

Concerned no doubt, lest the foregoing remarks should dissuade the potential visitor from coming to Weymouth, the editor of the guidebook stressed the 'healthfulness' of Weymouth and its vicinity, evinced by the general state of its inhabitants 'whose chearful looks and glowing cheeks bespeak the purity of the air they breathe . . .'

John Love, bookseller of Weymouth. He died in 1793 aged 41 and weighing 26 stone. In 1790 he published a collection of views of Weymouth by artists of the period.

The 'chearful looks' of the inhabitants are easily explained. Shops were thriving – and multiplying. In addition to the increased demand for food, drink and everyday commodities, there was also a growth in the sale of luxury goods and souvenirs not unlike those sold today. Shells and polished stones from Chesil Beach could be bought, as well as silks, ribbons, laces and trinkets, some no doubt finding their way into Weymouth illegally after being landed by local smugglers.

Sedan chairmen carried the well-dressed visitor around the town lest a silk dress should be muddied in the street. Carriages could be hired to take the visitors to local landmarks and beauty spots – to the ruins of Sandsfoot Castle, the sulphurous spring at Nottington, Maiden Castle or Abbotsbury. Sea trips could be enjoyed in fine weather, to explore Portland, Lulworth and Durdle Door. Libraries provided reading and the circulating library in St Thomas Street advertised its stock as 'rather calculated as a collection of books of elegant amusement than a selection for the use of the learned', whilst finding it proper to add 'that nothing licentious or immoral is admitted'. John Love's 'Repertory' on the Esplanade provided every periodical paper, both town and country, for perusal in the Library, as well as papers for sale. Love kept a *Correct Register* of all the Lodging Houses and a *List of Arrivals* so that visitors could be aware of who else was in residence.

Evening entertainment was provided at the Assembly Rooms, where Balls were held regularly, and also at the little theatre on Weymouth sea-front, built in the early 1770s, long demolished and now the site of the Weymouth Hotel. Presiding over the social scene was Thomas Rodber, in the prestigious post of Master of Ceremonies. To ensure the observance of strict etiquette at the Balls, he published the following:

RULES AND ORDERS

It being absolutely necessary in all polite assemblies to have some regulations established, without which no order or decorum can be observed, the company are humbly requested to comply with the following Rules:

I That Gentlemen are not to appear in the Rooms on Tuesday or Friday evenings, in boots, or Ladies in riding habits.

II That the Balls shall begin as soon as possible after seven o'clock, and finish precisely at eleven.

RATES of CHAIRMEN.

From any part of the town to the Aſſembly-Room,	— — —	1	0
From any part over the water,	—	1	6
Waiting an hour,	— — —	1	6
Every hour after,	— — —	1	0
A ſhort fare,	— — —	0	6

A list of fares issued by the Chairmen in the 1780s.

Fashionable ladies at the Assembly Rooms.

III That Gentlemen and Ladies who dance down a country dance, shall not quit their places till the dance is finished, unless they mean to dance no more that night.
IV That no Lady or Gentleman be permitted to dance in coloured gloves.
V That after a Lady has called a dance, and danced it down, her place in the next is at the bottom.
VI That no tea table be carried into the Card Room.
VII That Gentlemen will be pleased to leave their swords at the door.
VIII That no dogs are admitted.

As yet there were no buildings facing the sea beyond Stacie's Hotel (now proudly claiming in advertisements to be 'within a few doors of His Highness the Duke of Gloucester's'). The Hotel and Gloucester Lodge with its adjoining houses were separated from the town by the large garden of the Lodge known as 'The Shrubbery', occupying the land now filled by Royal Terrace and Frederick Place.

Thus Weymouth in the 1780s was already a thriving resort, enjoying the patronage of the Duke of Gloucester. In 1789 however, a visit took place that was to make it the most famous and fashionable watering-place in the country: George III, recovering from a bout of illness which had alarmed all who had seen him, was to spend a holiday by the sea – at Weymouth.

George III had come to the throne in 1760 at the age of twenty-two. His long reign was to see the growth of the British Empire in India and Canada, but also the loss of the American colonies, and it was this latter event which was to cause so much distress to the King and to become a major contributing factor to his breakdown in health. Modern research suggests that the King suffered from a then unknown illness called 'porphyria' in which defects in the body chemistry lead to an accumulation of toxins which damage the nervous system. The ensuing mental disturbances experienced by the King resulted in the notorious Dr Francis Willis being called in to treat the royal patient. Dr Willis was a clergyman, not a physician, who had made a special study of the insane. His harsh methods combined with the typical and barbaric 18th century medical practices such as bleeding and blistering to remove the 'ill humours', can have had nothing but detrimental effects on the health of his patient.

Rumours regarding the King's 'madness' had abounded, and the journey to Weymouth was made at a leisurely pace to ensure that all his loyal subjects had the opportunity to see that His Majesty was fully recovered and perfectly sane. George III, Queen Charlotte and three of their thirteen surviving children, the Princesses Charlotte, Augusta and Elizabeth, aged 22, 20 and 19 respectively, left Windsor on 24th June 1789, three weeks after the King's fifty-first birthday. At Weymouth, workmen from London were busy preparing Gloucester Lodge and the adjacent houses for the arrival of the royal party and the numerous companions, attendants and servants who accompanied them.

The journey to Weymouth for this first visit took six days and all towns and villages along the route were decorated with greenery, flowers and loyal mottoes, with cheering crowds lining the streets. As the coaches passed through Lyndhurst, Salisbury, Blandford and Dorchester the cheers of welcome grew louder, reaching a peak as the carriages approached the Weymouth Turnpike, at the entrance to the town, at 4 p.m. on 30th June 1789. Here a crowd thousands strong waited to see the King, and after a tumultuous welcome and a pause to greet the Mayor and Corporation, the entourage proceeded to Gloucester Lodge. Salutes were fired from the shore

Gloucester Lodge, as painted by John Upham in 1802. At this time the entrance was at the side of the building, whilst to the south were the enclosed gardens known as 'The Shrubbery'.

batteries at Weymouth, from ships in the Bay and from Portland Castle. Flags were hoisted all over the town, and at night illuminated transparencies were exhibited in the windows of local businesses and shops. Despite what must have been a fatiguing journey, the Royal Family walked on Weymouth Esplanade for about two hours after dinner, to the joy of the throng of people shouting 'God Save the King' and 'Long live Their Majesties'. It is recorded that on viewing the Bay of Weymouth for the first time, His Majesty exclaimed 'I never enjoyed a sight so pleasing'.

This first visit to Gloucester Lodge was to last for ten weeks. 'Royal Lodge' was not a large building and forms only part of the modern Gloucester Hotel. The main entrance at the front of the hotel did not exist in Georgian times, and the royal visitors entered the Lodge through doors at the side of the building. In 1862, a large new wing, part of which was designed to house the exclusive 'County Club' was added to the southern end of the hotel, and the front entrance is probably of the same date. The Gloucester Hotel was seriously damaged by fire on 3rd March 1927, but the outer walls remained intact. During the process of rebuilding, an additional storey was added to the original Royal Lodge, as well as an extra attic floor immediately beneath the roof. John William Upham's watercolour of 1802 was painted when the building was a royal summer home and the large ground floor windows shown are still an attractive feature of the building, although one is partly obscured by the modern verandah which has been added to the front of the hotel.

The original Gloucester Lodge is the part of the building immediately behind the main hotel entrance. The section to the left of the picture was built as the County Club in 1862, but later incorporated with the hotel. A comparison with the painting made by Upham in 1802 will show how the building has been altered over the years.

Fanny Burney, the well-known novelist and diarist, accompanied the royal party to Weymouth in 1789 in her capacity of a 'Keeper of the Queen's Robes'. Her record of the visit provides an entertaining and often ironic view of the life style in the town. She occupied one of the attic rooms at Gloucester Lodge – 'My bedroom is in the attics. Nothing like living at Court for exhaltation' – and she noted that even with the additional accommodation in adjoining houses, the Duke of Gloucester's home could not provide lodging for all the royal staff and a number of footmen were obliged to live some distance away.

On the day after the arrival of the royal family at Weymouth, the Mayor (John Arbuthnot) and Corporation presented the King with a lengthy and often flattering address. 'It is our anxious hope' reads one extract, 'that we shall not soon be deprived of that heartfelt joy which the presence of Our Beloved Sovereign everywhere diffuses. The sight of their Monarch is always grateful to a loyal people, but it is never more so, than, when laying aside the awful splendour of a throne, he condescends to appear amongst them, clothed in the more pleasing, because better known, character of domestic life'.

In her account of this event, Miss Burney clearly felt that the solemnity of the occasion was not all that it should have been.

> One thing however, was a little unlucky: – when the Mayor and burgesses came with the address, they requested leave to kiss hands: this was graciously accorded; but, the Mayor advancing in a common way, to take the Queen's hand, as he might that of any lady mayoress, Colonel Gwynn, who stood by, whispered, 'You must Kneel, sire!' He found however, that he took no notice of this hint, but kissed the Queen's hand erect. As he passed him, in his way back, the Colonel said, 'You should have knelt, sir!'
>
> 'Sir' answered the poor Mayor, 'I cannot'.
>
> 'Everybody does, sir'.
>
> 'Sir, – I have a wooden leg!'
>
> Poor man! 'twas such a surprise! and such an excuse as no one could dispute.
>
> But the absurdity of the matter followed – all the rest did the same; taking the same privilege, by the example, without the same or any cause!

A week after his arrival, George III bathed in the sea for the first time. Fanny Burney judged the event to be a great success and her letters of the period offer revealing glimpses of the general lack of sophistication in Weymouth society, a state of affairs confirmed by the cartoon 'Royal Dipping' published to commemorate the King's bathe:

> His Majesty is in delightful health, and much improved spirits. All agree he never looked better. The loyalty of all this place is excessive; they have dressed out every street with labels of 'God save the King': all the shops have it over the doors; all the children wear it in their caps, all the labourers in their hats, and all the sailors in their voices, for they never approach the house without shouting it aloud, nor see the King, or his shadow, without beginning to huzza, and going on to three cheers.
>
> The bathing machines make it their motto over all their windows; and those bathers that belong to the royal dippers wear it in bandeaus on their bonnets, to go into the sea; and have it again, in large letters, round their waists, to encounter the waves. Flannel dresses tucked up, and no shoes nor stockings, with bandeaus and girdles, have a most singular appearance; and when first I surveyed these loyal nymphs it was with some difficulty I kept my features in order.
>
> Nor is this all. Think but of the surprise of His Majesty when, the first time of his bathing, he had no sooner popped his royal head under water than a band of music, concealed in a neighbouring machine, struck up 'God save great George our King'.

The King and his family remained in residence at Weymouth until August 13th, when the entire royal suite moved westward to Plymouth for an official visit which lasted until August 27th. The following day they all arrived back at Weymouth where they remained until September 14th. The royal family followed various pursuits in Weymouth, and established a pattern for the visits which were to follow. With the exception of the Queen, all the royal party took their regular bathes in the sea, weather permitting. On these occasions the water was cleared of all other bathers, even though the use of the horse-drawn bathing machines enabled royal modesty to be preserved.

What is believed to be the actual bathing machine used by the King in 1789 continued to be used by members of the public until 1916, when it was sold and converted into a summerhouse. Presented to Weymouth Local History Museum in 1971, it has now been completely restored.

The King's daily programme was fairly strenuous, and his staff must have risen very early indeed as, following medical advice, he was sometimes in the sea by 7.30 a.m. Later in the day he usually went riding with his officers. There were frequent excursions in ships of the Royal Navy which were on duty in the Bay throughout the royal visits. A special cruise was made to see the spot where in 1786 the East-Indiaman *Halsewell* had foundered below the cliffs near St Aldhelm's Head with great loss of life. This visit prompted the Dorset poet William Holloway to write 'On their Majesties and the Princesses viewing the spot where the Halsewell was wrecked', a poem first published in *The*

'Royal Dipping' – the King takes his first bathe at Weymouth. The details in the cartoon differ slightly from those described by Fanny Burney, but it is obvious that the King had little privacy and the whole event is depicted as having something of a carnival atmosphere.

The bathing machine which by tradition was used by King George III on his first visit in 1789. This was the largest of the octagonal machines which were such a well-known feature of seaside Weymouth throughout the 19th century.

The improved bathing machine built for the King's second visit to Weymouth in 1791.

Western County Magazine in October 1789.

The King enjoyed his days afloat, but the Queen and Princesses were to tire of the regular routine of cruising in the Channel. The *Sherborne Mercury* later noted the frequent absence of Charlotte, the Princess Royal, and stated that she had developed 'an unconquerable aversion to aquatic excursions'. Another diarist of the royal visit, Elizabeth Ham, had seen the Queen and Princesses 'look very wet and bedraggled' on their return from a day's cruise. On more than one occasion anxious crowds were to gather on the pier scanning the horizon for the first sight of the frigate *Southampton* with the King on board, when boisterous conditions at sea delayed their return until late in the evening.

On one historic day during the King's first visit to Weymouth, there was to be a dramatic contrast between the lives of the royal families of England and neighbouring France, across the Channel. On 14th July, an angry mob stormed the Bastille in Paris, signalling the beginning of the French Revolution and the start of events which were to lead to the eventual execution of King Louis XVI and members of his family. That same day, King George III and his family were sailing off Portland, sure of an enthusiastic and friendly welcome from the crowds awaiting their return to Weymouth.

Visits to local country seats, including Lulworth Castle, Sherborne Castle and Milton Abbey enabled the visitors to see much of the Dorset countryside as well as giving the local gentry an opportunity to show their loyalty and outdo one another in the lavishness of their hospitality.

Special events such as pony racing on Weymouth sands were viewed with interest, whilst walking on the Esplanade was a regular pastime. In the Assembly Rooms the King and the royal family could see and be seen by other visitors to the town. They were regular worshippers at the Parish Church and occasionally services were held on board ship such as on 6th September, when the whole of the royal suite attended Church on H.M.S. *Magnificent*.

There were visits to the theatre in Augusta Place, where the standards were initially so low the manager was forced to hire performers of national repute to entertain his distinguished clientele. The presence of the royal family at Weymouth brought a great influx of extra visitors to the town making accommodation scarce. The price of food rose so high the royal family had their produce sent down from their own gardens at Kew and Windsor, somewhat to the annoyance of local traders. Just such inflation had been envisaged before the royal visitors had even arrived at Weymouth, some thirty local traders having taken space in the *Sherborne Mercury* to state:

Weymouth, June 15th, 1789.

TO PREVENT IMPOSITION

On account of Their Majesties honouring this place with their presence during the summer months, it may be suspected that the price of lodgings and every other article will be considerably advanced; in order to prevent such extortion, we whose names are undersigned are determined not to raise the price of our lodging-houses, or any other article we respectively deal in; and are resolved to use our utmost endeavours to prevent such artifices in others. As a better criterion references may always be had to a correct register of all lodging houses, with their prices at every different period of the year; a plan which had been adopted for these three years last past by J. Love, at his Circulating and Musical Library on the Esplanade.

H. Kellaway, brewer.
Joseph Bennett.
Robert Sexton.
Tim. Scriven.
Rachael Carridge.
W. Johns, Builder.

Proprietors of the Bathing Machines.

Mrs. Bryher, innholder.
Mr. Davis.
R. Wilkinson.
E. & C. Pearse, milliners.
M. Wicker.
J. Richards, joiner.

H. Thornhill.	D. Barlow, wine merchant.
John Dammon.	W. Corp, cabinet maker.
N. Marder, grocer.	Jane Mansell, milliner.
B. Russell, linen draper.	Mrs. Ford.
Mr. Read, miniature painter.	Mrs.Read.
S. Sly, baker.	James Saunders.
J. Love, librarian.	Richard Green, shoemaker.
J. Puckett, cornfactor.	Richard Bartlett, linen-draper.
Mrs. Garland.	B. Harvey, ironmonger.
Morgan Wallas, baker.	J. Gear, linen-draper.
R. Oackley, builder.	Emanuel Bartlett.

De La Motte's guide of the same year advertised hotels and boarding houses. As well as Stacie's, 'The King's Head', 'The Crown' (both now demolished), and 'The Golden Lion' were recommended. Across the Harbour at the Old Rooms where 'Care is also taken, that no improper company be admitted', terms were 16s. (80p) per week for Board (Wine, Tea and Sugar, not included) and 10s. (50p) a week for each Room. Out of season the room charges were halved, but 'Fire and Candle' were extra.

The King, Queen and Princesses left Weymouth on September 14th, 1789 and it must have been with some satisfaction that the town noted the comment when they arrived at Windsor '. . . it was with extreme pleasure that the health of His Majesty appeared to be completely restored . . .'

Although the King did not visit Weymouth in 1790, there was no fall in the popularity of the resort. His brothers, the Duke of Gloucester, builder of Gloucester Lodge, and the Duke of Cumberland, stayed in the town, and the nobility and gentry still crowded its streets. By the following year Mr Stacie's establishment had adopted a new title – 'The Royal Hotel and Assembly Rooms', a name which has survived to the present day although Stacie's Hotel was pulled down and replaced by a new building in the 1890s.

George III's serious illness did not recur until 1801 and his visits to Weymouth between 1791 and 1800 were primarily family holidays, although the enjoyment of the health-giving properties of sea bathing was still an important feature every day. The summer of 1791 was almost over when on 3rd September His Majesty, the Queen and the three Princesses once again arrived at Gloucester Lodge. On this occasion they made the journey in one day, in fact the speed of travel was such that friction in a wheel-bearing of the Princesses' carriage set it alight and they had to complete the journey in a carriage appointed for some of the equerries. In general the royal holiday followed much the same pattern as the first visit in 1789. However, the local bathing machine proprietors had taken the opportunity to build a much larger and better equipped machine for the use of His Majesty, a detailed description of which was later published:

The King's Bathing Machine is in the form of an oblong at its base, and painted white, with the panels blue and red cornices, but is destitute of lining. The outside, at the top, forms a semicircle, on the extremity of which stands upon a pole, of about two feet in length, the crown; and on the other, the British flag, on a pole, or standard, of about ten feet high; on the front is painted the King's arms.

The Queen having determined to try the effects of bathing, there has been a machine new painted and fitted up.

There is some uncertainty as to whether the Queen actually bathed, but it is recorded that one Tuesday Her Majesty and the Princesses enjoyed what was described as 'a curious marine excursion'. They entered the Royal Bathing Machine which was then drawn into the sea as far as the depth of water would permit. Here they sat for some two hours, viewing the surrounding scene

In 1792 Bennet's new Floating Bathing Machine was introduced to give complete privacy and shelter to the royal family when they bathed. It was moored alongside Weymouth Quay where it also served as a Landing Stage.

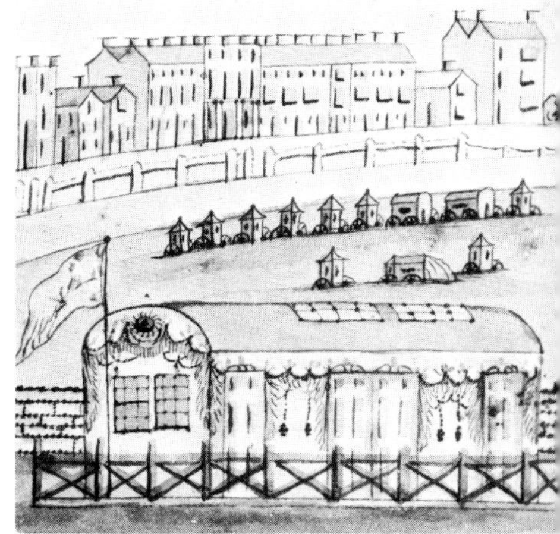

The Royal Barge leaving Weymouth Harbour, taking the King and royal family on one of their aquatic excursions. The far side of the harbour as seen in this view is now the site of Pulteney and Devonshire Buildings. From a painting by J. T. Serres (1759 – 1825).

through telescopes, whilst a large crowd gathered to watch from the shore.

The season was nearly over and there were no sea excursions, but the usual visits were paid to the local nobility and gentry, and the King took the opportunity to study Dorset sheep farming in some detail. He rode and hunted, and paid his first visit to Portland, visiting the quarries, castles, lighthouses and church. The visits to Portland became a regular feature of the King's annual stay in Dorset. He would dine at the 'Portland Arms' in Fortuneswell, now known as the 'Royal Portland Arms'. He was fond of Portland mutton, a local delicacy that always appeared on the menu when he visited the Island.

At Weymouth, on the occasion of the birthday of the Princess Royal, two prizes of ten guineas were awarded – one to be sailed for, the other to be rowed for. Royal birthdays and anniversaries were usually celebrated in some way, and the King's large family ensured that these events were regular occurrences.

Although the royal family returned to Weymouth in 1792, they failed to appear in 1793, the year that France declared war on England. Great concern was expressed over the lack of defences at Weymouth, especially by John Harvey, the proprietor of Assembly Rooms on the Esplanade, and 'Watchmaker and clockmaker to King George III' (one of Harvey's clocks being in use at Royal Lodge). He prepared a pamphlet urging the strengthening of the defences in the area by the building of a breakwater to form an enclosed harbour at Portland – although it was to be more than fifty years before the foundation stone of Portland Breakwater was laid.

In 1794 the royal visitors were back again, and this was to be the last time that Weymouth was to see Princess Charlotte, (The Princess Royal), who later married Frederick, Prince of Wurtemburg, and moved to Germany. Joining the royal party for the first time was Prince Ernest, the King's fourth son, who became a regular companion to his father on his daily walks and excursions on horseback. Later created Duke of Cumberland (and in consequence sometimes confused with his uncle who was here in 1790), he is now remembered locally by a road name on the Weymouth industrial estate.

The fear of a French invasion was by now acute and the concentration of troops in the area, which was to increase every year, saw the introduction of a new feature of the King's visits – the regular reviews of troops in camps and barracks in and around the town. Local volunteer forces were raised, and the variety of uniforms added colour and excitement to the daily parade along the Esplanade.

From 1794 onwards, the royal family visited Weymouth every year until 1802, and then again in 1804 and 1805. The visits followed a more or less set routine, with the occasional highlight to enliven what must have been a somewhat boring holiday for the younger members of the party. The domestic life of the royal family was a good subject for the pen of the cartoonist, whilst the Queen's continued objection to the high prices of food at Weymouth produced the following jingle:

The Mail arrives! Hark, Hark, the cheerful horn,
To Majesty announcing oil and corn;
Turnips and cabbages, and soup and candles;
And lo, each article Great Caesar handles!
Bread, cheese, salt, catchup, vinegar and mustard,
Small beer and bacon, apple-pie and custard;
All, all from Windsor greets his frugal Grace,
For Weymouth is a d----d expensive place.

The town's fame as a health and pleasure resort grew with each royal visit. The welcome given to the King on each occasion continued unabated. Crowds and a huge military contingent greeted him in 1795 and this year he again spent much time reviewing the troops at Southdown, Wyke Common, Radipole Hill and Dorchester Barracks. The royal holiday of 1796 also saw frequent reviews of the troops, and excursions from Weymouth to one of the camps nearby became an almost daily occurrence. The grand review held at Maiden Castle in September even included a mock battle between the Light and Heavy Cavalry.

The 1797 visit began in a heatwave but was later marred by rain and storms. Despite the changeable nature of the English climate, royal birthdays continued to be a good excuse for a celebration; and in the following year, that of Princess Charlotte, Duchess of Wurtemburg, was marked (in her absence) by general festivity at Weymouth and rural sports at Maiden Castle. The sports were attended by the King, Queen and all the Princesses, with a number of the nobility, the various contests being of a somewhat rumbustious nature if the printed programme is any indication.

All persons of jovial, friendly, and loyal dispositions, are invited to be present at, and to partake of the undermentioned country sports, which with others, to be declared upon the ground, are intended, if the weather is fine, to be exhibited at Maiden Castle, near Dorchester, this day, September 20, at 11 o'clock in the morning in honour of the Birthday of Her Royal Highness the Duchess of Wurtembergh: –

To be played for at Cricket, a Round of Beef – Each man of the winning set to have a ribband.
A Cheese to be rolled down the Hill – Prize to whoever stops it.
A Silver Cup to be run for by Ponies, the best of three heats.
A Pound of Tobacco to be Grinned for.
A barrel of beer to be rolled down the Hill – Prize to whoever stops it.
A Michaelmas-day Goose to be Dived for.
A good Hat to be Cudgelled for.
Half a Guinea for the best Ass in three heats.
A handsome Hat, for the Boy most expert in catching a Roll dipped in Treacle, and suspended by a String.
A Leg of Mutton, and a Gallon of Porter, to the winner of a Race of 100 Yards, in Sacks.
A good Hat to be Wrestled for.
Half a Guinea to the Rider of the Ass, who wins the best of Three Heats, by coming in last.
A Pig – Prize to whoever catches him by the Tail.

Royal economy was good material for the cartoonist – 'Frying sprats' and 'Toasting muffins' suggest one way in which the King and Queen faced up to inflated prices!

The King walking on Weymouth Esplanade in 1797. It has been suggested that the man leaning on his stick on the right was the Mayor of Weymouth!

The highlight of the visit of 1798 however, was the announcement of Admiral Nelson's victory at the Battle of the Nile on 1st August. A messenger from London brought word of the victory to the King on the evening of 2nd October, and it was conveyed almost immediately to the company attending the customary Tuesday evening ball at Stacie's Assembly Rooms, who greeted the news with cheers. Next day crowds thronged the sea-front and saw victory salutes fired by the ships in the Bay and repeated by the troops lined up on the sands – men of the Third Guards, the Berkshire, the Shropshire, the North Hants and the Cheshire Regiments, as well as the Weymouth Volunteers. The King personally acquainted several people with Nelson's triumph before embarking for a day's sailing.

There were further celebrations in the evening when the royal family visited the theatre, where the entertainment commenced with a long oration delivered by Mr Fisher. Its contents can be summed up by the first four lines:

> Another Conquest swells Britannia's fame!
> Let grateful memory wait on Nelson's name;
> In distant seas the conquering hero shows,
> How vain the projects of our Gallic foes.

One day when out riding near Weymouth, the King observed a lone woman working in a field. Pausing to ask her why she had not gone to town to see the King, he was told that 'somebody had to stay and get on with the work'. She was rewarded with a guinea for her industry, and only then realised the identity of her distinguished visitor.

Before the evening was over, a band had played 'Rule Britannia', the royal family and clowns had been decorated with wreaths of oak and laurel, and a Mr Penley had given a dissertation on hobby horses. Later, much of the audience trooped through the illuminated streets to a dinner for 200 at Stacie's Hotel. It must have been quite an evening!

At Mr Wood's Library on the Esplanade, a subscription was opened for 'the wives and orphans of those brave men who so gloriously fell in the ever-memorable action of the mouth of the Nile', to which the proceeds from two performances at the theatre were donated by royal command, as were the proceeds from a ball at the Assembly Rooms.

By 1799 Weymouth was at the height of its fame as a resort, and the *Sherborne Mercury* announced that the town '. . . had seldom heretofore had to boast of a greater assemblage of rank, beauty and fashion than at present . . .' and so many fashionable families had arrived '. . . that every house is crowded'. More buildings were now being erected along the seafront and Royal Crescent beyond Stacie's Hotel was under construction. Original plans show a slight curve to the intended terrace of forty-nine houses, but although the Crescent kept its name, it was built as a straight row and is only one third of its planned length. The back yards at the southern end of the Esplanade became the site of seaward facing houses, as Clarence Buildings, Augusta Place, Charlotte Row and the other regally named terraces were fitted in – their names now, alas, lost in the modern renumbering of the Esplanade.

Walling of the Esplanade itself, which was previously faced with turf, began in 1800, the contractors being James Hamilton and Robert Vining. The wall was to be six feet high and two feet thick and it was stipulated that 'such wall to be warranted to stand against the force of the sea for ten years from completion'. The names of Hamilton and Vining become very familiar to anyone studying the Georgian architecture of the town. Hamilton was the better known and his work outside Weymouth included the design and erection of the obelisk to the memory of James Frampton at Moreton, and work on Bridport Town Hall and the Cobb at Lyme Regis. A fine monument at All Saints Church, Wyke Regis, commemorating the loss of the ship *Alexander* on Chesil Beach in 1815 is also Hamilton's work.

There were plans to embank the Melcombe Regis shore of the Backwater and to construct a road to carry traffic clear of the town to the bridge, away from the elegant Esplanade where the visitors walked or rode in their carriages. One building lost to the town in 1800 was the barracks on the Nothe, destroyed by fire and replaced by the present Red Barracks overlooking the harbour.

There were three main army barracks built at Weymouth to accommodate the troops stationed in the town because of the presence of the royal family. In addition to one on the Nothe there was the Cavalry Barracks at the western end of Coneygar Lane (now Lower Bond Street), adjoining the Backwater, and Radipole Barracks to the west of the main Dorchester road at Lodmoor Hill. The Cavalry Barracks was later converted to a tenement block and was known throughout the 19th and early 20th centuries as 'Burdon's Buildings', whilst Radipole Barracks has almost disappeared beneath the housing developments of Westbourne Road, Grosvenor Road and Alexandra Road.

Two well-known names in the town's social life – John Harvey of Harvey's Library and Card Assembly and John Love of Love's Repertory and Library were publishing descriptions of Weymouth during the Georgian period. Harvey's *Improved Weymouth Guide* of 1800 must have been an invaluable companion for many a visitor and John Love's collection of *Picturesque views of the Countryside in and around Weymouth* are an attractive record of the area at the time of the royal visits. Harvey claimed to provide 'an account of the many alterations this salubrious spot has recently undergone'. His description of the sea-front in 1800 is an interesting one:

> The Esplanade, which even boys remember to have been nothing but a place where the inhabitants deposited all the rubbish of the town, is in so short a space converted into one of the most charming promenades in England, and adorned by a range of handsome edifices, which though not regular, altogether forms a very genteel appearance; beyond this is a regular row of elegant buildings called Gloucester Row, from whence to the turnpike the range of houses are to be continued, which from the bottom of the Esplanade, will extend nearly a mile in length.

Harvey was not modest in advertising his own premises:

> The principal Library is built in a very elegant style, delightfully situated about the center of the Esplanade; where there is a commodious room to read the Newspapers, &c. with every suitable

accommodation to make it agreeable to the Nobility and Gentry who continually resort to it. The Card Room over the Library is 45 feet long, 23 wide and 16 feet high, and is very handsomely furnished. It may not be presumptious to say that it deserves to be ranked among the first Libraries in the Kingdom.

The building is certainly an impressive one with its colonnaded front, now No. 51 The Esplanade.

More than thirty bathing machines were available for hire, each supplied with two towels 'perfectly clean and dry'. 6d (2½p) hired the machine, but if attendants were required there was a charge of 6d. (2½p) each. Umbrella machines, fitted with a large hood which could be pulled down when the machine reached deep water, enabled the bather to take his dip in complete, if somewhat claustrophobic privacy, and were more expensive at 1s.0d. (5p) per hiring. The Hot and Cold Sea Water Baths were costly – 3s.6d. (17½p) per person before six o'clock in the evening and 4s.0d. (20p) after six; whilst ladies bathing in the evening with a guide paid 4s.6d. (22½p). Harvey slipped in another advertisement here – bath caps could be had at his Library on the Esplanade. The Queen certainly bathed during the royal visit of 1800 – the papers reported that she used the Warm Bath 'every other night'.

Weymouth Bay in 1812, a pair of views by John W. Upham.

The main talking point of the visit of 1800 was the 'indisposition' of

twenty-two-year-old Princess Sophia, the King's fifth daughter. The Princess was ill at the time of her arrival, and the local gossip insisted that she had given birth to a child shortly afterwards. Attention focused on a new-born baby boy who had been deposited with the wife of a tailor named Sharland, and there was much speculation regarding the identity of the father. The child remained with the Weymouth family until he was about four years old, when he was taken by General Garth of Ilsington Manor, Puddletown, and brought up as his own son. Garth, an equerry in attendance on the royal family at the time the baby was born, was believed to have been Sophia's lover.

A very young visitor accompanied the family on their holidays in 1799 and 1800 – baby Princess Charlotte, daughter of the unhappy marriage between the King's eldest son, George, Prince of Wales, and Caroline of Brunswick. Rather charmingly, the *Gentleman's Magazine* reports a visit by the Queen (her grandmother) and the Princesses to Mr Ryal's toyshop in Weymouth to purchase toys to entertain the little girl.

Joe Grimaldi, the famous clown, was a regular visitor to the Theatre Royal at Weymouth, and on one occasion interrupted his normal act to recite the following lines of doggerel,believed to be his own work. Whilst by no stretch of the imagination a work of great literary merit, it does give a light-hearted glimpse of Georgian Weymouth.

Many towns I have oft heard extolled
For their cleanliness, beauty and trade,
Their churches and buildings so old,
And their streets so completely well made.

But the place of all places for me,
Is Weymouth, so handsome and gay,
Where you sniff the salt air of the sea,
And drive your complaints all away.

On the grand esplanade you may walk
Where Beauty and Fashion combine;
There you hear the Nobility talk,
Lord, Chancellor, Duke and Divine.

On the sands see the curricles roll,
Gay chariots and tandems beside,
And ladies – between pole and pole –
By the help of two men take a ride.

There are Bathing Machines in a row
That you ride in to pickle your skin,
(Kept by Scriven, Ford, Saxon & Co.),
They will cleanse you of all but your sin.

Then the baths you may try, cold and hot,
If your health is not utterly spoiled,
Where, whether you like it or not,
They'll keep you until you are boiled.

Then to Portland for pleasure you go,
Where the natives don't trouble a button
For you or for all that you know,
They're so proud of their stone and their mutton.

Can Weymouth be equalled? Oh no!
And here is a proof I will bring,
For beside these delights it can show
That it adds to the health of our King.

It was not until 1801 that the King purchased Royal Lodge from his brother and marked the occasion by spending the longest period ever in residence, 3rd July to 1st October. This year had seen a decline in the King's health and a recurrence of the distressing symptoms which so alarmed his Court in 1788.

Although a visit to Weymouth in 1803 had to be cancelled due to the

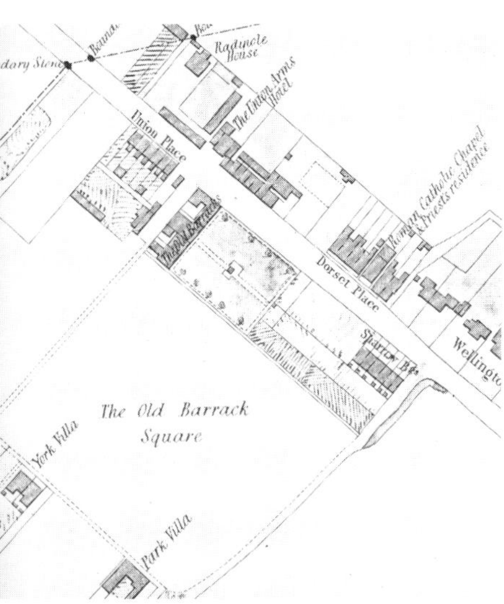

Plan of Dorchester Road area in 1857, showing the site of the former Radipole Barracks, now enclosed by Westbourne and Alexandra Roads.

invasion scares which marked the renewal of the war with France, the 1804 summer holiday went ahead. As was usual, the Army was much in evidence, leading to endless inspections and parades. Because of the renewed threat from the French, the number of troops stationed in the area had greatly increased. George III himself had expressed anxiety about the security of the coast and had prepared a scheme for the concentration of local troops. Frederick, Duke of York, the King's second son had been promoted Commander-in-Chief of the Army in 1798, and he joined the royal family at Weymouth on 1st September, 1804, to attend yet another 'Grand Parade', accompanied by his younger brothers, the Dukes of Kent, Cambridge and Sussex.

That summer, two regiments of King George III's Hanoverian troops were stationed near the town; one regiment at Dorchester and the Brigade of German Light Dragoons at Radipole Barracks. Other regiments were stationed in the temporary camps around Weymouth.

Much of the preparation for defence against invasion was in the hands of the local volunteer forces, and from 1798 onwards, in addition to the Dorset Yeomanry, many Dorset towns had their own volunteer corps. The arrangements for mobilising the volunteer forces and the evacuation of non-combatants was planned in great detail, the county being divided into ten geographical divisions. Extensive surveys were made of each of these divisions and lists prepared showing the availability of supplies, food stocks, livestock and transport, together with the numbers of able-bodied men and women, those who could bear arms and those who would require help in the event of an invasion. Signal stations and a network of hill-top beacons were set up along the coast to warn of an enemy's approach.

The activities of 1804 are particularly well recorded in the diaries of a Captain Landmann, a fortifications expert who was stationed at Weymouth to advise on coast defence. Landmann appears to have had a natural aptitude for doing the wrong thing. The poor man not only collided with the Queen whilst walking on the Esplanade, but also distinguished himself by trying to arrest Lord Hawkesbury as a vagrant. On a visit to Portland with the King and senior officers, he added to his escapades by letting his horse get out of control and leaping with it right over the edge of the cliff. Landing on a ledge a few feet down, Captain Landmann records how, on getting to his feet again and quietening his horse, he looked up to see a very worried royal face peering down at him from the clifftop above.

Weymouth's years as England's most fashionable resort were now drawing to a close, for the King's health was worsening. 1804 marks its peak, for 'The town was never more crowded since His Majesty has done it the honour to visit it, nor was the rent of the houses ever higher'.

The final visit of George III to Weymouth took place in 1805, when he arrived on 13th July. His Majesty was seen to be wearing a green eyeshade and there was concern about his sight. The greatest number of troops ever seen in the Weymouth area were on duty, a garrison of over 10,000 men, with an entire regiment piquetted on the Esplanade every night.

During the last visit of the royal family to Weymouth, one of the sights of the town was the wreck of the East Indiaman *Earl of Abergavenny*, which had foundered two miles out in Weymouth Bay earlier in the same year. On her fifth voyage, in convoy, for Bengal and China, under the command of Captain John Wordsworth, the ship carried more than 400 passengers and crew. On 5th February, in increasing bad weather, the signal was made that

Survivors of the wreck of the Earl of Abergavenny *being rescued by a Weymouth vessel, 5th February 1805.*

Weymouth Esplanade and Harbour mouth, 1821. The pier on the Melcombe side extends only just beyond Devonshire Buildings. Painting by J. W. Upham.

the eight ships sailing in convoy should make for the shelter of the nearest port. The *Earl of Abergavenny* headed for Portland Roads, but according to contemporary sources 'having on board a pilot who did not seem well acquainted with the coast', she struck hard on the Shambles Bank. The extent of the damage the ship had suffered was badly underestimated and initially no distress guns were fired as attempts were made to get her off. Captain Wordsworth decided to run for Weymouth but it soon became obvious that the ship could not last – water was pouring in and the pumps were unable to cope.

The *Earl of Abergavenny* sank in the late evening, just over two miles out in a line from where the Jubilee Clock now stands on Weymouth Esplanade. More than three hundred people drowned that night; many who clung to the rigging lost their hold in the freezing gale before rescuers could reach them. The bodies which were washed ashore were buried in the local churchyards, and the Poet Laureate, William Wordsworth, dedicated his 'Elegiac Verses' to the memory of his brother John, who died 'by calamitous shipwreck' at Weymouth.

Peter Green, a sailor, who as a child kissed George III and later served on H.M.S. Victory *at Trafalgar. Photographed on the Quay in about 1865.*

The masts of the wrecked East Indiaman showed above water, and sightseers visited the spot by boat. For the royal party, shipwreck sites had featured as part of both their first and last holidays at Weymouth.

On 26th August, the King received the news of the death of his brother the Duke of Gloucester, the builder of Gloucester Lodge. There was a week of mourning in Weymouth and great distress in the town, which looked upon the Duke of Gloucester 'as their first patron and benefactor and as the sole means of introducing his royal brother here'.

The royal family left Weymouth on 4th October. On that same day, Admiral Lord Nelson, cruising off Cadiz with the British fleet, laid before his officers a simple plan of attack, which two weeks later was to result in the total defeat of the French and Spanish fleets at the Battle of Trafalgar.

The following year the *Sherborne Mercury* reported from Weymouth, 'It is with much concern we now generally believe that His Majesty and the royal family will not honour this place with their presence this season . . .'. They were never to return again as a family.

The health of the King continued to deteriorate, until in 1811 a Regency was declared. The old King lived on, a recluse at Windsor, until his death in 1820. Because his illness was so completely misunderstood at the time, history remembers him as 'mad King George', and it is no wonder that he welcomed the peace of the Dorset countryside. There can be no denying that his regular visits to Weymouth established the fortunes of the town as a health and pleasure resort. He was the first of the Hanoverian Kings who could be considered English, and was never happier than when engaged in his rural or seaside excursions, which had included fourteen long holidays at Weymouth.

EIGHT

Consolidation

The 'Grateful Inhabitants' of Weymouth resolved in 1803 to commemorate the royal patronage which had resulted in the town's rise to fame by erecting a statue of George III. This tribute to the resort's most illustrious visitor was commissioned from Coade and Sealy's Ornamental Stone Manufactory in Lambeth. It was to be made in artificial Coade Stone, and was finished and shipped to Weymouth in October, 1804, the manufacturers charging 200 guineas for:

Modelling Statue of His Majesty in his royal robes decorated with the Order of the Garter – an antique Table supported with Lyons legs behind him bearing the Crown on his right and books of the Constitution of England on his left – Against the table is a very bold Cornucopia with the Arms of Great Britain and Ireland. In His Majesty's right hand, the Sceptre, At his left, the Sword, Whole Extent abo' 14 feet by 19′3″ high.

The £210 had also paid for 'the Lyon and Unicorn' and the remainder of the £254.8s. (£254.40) bill was for making preliminary drawings of the proposed statue (which had to receive Royal approval before work could commence) and for the enormous quantity of deal required to fashion the wooden cases into which the figures were carefully packed for the voyage from London to Weymouth.

The King's Statue was not erected on its present site until five years later, when the leading townsmen who had commissioned it presented the Statue to the Borough in celebration of the King's Golden Jubilee. On 25th October 1809 the foundation stone was laid at the entrance to Weymouth's main streets – St Thomas Street and St Mary Street. The inscription on the monument is a simple one:

The *grateful* Inhabitants
TO GEORGE THE THIRD
On His entering the 50th Year
Of his REIGN
J. HAMILTON
ARCHT.

Inscribed on its reverse is a long record of the manner in which the town celebrated the occasion. As well as the presentation of the customary 'Congratulatory Address' to the King, there was a more charitable aspect to the event, for at a public meeting it had been decided that as 'Dinners and general illuminations are ill-adapted to this occasion or to the awful times in which we live' alms would be given to the poor and money used for the relief of the townsfolk then held prisoners of war by the French.

Although George III never saw the monument which Weymouth erected in his honour, others of his family did witness the laying of the foundation stone. In the autumn of 1809 three of the King's children came back to Weymouth, staying from September to early November. The Princesses Mary and Amelia arrived first, and were joined about a week later by their brother Adolphus, Duke of Cambridge. This was a quieter visit than the previous royal holidays for twenty-six-year-old Amelia was seriously ill. The local press reported that

The King's Statue about 1900. The 'round houses' between St Thomas and St Mary Street had yet to be converted to shops.

she benefited from her stay, and she was taken out into the Bay in a bathing machine 'for the purpose of inhaling the sea air in its greater purity'. Mary and Adolphus attended the stone-laying ceremony, but there is no record of any member of the King's family being present when the Statue was unveiled a year later on 25th October 1810. Their absence was no doubt due to the fact that Princess Amelia, George III's beloved youngest daughter, now lay dangerously ill at Windsor – she died just a week later.

Weymouth has grown used to its rather gaudy tribute to King George III, although the statue was not painted in its present heraldic colours until 1949. The lettering of the long account of the Jubilee celebrations on the reverse of the plinth, and the list of those who subscribed to its erection has been so weathered by the salt air as to be almost indecipherable. In recent years this inscription has been copied on a small stone plaque which is now placed at the base of the front of the Statue.

The monument has had a variety of settings over the years; the Victorians surrounded it with evergreen shrubs and railings, whilst more recently, His Majesty has overlooked a collection of bus shelters and the gardens of the traffic roundabout. There have been a number of attempts to alter or re-site the Statue. In the 1880s a ten guinea prize was offered for the best scheme submitted 'for the improvement of the King's Statue' on the grounds that it was 'unsightly', 'hideous' and 'only a mass of pottery'. In 1938 it was thought that the King should give way to the motorist, whose view, it was felt, the Statue dangerously obscured. These ideas, and others, were eventually dropped and it now seems likely that King George III will forever gaze along the sea-front he made famous.

Weymouth's other landmark commemorating the royal visits, the White Horse at Osmington, is fittingly carved in the chalk of the hills where the King so much enjoyed riding with his officers. The equestrian figure on the slope of the hill facing Weymouth Bay was carved during the summer of 1808 and a contemporary account recorded that 'the likeness of the King is well preserved' in the chalk cutting, 280 feet long and 323 feet high. There is a popular but incorrect local legend that George III objected to the White Horse because it showed him riding away from Weymouth and in consequence he never visited the resort again. The truth is that the King never saw the chalk

The owld White Harse wants zetting to rights,
If some un ull promise good cheer,
They'll gee un a scrape to kip un in zhape,
And a'll last for many a year.
Jarvis Harker, c1877.

figure since it was not cut until three years after his last visit to the town. The cutting of the White Horse was a private venture paid for by John Ranier and the work was directed by Weymouth bookseller John Wood who owned the land at Osmington.

A boat trip to see the White Horse, 'as from the Bay its view is more complete', was one of the outdoor excursions which could be enjoyed by the visitor to Weymouth. In the evenings, while the wealthy danced and socialised in the fashionable Assembly Rooms, there is evidence that some of the local inhabitants were disporting themselves in a less genteel manner, as recorded by the Corporation minutes of 1812:

> It appearing that there are frequently public dances in the Inns and Public Houses of this town which are attended by apprentices, servants of both sexes and other young persons in the lower rank of life, and are continued to late hours of the night, whereby debauchery is greatly increased and other vices and crimes are much promoted amongst persons in dependent situations, this meeting taking the same into their serious consideration have determined that public and general notice shall be given that the licence of any innkeeper or victualler who shall permit such dances or assemblies shall not on any account whatsoever be hereafter renewed.

In 1810, 'An act for more effectually cleansing, lighting and watching' the town found the previous similarly-titled Act of 1776 'insufficient and defective' in its provisions. One of the main objects of the new Act was to increase the rates which provided the necessary revenue for any improvements. There were to be more street regulations: the names by which streets, ways, lanes, passages and public places were usually known were now to be 'placed, marked or painted on some conspicuous part of some house or building at or near each end, corner or entrance of the said streets', and buildings in the streets were to be individually numbered. Owners and occupiers were required to sweep the public pavement around their properties every day between 7 a.m. and 10 a.m. and anyone leaving a pile of building materials in the street, or causing a hole to be dug in the street had to affix a light to the obstruction to prevent accidents to passers-by. Among a long list of acts not to be committed in public places, it was forbidden to 'let off or fire any Crackers, Squibs or other Fireworks'; or 'ride or drive any Horse, Cattle or other Beast within the said Borough and Town, so furiously or carelessly as thereby to cause a personal Danger to any one whomsoever'; or to 'bathe in any Manner than by means of a Bathing Machine upon the Sea Sands, or in the Harbour, or Back Water within the said town'.

More bye-laws regulated the tradesmen who plied for hire – the sedan chairmen, bathing machine proprietors, pleasure boat owners and others. It would appear that some of the watchmen and beadles who policed the Borough perhaps neglected their duties, for the 1810 Act makes provision for the immediate dismissal plus a fine of up to £1 for any such official's misbehaviour, as well as fixing the same fine on any 'Victualler, Publican or any other Person selling Spirituous or other Liquors' who should 'entertain or harbour in his or their House or habitation or Shop any Watchmen . . . during any of the Hours or Times appointed for such Watchmen to be on Duty'.

Although the heyday of Royal Weymouth was really over, there were still occasional visits by members of the King's family. The Prince of Wales (Prince Regent from 1811 onwards) had no affection for Weymouth, preferring the attractions of Brighton, but his daughter Princess Charlotte of Wales, who had accompanied her grandparents to the town as a small child, returned to Weymouth in 1814 and 1815 to spend long holidays at Royal Lodge.

Despite, on one occasion, having referred to Weymouth as '. . . this odious place', the Princess clearly enjoyed the benefits of sea bathing and was popular in the town. As her grandfather had done, she visited villages in the neighbourhood, stopping to talk to the local inhabitants as well as visiting the homes of the local gentry. Charlotte had inherited the old King's love of the sea and used the naval guardship as a Royal Yacht whilst in Weymouth. The success of her visit in 1815 led the author of Kay's *Weymouth Guide* to forecast that 'It is generally believed that Weymouth will be the future summer residence of Her Royal Highness'. This, alas, was not to be, for Princess Charlotte Augusta died in childbirth in 1817, just over a year after her marriage to Prince Leopold of Saxe Coburg. Leopold stayed at Royal Lodge after her death, but he was grief stricken and withdrawn, shunning the social life of the town.

William Frederick, Duke of Gloucester, son of the builder of Gloucester Lodge, had married Princess Mary, daughter of George III, and the couple were staying in Weymouth when Charlotte's death was announced in November 1817. The Duke and Duchess left for Windsor immediately, ending the last royal visit which can be directly linked with the family of King George III.

Following the death of the King, the contents of Royal Lodge and the adjoining properties were auctioned in a six-day sale commencing on 15th July 1820. A handsome catalogue listed over two thousand lots ranging from 'A mahogany four-post bedstead and cornice, with white dimity and blue flower border fringed furniture' from Her Majesty's Bedroom, and 'The late King's Writing Table, with double elevating desk, brass rack work and two drawers, on castors' to the everyday items in the Steward's Room – 'Three tin cans,

THE
RESIDENCE AND FURNITURE,
CLOCKS, GLASSES, &c. &c. of
HIS LATE MAJESTY'S,
At Weymouth.

A
CATALOGUE
OF THE ENTIRE ASSEMBLAGE OF
HOUSEHOLD FURNITURE,
OF
Gloucester Lodge, and Four Houses adjoining;
COMPRISING
BRILLIANT PLATE GLASSES,
Valuable and excellent Clocks, by Vulliamy, Harvey, Recordon, and Others;
PIANO-FORTES AND HARPSICHORDS, BY KIRKMAN AND OTHERS.
BAROMETERS & THERMOMETERS, BY FRAZER, WATKINS, ADAMS & OTHERS;
Upwards of One Hundred Bedsteads and Feather Beds, suitable Mattresses and appropriate Bedding;
WARDROBES AND CHESTS OF DRAWERS,
AND A PROPORTIONATE NUMBER OF DRESSING TABLES AND GLASSES,
And every other Chamber Requisite;
DINING, SOFA, CARD, PEMBROKE AND OCCASIONAL TABLES,
CARPETS AND DRUGGETS,
A Variety of Sofas and Chairs of various Classes: Chintz and Dimity Draperies;
BOOKCASES, CABINETS, WRITING TABLES, GLASS WARE, CHINA;
An extensive Assortment of Copper Appendages for the Kitchen and Confectionary;
TWO WATER CARTS, & MISCELLANEOUS ITEMS OF UTILITY & ORNAMENT.

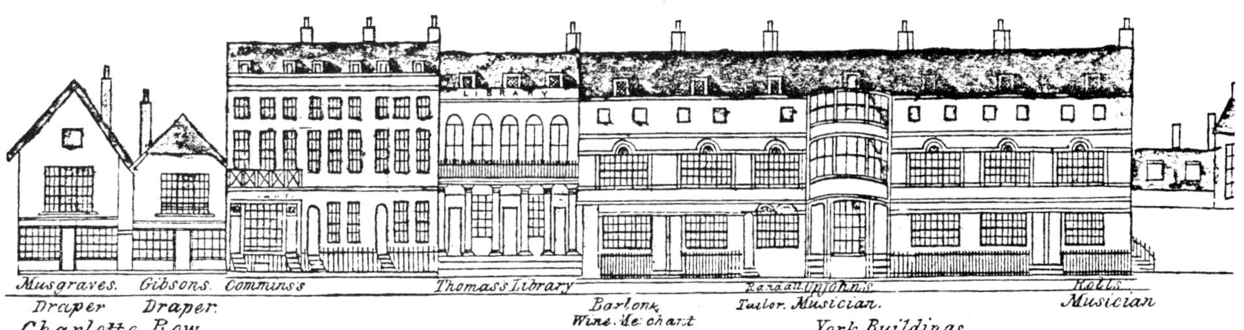

Charlotte Row and York Buildings on Weymouth Esplanade, part of a panoramic drawing of the early 19th century. York Buildings, completed in 1783, was the first terrace built facing the sea.

four tin coffee pots, four iron candlesticks, egg boiler, and three pairs of snuffers' – and Kitchen – 'Twelve saucers and nine cups, fourteen blue and white coffee cups, two basons and two odd saucers'. A contemporary guidebook commented that 'the furniture was purchased at an enormous price, each piece being looked upon as a relic of departed royalty'. Gloucester Lodge itself was bought by William Young for £4000 and the 21 seat royal pew in St Mary's Church fetched £220.10s. (£220.50).

Writing in 1829, George Alfred Ellis, a Weymouth surgeon, stated:

> . . . the Royal Family have not intimated any inclination to revisit this place as a residence. It is now the resort chiefly of those who wish to invigorate their system by bathing in a spot which cannot be equalled by any place in the empire, for the security of the sands, the translucent state of the water, and for the comfort and convenience of the bathers.

The expansion which had begun in the days of 'Royal Weymouth' was to continue throughout the 19th century. Thomas's *Weymouth Guide,* published in 1815 observed that 'the inhabitants by such an influx of money, have been encouraged to rebuild, beautify and greatly enlarge the town: which, in little more than twenty years, has undergone a considerable transformation.'

In 1811 seven houses in Johnstone Row were completed, with the 'roundhouses' added to this and Coburg Place about 1815. Although Royal Lodge was not sold until 1820, some of the adjoining land used as gardens must have been disposed of earlier, as Royal Terrace was built on this site during the years 1816-1818. The four houses in Gloucester Row between Royal Lodge and the Royal Hotel had been built at the time of the King's first visit in 1789 and were used to accommodate members of the royal entourage. Royal Crescent (not a 'crescent' but a straight terrace) was built during the period of the royal visits and was completed about 1805. Belvidere was not commenced until 1818 and its construction spread over many years, the last house not being completed until the 1850s. Brunswick Buildings (now Brunswick Terrace) was completed about 1827 having taken some five years to build, whilst Waterloo Place dates from about 1835. Frederick Place at the northern end of St Thomas Street dates from the 1830s and, like Royal Terrace, was built on what was once the garden of Royal Lodge.

At the southern end of the Esplanade, Pulteney and Devonshire Buildings had been built during the years 1812-1819, on land reclaimed from the sea. The final house in Devonshire Buildings was altered so that it could be completed in a rounded form matching in many ways the roundhouses in the vicinity of the King's Statue and the one planned for the southern end of Brunswick Buildings. Thus, the growth of the Esplanade terraces which had begun during the period of the King's visits was to continue after the end of 'Royal Weymouth', but there was some slowing down in progress during the

No. 1 Frederick Place, on the corner of Westham Road, now converted to 'Forte's Restaurant'.

Victoria Terrace and the Burdon Hotel, completed about 1855. The Dorset Yeomanry were regular visitors to the town in the early years of the 20th century.

1830s and 1840s. The final terrace of the Esplanade, Victoria Terrace, with its central feature the Hotel Burdon (now the 'Prince Regent') dates from 1855 although the style of architecture is in keeping with the Esplanade's Georgian buildings. Modern street numbering has replaced the old terrace names, but full details are given in Appendix G.

Today, the houses on Weymouth Esplanade are almost without exception hotels and boarding houses, but when first built they were for the most part private dwellings. A number were let as 'apartments' during the season, but those used as guest houses were comparatively few until after the arrival of the railway in 1857. Some of the houses on the Esplanade were used as 'summer residences', a reminder that in these early days of Weymouth as a resort it was only the wealthy who could afford extended seaside holidays.

Some idea of the growth of Weymouth during the years following the royal visits can be obtained from the Census returns. In 1811, the first count made after the King's final holiday of 1805, the population was 4,732. Ten years later in 1821, it had risen to 6,622, an increase of 40%. By 1831 the population was 7,655, an increase in the previous ten years of a further 15%. All these extra people had to be housed and whilst the most spectacular building project was the terraces facing the sea, smaller houses were squeezed into the existing town area, whilst the first expansion north from old Melcombe Regis (which prior to 1770 had not extended much beyond modern Bond Street) began with building behind the Esplanade.

The Esplanade itself, the embanking and walling of which had begun in 1800, was 'The pride of Melcombe' until the night of 23rd November 1824, when a near hurricane struck the south coast of England. The 'Great Gale' is most remembered in this area for the awful damage caused at Portland when the sea overflowed the Chesil Beach, drowning more than twenty people and destroying many houses in the village of Chiswell. At Fleet, the sea knocked down several cottages and most of the village church, and the storm caused numerous shipwrecks along the Dorset coast.

There was tragedy at Weymouth too. The sea swept over the spit of land which then separated the Bay and the Backwater at a place called 'the narrows' (the site of the Prince Regent Hotel of today) and drowned two men attempting to cross there. The Esplanade, with its stone posts and iron chains was completely destroyed, the piers were damaged, and vessels, boats and small craft were either driven into the centre of the town, sunk, destroyed or carried out to sea. An inscribed stone post preserved from the old Esplanade has been built into the wall of a raised flowerbed near the Alexandra Gardens.

Even today storms and high tides can cause damage, although since the building of the Portland Breakwaters in the latter half of the last century, the damage has been confined to the northern part of Weymouth bay – the sea wall between Greenhill and Overcombe.

The years which brought the spectacular rise to fame of Weymouth as a holiday resort also saw the revival of the town's importance as a port. It offered the shortest sea route to the Channel Islands and was chosen by the Post Office for the introduction of its Packet Service to Jersey and Guernsey in 1794. The growing importance of the harbour in the early 19th century helped to offset the inevitable slight falling off in popularity as a holiday town, when the ending of the King's visits lost Weymouth the right to the title of 'most fashionable resort'. Initially the mail service ran once weekly, on Thursdays, two 70 ton ex-Dover packet boats *Rover* and *Royal Charlotte* carrying the first mails. A single letter cost 2d. from Weymouth to the Channel Islands and 5d. from London to Weymouth. The packets were not permitted to compete with cargo carrying vessels, but they did take passengers to Jersey and Guernsey. In 1806 sailings from Weymouth were increased to two per week and after the introduction of steam vessels on the service in the late 1820s an experimental thrice-weekly service was tried, but later discontinued.

During this period of increased port trade a new Town Bridge was constructed across Weymouth Harbour in 1824. The former bridge of 1770 had been built opposite the end of St Nicholas Street some 70 yards west of the traditional spot, but although providing a larger harbour area and additional quay space, it was an unpopular site. The new bridge once again crossed the water at the end of St Thomas Street, as its successor does today. Early in 1821 it had been decided to demolish a number of houses on the Weymouth side of the harbour to provide approaches to the new bridge. In one of these buildings large jars filled with silver coins were found, possibly hidden there during the Civil War. The spectators who gathered to watch the removal of the coin hoard soon turned to treasure hunting when a number of jars fortuitously broke while being carried away, spilling their contents.

A link with the gale of 1824 – the original inscribed stone pillar, now built into the wall retaining an Esplanade flower bed.

The last wooden Town Bridge across Weymouth Harbour, 1770 – 1824, and the only permanent bridge built opposite the end of St. Nicholas Street.

The first stone Town Bridge completed in 1824. Partly rebuilt in 1880, the basic structure of this bridge remained in use until 1928.

The original wooden Ferrybridge of 1839, photographed about 1860.

Surprisingly, the 1824 Town Bridge was the first to be made of stone, with a central cast-iron swing section which enabled ships to pass up harbour; all previous bridges had been built of timber, although the possibilities of using stone had been discussed as early as 1669.

Later in 1824 another bridge was under discussion, following the destruction of Smallmouth Ferry in the Great Gale. This tethered ferry was the only link between Portland and the mainland at Wyke Regis, and, as the ferryman had been drowned and the ferry house destroyed in the gale, it provided an ideal opportunity to re-introduce earlier proposals for the provision of a bridge to Portland. The *Dorset County Chronicle* of November 1827 commented: 'Portland Fair, on the 5th inst., in consequence of the fine weather, was numerously attended. There were about 60 head of cattle, and a good supply of pigs and sheep. It is much to be regretted that there is not a *bridge* at the ferry, or a causeway higher up, (so easily to be accomplished). The cattle were swam over the ferry, the pigs and sheep conveyed in the ferry boat. Portland suffers in every point of view from the want of land conveyance'. This report is typical of a sustained campaign in the local press, although the first bridge between Wyke Regis and Portland did not open until 30th January 1839.

The local newspapers continued to head their Weymouth news columns with weekly lists of 'Fashionable Arrivals'. *Benson's Guide* of 1828 claimed that 'nearly the whole town is devoted to public accommodation', with 'numerous commodious and well furnished houses fronting the sea and on both sides of the harbour'. Visitors enjoyed much the same attractions that had pleased George III, with the addition of some new events – including an annual regatta and the three day Weymouth Races held at Lodmoor in August/September. A short-lived but popular tourist attraction from 1826 onwards was a trip by boat to view the 'Burning Cliff' at Holworth, where shale exposed in the cliffs caught fire spontaneously and burned for a considerable period. The dramatic fire caused the curious to experiment with its powers, and in 1827 a local boatman, Peter Green, removed a small quantity of the earth and 'by the heat then existing, broiled a mackerel, fried a slice of bacon and boiled an egg in the ordinary time required over a kitchen fire'.

The columns of the local newspapers also devoted much space to a thriving but strictly illegal 'industry' – smuggling. Faced with gangs of armed smugglers the length of the coast, and the belief by even the most respectable members of the local population that once the goods were ashore it was quite in order to profit from them, the preventive men had an almost impossible task. Smugglers themselves were not considered as wrong-doers as William Lewis's headstone in Wyke Regis Churchyard testifies:

> Of life bereft (by fell design)
> I mingle with my fellow clay,
> On God's protection I recline
> To save me on the Judgment day:
> There shall each blood stain'd soul appear,
> Repent, ah! ere it be too late,
> Or else a dreadful doom you'll hear,
> For God will sure avenge my fate.

Surmounting the inscription is a carving which depicts the *Pigmy* schooner, from which the shot which killed Lewis in 1822 was fired, chasing Lewis's vessel as the smuggler tried to evade capture. These were violent times. James Eaton Robens, born in Weymouth in 1814, recalled the following incidents from his boyhood:

> Smuggling was very rife in the town and neighbourhood and all round the coast. No one was thought worse of for being a 'fair trader'. People in good positions did not scruple to engage in what was very lucrative, if not found out; but risks were heavy. Sometimes fights between the Coastguard and smugglers had tragic endings. I remember seeing a cart being driven into the town containing a lot of kegs which had been captured; but on the top of them lay two corpses. A vessel called the *Good Intent* came into Weymouth Harbour, apparently laden with brooms; these, however, had kegs of spirits concealed beneath. Her owner audaciously anchored her alongside the Customs House, but the cargo was discovered and confiscated. The ship was sold and the prize money came to the men who discovered the fraud. Men taken in the act of smuggling were promptly sent to sea in a man-of-war.

Sentences on captured smugglers could include five years impressment on a man-of-war, heavy fines and the forfeit of their vessels: it is not surprising that the majority attempted to fight their way out of trouble. Letters received by one of Weymouth's long serving Customs Officers, Richard Wilkinson, give some idea of the intelligence service which operated when suspect vessels were in the vicinity. One warned of a Weymouth brig, supposedly bound from Alderney for Lisbon with coal, attempting to land brandy by means of boats and small kegs. The letter ended with a detailed description of the black and white-straked brig 'which you will use your utmost vigilance to detect and seize'.

A typical smuggling incident, which took place on Weymouth sea-front, was reported in the *Dorset County Chronicle* of 1827:

> 2nd September. Early in the morning a large party of smugglers assembled on the Esplanade near Brunswick Terrace, for the purpose of landing foreign spirits from a boat near the shore. On the Preventive Service Boatman (who saw the assembly of smugglers) firing his pistol as a signal to the other Customs Officers, the smugglers violently assaulted him, knocking him down and beating him, and took away his pistols and cutlass. The Commissioners of Customs offered a reward of £100 for the discovery of the offenders.

In March 1829, the Commander of the *Eagle*, revenue cruiser, detained 'after a spirited chase' the French sloop *La Concorde* and discovered the crew attempting to throw her contraband cargo overboard. An examination of two of the casks subsequently picked up revealed one thousand yards of smuggled silk. Under the command of Lieutenant Knight, the same cruiser arrested a boat near Osmington Mills, finding three Englishmen and two Frenchmen onboard, together with 94 casks of spirits. Lieutenant Knight fell victim to a gang of smugglers in 1832 whilst on duty with one of his men near Lulworth. The two preventive men were armed but outnumbered: they were beaten senseless and Lieutenant Knight was thrown over the cliffs. Doctors from Weymouth and Wareham were summoned, but he died from his injuries the following day, leaving a widow and five children. The funeral in Weymouth was impressive, a procession of boats from all the local Preventive Stations accompanying the body by sea from Lulworth. A solemn processon walked through the town, where Knight was buried in the little graveyard in Bury Street. His headstone can be seen in Weymouth Museum, the burial ground having disappeared beneath a modern shopping and car park development.

Regular auction sales of contraband goods which had been seized were held at the Customs House in Weymouth. One sale in 1832 included 1501 gallons of brandy, 263 gallons of Geneva and quantities of rum, currants, sugar, silk and numerous smaller items.

PORT OF WEYMOUTH.

By Order of the Honourable Commissioners of His Majesty's Customs.

On TUESDAY, 7th of Sept., 1830, at Eleven o'clock in the Forenoon, will be exposed

TO PUBLIC SALE,

At the CUSTOM-HOUSE, WEYMOUTH, (at a Price not less than the Duties,)

652 Gallons BRANDY, 72 Gallons GENEVA, fit for Dealers; 25lbs. Currants, 1 Bottle Eau-de-Cologne, 1 Glass Tumbler, 28lbs. Soap, 4lbs. Sugar, 1lb. Chocolate, 10lbs. Coffee, 56lbs. Rope, 1 Bottle Rum, 1 Fathom Firewood, 2 Open Boats, and the Broken-up Hulls of 4 Ditto, with their Materials.

For Exportation.—1 Clock Stand of Or-molu, 1 Pendulum, 1 Glass Shade, 1 Pair Silk Braces, 2 Silk Cravats.

For the Duties.—21 Yards Printed Cotton, 46 Dunnage Mats, 11 Yards Paper Hangings, 1 Bottle Eau-de-Cologne, 1 Glass Figure, 2 Pair Clogs, 28lbs. Soap, 3lbs. Sugar, 4lb. Marmalade, 12lbs. Wax Candles, 4 Bottles Brandy, 1 Bottle Geneva.

A Quantity of old unserviceable Coast-Guard Stores, consisting of Rope, Sails, Blocks, Broken-up Boats, &c. &c.

☞ The Goods may be viewed by applying at the Custom-House two days prior to the Sale only.

Notice of the sale of confiscated goods taken by the Preventive Men, from the Dorset County Chronicle, *August 19th 1830.*

The Customs men were not only looking for smuggled goods when they searched the vessels which came into Weymouth Harbour: cases of sickness onboard also had to be investigated. Impure water supplies, unsatisfactory drainage and overcrowded living conditions were sure ways to spread the diseases such as typhoid and cholera which were still endemic in the 19th century. The progress of epidemics was closely watched and precautions were taken to prevent disease coming ashore – a task made more difficult by the arrival and departure of many visitors. During the cholera epidemic of 1832 on the Channel Islands, a small vessel arrived off Weymouth 'with a number of women and children, and was immediately boarded by the Customs and not allowed too near the shore, as a suspicious case lay on board. An old woman was reported to be extremely ill – she died in the course of the day – was sown up in a hammock filled with stones – taken off to sea and sunk. The vessel was immediately sent to the quarentine ground at Plymouth.'

The French wars of the early years of the 19th century affected the everyday life of a seaport such as Weymouth in many ways. Local seamen were away serving in the navy, and coastal trade was affected to varying

The Post Office Steam Packet Flamer *in Weymouth Bay about 1835. Her normal passage time to Jersey was about 14½ hours.*

degrees. Whilst increased smuggling imported luxury goods, everyday commodities were often in short supply, and in September 1812 the Corporation decided to take action over the high cost of bread in the town by appointing a Mr How to buy 'loaves of good wholesome bread' in Dorchester and elsewhere for sale to the poor.

The 1830's were a period of considerable change for Weymouth. The physical shape of the town was to be radically altered, whilst in Parliament the Whig reformers were introducing laws affecting parliamentary and municipal elections and the provision of relief for the poor. By the end of the decade there were real fears that Southampton might well take over the Channel Islands Packet Service, and as railway lines snaked their way across the country it became obvious that other seaside resorts would soon be well placed to compete for the holiday trade, although as early as 1833 Weymouth was encouraged to hope for its own rail link.

On the passing of the Reform Act of 1832, Weymouth and Melcombe Regis lost its ridiculous and much abused privilege of sending four representatives to Parliament. The corruption which had characterised elections in the town in the previous century had continued into the 1800s as candidates bribed and cheated their way into Parliament. The fraudulent and temporary division of freeholds to obtain extra votes was common practice and money and gifts were freely distributed by prospective M.P.s to ensure they were duly elected. Treating with free beer was probably the most popular and successful bribe, and over-indulgence led to some ugly scenes at the local elections.

The most notorious parliamentary election took place in June 1826, when there were scenes of 'wild anarchy, riot and confusion' in the town as a mob broke into the old Guildhall, knocked down the chief magistrate, took the hall by storm, destroyed the polling books and closed the poll. The main trouble arose from the violence of a mob, largely of Portlanders, who had been hired by one of the candidates, attempting to physically prevent supporters of his opponents reaching the poll. Some voters had their clothes ripped off as they ran the gauntlet, and the military had to be called in to restore order.

From 1832-1885, Weymouth and Melcombe Regis, formerly the most discredited parliamentary borough in England, was permitted to elect only two M.P.s. The Redistribution Act in 1885 took away even this right when all boroughs of less than 15,000 inhabitants were disfranchised and Weymouth became part of the parliamentary constituency of South Dorset.

A degree of apathy affected the work of the Corporation for several years during the 1820s and 30s. Until 1821 they had met regularly to conduct the affairs of the Borough, but from then on 'Insufficient attendance to conduct business' was recorded on numerous occasions. In 1822 the mayoral election was held three months late and no such election took place at all in 1825, 1831 and 1832. Yet, from 1833 onwards, there was considerable suspicion regarding the work of the Municipal Corporation, Commission, and a motion agreed 'to defeat any design that may be in contemplation for wresting from them their ancient Charters, Franchises and Liberties'.

In 1835 the Municipal Corporations Act laid the foundations of the system in use today. The Borough was divided into wards and male ratepayers were to elect the Town Council, its members each serving for a term of three years. The new Weymouth and Melcombe Regis Corporation which took office on 1st January 1836 no longer included the ancient office of Bailiff. (There had been two Bailiffs, one for Weymouth and one for Melcombe Regis, from the inauguration of the combined Borough of Weymouth and Melcombe Regis back in 1571, the office almost certainly having been created in an attempt to placate the old separate Borough of Weymouth, which prior to the union had been led by two Bailiffs instead of a Mayor.)

The same Act required the establishment of regular police forces in the borough; the policing of Weymouth at this date being carried out under the provisions of the 'Watching, Lighting and Paving' Acts of 1776 and 1810. Weymouth Police Force was established in 1846, when an Inspector was appointed, with a force of eight constables. In the years which followed, the force was first increased by the appointment of a sergeant and two extra constables, and by the end of the century additional duties and responsibilities had led to it employing a total of thirty-one officers and constables.

The passing in 1833 of the Act for the abolition of the Slave Trade, although in no way directly concerned with Weymouth, was the result of a long campaign by the Anti-Slavery Society led by William Wilberforce. One of the M.P.s who took a prominent part in the anti-slavery lobby was Thomas Fowell Buxton of Weymouth, a man of integrity who had actually been elected to Parliament in the infamous election of 1826. The Buxton family had built Belfield House, an elegant mansion set in acres of rolling parkland, just south of the main road from Weymouth to Wyke Regis, and it was here that they had entertained royal visitors in George III's day. John Crunden designed the house in the 1770s – today it stands hemmed in by the housing built over its once extensive park. Buxton Road, leading from Rodwell to Wyke Regis, commemorates the name of the family who built one of Dorset's most attractive 18th century houses.

An early view of Belfield House.

Another large 'house' was to be built on the road leading to Wyke Regis and Portland, but the 'Union', on Wyke Road at the top of Boot Hill, was no graceful country mansion. The austere, Portland stone facade of Weymouth Workhouse is typical of the institutions built after the Poor Law Amendment Act became law in 1834. In general, the administration of poor relief during the early years of the 19th century had been rather haphazard, and varied from parish to parish. The Poor Rate was distributed largely as the overseers thought fit, and these officials were often quite unsuited to the job, which was frequently unpaid. Poor relief could be granted in cash, a weekly payment in the 1830s in Melcombe Regis could be a shilling or two, sometimes supplemented by a bread allowance. There was also money available for specific needs – burial expenses, for example – whilst the orphaned, the aged and the sick were usually admitted to the parish poorhouse. The former Melcombe Regis Poorhouse stands at the junction of Commercial Road and Lower St Alban Street and is now owned and used by a boatbuilding company. Weymouth Poorhouse stood on the site where the new Workhouse was built in 1836.

Other help for the poor came from the town's charities, the earliest of which was a £50 bequest by Lady Browne in 1652 for the repair of the church and the care of the poor of Weymouth. Perhaps the best known charity is that founded by Sir Samuel Mico in 1665, when he left ten pounds and his house 'The George Inn' on Melcombe Quay to the Corporation of Weymouth and Melcombe Regis, from the profits of which they were to apprentice three poor children. A further £500 was to be spent on the purchase of lands, the profits from this to be used to pay 20s. a year to a 'good divine' for preaching a sermon in Melcombe Regis Church on the Friday before Palm Sunday; and the rest to be distributed between 'ten poor decayed seamen of sixty years and upwards, belonging to Weymouth and Melcombe Regis' with the proviso that the seamen, 'or as many of them as are able', should attend the sermon. Contrary to the directions of the will, the £500 was let out on loan for several years, but in 1718 an estate at Osmington was purchased and sub-let. Records of the 19th century show that there was always an applicant ready to take the place of a deceased recipient and this charity has survived down to the present day. The trustees, apprentices and 'decayed seamen' process to St Mary's Church every Friday before Palm Sunday to listen to a sermon by a 'good divine'.

Jonathan Taylor, by a will dated August 24th 1753, gave a sum of money to purchase twelve penny loaves of wheaten bread, for fifty poor men and women of Weymouth and Melcombe, who receive no alms from the parish; to be distributed at the discretion of the Minister, Mayor and Churchwardens of Weymouth, in whom it was vested.

Charities and small parish workhouses found it difficult to cope with the increasing numbers of people seeking relief and the legislation of 1834 set out to organise the poor rate systems with greater economy. Parishes were now permitted to form 'unions' and build large workhouses where paupers could be more economically housed and contribute to their upkeep. The workhouses became notorious for the harsh conditions which prevailed inside their walls and the instances of family separation, overcrowding, poor food and stern discipline are well documented.

Weymouth Workhouse was built in 1836 to serve a union of eighteen local parishes. The 19th century records of the day-to-day life of the poor who dwelt there no longer exist, but certainly the only minutes which have survived – for the 1920s – suggest a strict regime even at this late date. Portwey Hospital now occupies the Union buildings and Union Road at Chapelhay was renamed St Leonards Road as early as 1872.

On the day of Queen Victoria's coronation, 28th June 1838, the town's new Guildhall opened at the lower end of St Mary Street, and on the site of the former Town Hall buildings. New parish churches had been consecrated on both sides of the Harbour. Holy Trinity, the first Anglican Church to be built

The former Weymouth Workhouse on Wyke Road, built in 1836 and now 'Portwey Hospital'.

Holy Trinity Church, opened in 1836. The old houses to the right of the picture were demolished in the 1880s when Chapelhay Steps were built and the church enlarged.

An early drawing of the second St Mary's Church in Melcombe, opened in 1817. All buildings adjoining the church have long since been demolished and replaced.

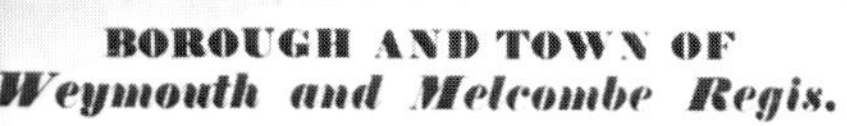

BOROUGH AND TOWN OF
Weymouth and Melcombe Regis.

On WEDNESDAY, the 31st AUGUST, 1831,
WILL BE SUBMITTED TO

AUCTION,

AT THE

Guildhall, in Melcombe Regis,

BY ORDER OF THE MAYOR AND CORPORATION.

By Messrs. Hancock & Son,

AT ELEVEN O'CLOCK IN THE FORENOON,
Subject to Conditions which will be then and there produced,

SEVEN LOTS OF

LAND

TO BE ENCLOSED FROM THE BACKWATER.

Extending from the Pipe Yard, now in Occupation of the Weymouth Water Company, on the South, to the extremity of, and in a Line with the Road which runs between No. 1, Royal Terrace, and Gloucester Lodge on the North, and which will be Sold for an absolute Term of 100 Years, subject to a Ground Rent on each Lot of Twenty Shillings per Annum.

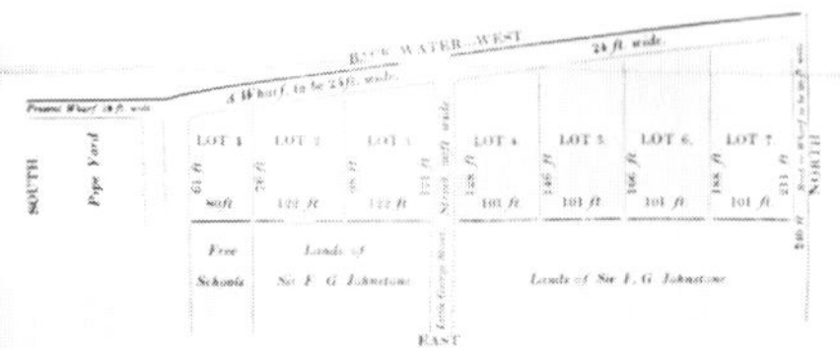

One step in the development of Commercial Road – the original sale of land between modern Westham Road and Gloucester Street, 1831.

Gloucester Street Congregational Church, 1864 – 1971. The wood in the foreground was floating in a timber-pond, adjoining the Backwater.

in Weymouth parish, opened in 1836, having been built at the sole cost of the Reverend George Chamberlaine, Rector of Wyke Regis. In Melcombe, the little 17th century parish church of St Mary was too small, and by the early 1800s, very much dilapidated. The collapse of the ceiling one Sunday in 1815 had not only covered the congregation with plaster, but also resulted in the final closure of the old building and the announcement of a competition for the design of a new parish church for the site. James Hamilton's plans were chosen and the present St Mary's Church opened in 1817. The great altar painting by Sir James Thornhill, designed for the original church, was preserved and moved to the new building.

The spiritual needs of the growing town led to the building of a great number of churches and chapels in the 19th century, whilst the education of the growing numbers of children in the area was much improved during the same period as National Schools and British Schools opened in the borough. (See Appendix E)

The need for more land for commercial use and for housing within the Melcombe Regis area had led to the reclamation of much of the Backwater, along the foreshore at the rear of the town. As early as October 1804, a plan had been approved for embanking ground from the vicinity of the town bridge, westward then northward along the shore of the Backwater. Lots were sold on the understanding that the purchasers would reclaim land from the Backwater, not only to enlarge their own sites, but also to provide sufficient ground for a new road to be built from the Quay to the western end of Coneygar Lane (now Lower Bond Street), this new road to be called Commercial Road. The decision that the Quay should officially end at Ferry's Corner and Commercial Road commence from that point was not made until 1872, long after the new road had been extended as far as modern King Street.

The new road had been designed to relieve traffic pressure in the town centre and on the Esplanade, and by 1831 had already extended beyond Coneygar Lane, as in that year seven new 'lots' were advertised for sale taking the road as far as the end of Gloucester Street. The decision to extend again beyond this point and to build a retaining wall as far as Black Rock was made in February 1834, and later the same year authority was given for the reclamation of land on the Backwater side of Commercial Road at a point opposite the end of Coneygar Lane. These two decisions had long reaching effects, the first resulting in the reclamation of land which would eventually become the Park District and the second in the extensive reclamations from the Backwater on the western side of Commercial Road carried out during the remainder of the 19th century and up to the present day. The site of Weymouth Museum was reclaimed between 1904 and 1905, and the area of Melcombe Regis Gardens as far north as the Railway Station during the early 1920s. Radipole Park Drive and Radipole Gardens followed in 1926, and what to date are the final reclamations in this area, the extensive car parks beyond where the old railway viaduct stood, were completed in the early 1950s.

The most important event in the town planning of the 1830s was the construction of a wall from the 'termination of the lately embanked ground' as far as the Black Rock, thus reclaiming some 50 acres of marshy land from Weymouth Backwater to provide a fashionable park with extensive rides and drives, to be entered via two handsome entrance lodges. With its new park, the *Dorset County Chronicle* proclaimed that Weymouth would become 'the most perfect complete and delightful watering place in the empire'.

The Black Rock can be identified as the high land at the western end of what

is now Cassiobury Road, and on 4th June the Corporation attended in state the ceremony of laying the foundation stone of the embankment wall for the new park. The celebrations were witnessed by a crowd estimated at eight or nine thousand, and the intended park was certainly launched in fine style. A Civic procession preceded a service at the parish church, bands played at the King's Statue, salutes were fired, speeches read and after the foundation stone was laid the dignitaries enjoyed a sumptuous dinner and ball in the evening. Even the residents of the poor houses were not forgotten, being treated to 'an abundance of prime roast beef, plum pudding and a pint of strong beer each'.

Laying the foundation stone of the Park Wall, 4th June, 1834, as recorded by the artist Haseler.

It was a spectacular beginning, but the proposed park never materialised. It was soon realised that the intended wall would not be high enough and in 1835 it was agreed that the new Park Wall be raised by two feet to prevent the Backwater from overflowing. One of the final actions of the old Weymouth Municipal Council, on 16th December 1835, was to seal a lease of Victoria Park for grazing, thus initiating twenty years of complicated and costly litigation. The involvement of certain civic leaders in the affair did not bear too close an examination, and an attempt to sell off the entire property for £162.15s. (£162.75) was only foiled by the action of a few public-spirited citizens. Eventually the Corporation sold the land and cleared £3370.8s.9d. (£3370.44) when legal costs were met. In his *Recollections* James Eaton Robens stated that 'The persons whose corrupt bargain was thus foiled were naturally indignant, one saying with certain profane additions that it would have been £20,000 in their pockets but for the fuss made'.

James Eaton Robens, J.P., one of the leading Weymouthians of his day. An active reformer, his Recollections *give all too brief a glimpse of life in 19th century Weymouth. He died in 1910 at the age of 96.*

With the arrival of the railway and the building of the station on part of the reclaimed area, the idea of a public park was finally abandoned, but the name has survived. Today the names of Park Street leading to the railway station and the densely-packed terraced housing of the Park District remain to remind us of a grandiose scheme which never materialised.

On 12th August 1842, Mr Green and Captain Currie ascended from Lodmoor in the Albion balloon. After passing over the Esplanade, they eventually landed near Bere Regis. The original painting was by Henry Burn.

The St Thomas Street entrance to the Royal Baths, built in 1842 and demolished in 1927. This photograph taken about 1860 shows the small cottages adjoining the Baths, which, converted into shops, have survived until today.

NINE

The Railway Arrives

After a thirty year revival in harbour trade, Weymouth was now being overtaken by Southampton and Portsmouth, both of which had been operating commercial steamship services to the Channel Islands since the mid-1820s. Passengers had been lost to these rival routes, and in 1845 it was announced that Weymouth was also to lose the mail service to its great rival port, Southampton, which, since 1840 had benefited from its rail link with London. There were proposals for a railway line to connect Weymouth and Bath in 1836, but these were later abandoned, and despite various schemes aimed at putting Weymouth on the railway map during the 'Railway Mania' period of the 1840s, nothing was done. The Great Western Railway's broad gauge line stopped at Westbury and although the London and South Western Railway's line to Dorchester was opened in 1847, it was to be another ten years before trains reached Weymouth.

Weymouth was also in danger, by virtue of its distance from the large centres of population, of being left behind in the holiday trade. James Silk Buckingham's guidebook of 1842 had sounded a warning regarding the growing popularity of other resorts. According to Buckingham, the town was 'less frequently visited by families from the metropolis than Brighton, Hastings, Dover or Broadstairs; but this very circumstance renders it a more agreeable place of sojourn than either of these crowded watering places . . .'

Buckingham found plenty to describe; seaside activities changed little over the years and the guidebooks spanning a century since the first was published in 1785 were fairly repetitious, each one adding one or two new attractions to those listed in its predecessor. In 1842 there were the handsome 'new hot-air, tepid and shower baths' in a colonnaded building at the top end of the main streets, and an extended pier to stroll on. Visitors in 1846 could enjoy a trip to Lulworth on the paddle steamer *Rose*, the first of numerous pleasure boats which were to provide trips along the coast for more than a century. From 1849 the steamers were to ferry passengers out of the harbour to see the most unusual tourist attraction of all – the great Portland Breakwater under construction, an exciting sight indeed.

When the plans to enclose Portland Roads were first put forward there had been some alarm in the genteel holiday resort of Weymouth. Across the water there would be the continued noise of pile-driving, steam engines, stone hauling and all the associated din of a major civil engineering project. The proposed prison, housing hundreds of convicts, a rough bunch awaiting transportation, spending their time at Portland working on the Breakwater before being sent to Van Dieman's Land to complete their sentences, would be uncomfortably close. It was feared 'that some interruption might be caused to the fashionable visitor to Weymouth', but eventually it was decided that the breakwater would be too far distant to cause severe inconvenience, although not, it was hoped, 'too far off for the tradesmen of the town to reap much pecuniary advantage from it'.

Many years had passed and much discussion had taken place since 1794, when John Harvey first set forth his proposals for the enclosure of Portland Roads. Not until 1849 did work commence on the construction of two massive breakwaters designed by James Meadows Rendel, which were envisaged as the complete project at that time: the two additional breakwaters which now complete the enclosure of Portland Harbour from the Weymouth side were not begun until the 1890s, long after the final stone of Rendel's work was laid in 1872. Rendel died only a few years after building started and his successor as Engineer-in-Chief was John Coode, whose name became well-known locally during his years in charge of the Breakwater works. He published papers on various local topics, including his observations on the formation of the Chesil Beach and the movement of its shingle, and drew up plans for drainage works at Weymouth.

The construction of Portland Breakwater brought great social change to Portland in the second half of the 19th century. The Island, joined to the mainland at Wyke Regis only since 1839 when the first Ferrybridge was built, now began receiving hundreds of new residents, albeit most of them unwilling visitors, as the work progressed. The shape of the top of Portland was completely changed when the Verne Citadel was constructed in the 1850s. Associated defence works in the area included a fort on the Breakwater and the Nothe Fort at Weymouth. Before the breakwaters were built, the shoreline between Bincleaves, just south of Weymouth Harbour, and Smallmouth, where Ferrybridge crosses the water, was a long expanse of golden sand, superior in the opinion of some observers to the sands of Weymouth itself. By 1864, with the Breakwaters not yet complete, the whole of this sand had been swept away, leaving the rough stone ledges which are still visible at low water today.

Prince Albert laid the foundation stone of the great works on 25th July 1849 and concluded his speech on the occasion with a reference to previous royal visitors:

> The work, of which I am about to lay the foundation stone, whilst it is of great national importance as forming a secure Harbour of Refuge for ships of the Royal Navy, and for merchant vessels freighted with the commerce of the whole world, will, I trust, be also of especial service to this neighbourhood by increasing its trade, and spreading employment among its labouring population. Her Majesty the Queen in passing along this coast has always viewed the Isle of Portland and the town of Weymouth with particular interest, from the associations connected with it.

Queen Victoria had in fact landed briefly at Weymouth three years earlier in the summer of 1846, the only time she visited the town during her long reign.

The six million or so tons of stone used in the construction of Portland Breakwater – much of it the waste 'cap' stone from the upper levels of the quarries and unsuitable for architectural purposes – were conveyed out to sea in wagons drawn by steam engines along rails laid on a massive timber staging. The staging itself was built on 100 feet piles made of baulks of timber banded together which had a large iron screw at the lower end. The screw principle allowed the piles to bite into the firm clay of the sea-bed to a depth of 6-8 feet. Upon this foundation the railway was laid, holes between the rails allowing the wagons to be placed so that the trap-doors in their bases could be opened and the stone deposited straight into the sea. Visitors to Weymouth and Portland were naturally interested in the building works and it would appear that sightseers were not discouraged from viewing the Breakwater, since contemporary drawings show crinolined ladies strolling apparently quite unconcerned between the railway lines on the wooden staging. What appears to be a somewhat perilous walk is described in a contemporary account as being '. . . between two of the five broad-gauge roads which run to the end of the Inner Breakwater . . . the heavy four-wagon trains flit by us . . . the large blocks of heaped stone soon become dashed with surf, which if the day be at all fresh, will give the visitor a sprinkling . . .'.

The construction of the railway for the Breakwater served only to highlight the fact that Weymouth was still cut off from the national railway network. Although there were great plans for a line to Weymouth in the 1840s, funds ran low and work on the Wilts, Somerset and Weymouth Railway, scheduled to leave the G.W.R. main line near Chippenham and to reach Weymouth by way of Westbury, Yeovil and Dorchester, was long delayed.

Sherren's Guide to Weymouth of 1844 was over-optimistic in featuring on its front cover and title-page an engraving of a train emerging from a tunnel and presumably steaming towards Weymouth – this was three years before even the Southampton-Dorchester line opened! Inside the guide were details of the coach services from Weymouth, more aptly illustrated with an engraving of a coach-and-four, and which then included a daily service to London and regular services to Southampton, Exeter, Bath and Bristol.

Great confidence was expressed in the mid-1840s on the subject of the 'new era' about to open in Weymouth with the simultaneous construction of the Breakwater and the railway. The *Dorset County Chronicle* had reported early in 1846 on both proposals, predicting that 'brighter days' lay ahead for Weymouth and quoting Brunel's belief that 'he had not seen any place that nature had endowed with so many natural resources as Weymouth, which would one day become, in a maritime point of view, a port of the greatest consequence in the West of England'.

For the next few years, despite seemingly endless discussions and delays, Weymouth remained certain that the opening of the railway line was imminent. So great was the optimism that in 1851 the churchwardens of Melcombe Regis announced that the town clock was to be regulated to keep Greenwich Mean Time, or 'Railway Time', instead of local time.

The town kept 'Railway Time' for five years before the first train left Weymouth station on 20th January 1857, and ran to Yeovil and back. Surprisingly, after the long wait, the event was not marked by local celebrations on the day. 'No "salvo of artillery", no band with joyous music announced the fact that Weymouth at last had a railway, and may now be said literally to have entered the path of prosperity' commented the *Dorset County Chronicle*, blaming the apathy on the short notice of the official opening given to the Town Council by the railway company and inclement weather on the day. A week later there was a public holiday to commemorate the opening of the railway, coupled with the customary processions, speeches and dinners, and a free return trip to Yeovil for the recipients of three hundred complimentary train tickets distributed by the Great Western Railway Company.

Two railway companies were running trains to Weymouth from the junction at Dorchester, where the Great Western Railway's line from Yeovil joined the London and South Western Railway's line from Southampton. Consequently the track from Dorchester to Weymouth was mixed gauge to accommodate the 7 feet G.W.R. and 4 feet 8½ ins. L.S.W.R. gauges, and remained so until 1874. Weymouth's large timber-built railway station with its huge overall roof, although rather dark, was an impressive and interesting example of Brunel's designs for the Great Western Railway. However, since

MELCOMBE REGIS.

It having been represented to us, the CHURCHWARDENS OF THE PARISH OF MELCOMBE REGIS, within the Town of WEYMOUTH, that much inconvenience is felt from the Town Clock not being in accordance with Railway Time; and having ascertained from undoubted authority, that the Completion of the Railway into this Town may be looked forward to at no distant period:

We Hereby Give Notice,

that on and after the FIRST DAY OF JANUARY, 1852, the Town Clock will be regulated and kept by GREENWICH TIME, more commonly known as "*Railway Time.*"

R. COMMINS,
J. MAUNDERS, CHURCHWARDENS.

N.B. The alteration will be about Ten minutes in advance.

Weymouth, December 23rd, 1851.

There is good reason to believe that this photograph of Weymouth Station was taken on the opening day in January 1857. The large roof spanning four tracks survived until after the Second World War.

WEYMOUTH RAILWAY

TRAINS BY THE GREAT WESTERN

LEAVE FOR

DORCHESTER, YEOVIL, BRISTOL, CHIPPENHAM, AND PADDINGTON, at 6.0 9.0 12.50 and 3.45 and 5.45

TRAINS BY THE GREAT WESTERN

ARRIVE AT WEYMOUTH

At 10.50 12.55 2.30 5.20 and 10.0

A Train to Dorchester at 8.0 p.m., returning at 9.0 p.m.

TRAINS BY THE SOUTH WESTERN

LEAVE FOR

DORCHESTER, POOLE, SOUTHAMPTON, AND LONDON, at 6.25 8.40 12.20 4.50 5.30 and 9.30.

TRAINS BY THE SOUTH WESTERN

ARRIVE AT WEYMOUTH

At 9.20. 1.28 4.0 8.0 and 10.5

the removal of the entire wooden roof in the early 1950s, the buildings retain little of architectural value.

Amongst those who had eagerly awaited the opening of the railway was Mr D. Archer, proprietor of the Royal Library. Archer delayed publication of his new illustrated guidebook until after the event and his remarks in its preface are an accurate forecast of the changes which the arrival of the railway was to bring:

> The Directors of the Great Western Railway liberally permit visitors from London, Bath, Bristol and intermediate places, at the cost of a few shillings, to visit our town and surrounding objects of interest; and enable them to return to their homes with recruited health and spirits even by a two days' visit, and to encourage their friends to see for themselves by next cheap excursion.

For Weymouth, the era of long, leisurely holidays by the sea for the wealthy visitor was coming to an end: the new age of the 'tripper' was not far away.

Archer's guidebook had a cumbersome title: *Weymouth as a watering place: with a description of the town and neighbourhood, the breakwater and its construction, the Portland quarries, the Chesil Beach, etc., etc., for the use of intending and actual visitors*, but it is one of the most entertaining of the numerous similar 19th century publications. Some of the author's pithy comments on a wide range of local topics would seem to do little to attract the 'intending visitor':

> With few exceptions, the houses in Weymouth (i.e. Weymouth proper, on the south side of the harbour) are old fashioned, inconvenient, kept in bad order, and seemingly doomed to remain in this condition . . . we will just remark that the same Nothe we have been describing and you have been visiting, owes all it is or seems to Nature herself; not one shilling is laid out upon it either to improve or adorn it . . .
>
> In no town in the Kingdom are abuses and nuisances better protected and more obstinately defended, or less encouragement for private enterprise in attempting improvements; hence so little is done, or even attempted. Let a steam boat be required, no one who knows the town will attempt its introduction; but woe to the stranger who calculates on encouragement in the dilemma; he will find, to his cost, the full tide of opposition from the day he makes the venture. The only things likely to be unmolested are those whose opposition would be a benefit to the town; but let it be proposed that the town be thoroughly drained; a market house erected; a piece of sea wall properly and economically built; the Esplanade permanently repaired; and obstacles of one kind or another will overpower the proposer, until human endurance is exhausted. Frequently the plea of ECONOMY is carried out against some proposal AT A COST EQUAL OR GREATER THAN THAT OF THE THING OBJECTED TO.

Sanitary conditions in mid-19th century Weymouth, as in many other 'health' resorts, were appalling. Consider this extract from a letter published in the *Dorset County Chronicle*, and headed 'Weymouth, August 4th, 1846':

> Sir, *Open Sewers*. I am glad to find that these public nuisances are beginning to attract the attention of the Press. I wish particularly to draw your notice to the disgusting state of the sewers in Weymouth – the stench from the open sewers in St Mary Street, St Thomas Street and the entrance from that beautiful drive to the Smallmouth Sands, is intolerable. At a time when Weymouth is crowded with company, a nuisance so dangerous to health ought immediately to be remedied.

High West Street, Weymouth, about 1880.

The issue of public health had been seriously considered by central government during the severe cholera outbreak of 1831-1833, but interest had waned when the epidemic was over. Not until 1849 (the year of another cholera epidemic) did George T. Clark, Superintending Inspector of the General Board of Health, make his report in a *Preliminary Inquiry into the Sewerage, Drainage, and Supply of Water, and the Sanitary Condition of the Parish of Melcombe Regis, in the County of Dorset*. Although the statutory 10% of the population had petitioned for the inquiry, a counter-petition was produced following a public meeting, signed by those who did not wish to have matters of public health investigated, and allegedly, including the names of some individuals who had changed their minds after signing the original petition!

The Parish of Weymouth showed no interest at all, but although he was not required to do so by law, Mr Clark took it upon himself to inspect streets on both sides of the harbour and the resulting report provided an excellent portrait of the mid-19th century town, with its crowded tenement blocks and narrow alleys. The population numbered about 8000 and although the mean annual mortality of the borough was 21.2 per thousand, in Weymouth parish the figure was averaging 25.4 in the thousand as compared with only 17 in the thousand for the full registration district, which extended as far as Beaminster and Bridport.

The reasons for these high mortality figures are not hard to find. There was an almost total absence of sewers and even the provision of a cesspool was something of a luxury. In Helen's Lane and other properties near the Harbour, soil was collected in a tub and emptied over the quay wall at night. In many streets open gutters intended for storm water were used as sewers, receiving nightsoil deposited secretly, because in many small houses and cottages there were no privies at all. Six of the seven houses in New Court had no sanitary provision, and these residents also enjoyed the aroma of a neighbouring slaughter-house and a tallow works. Almost any open space became a dumping ground for all kinds of filth.

The Inspector's comments on conditions in King Street and its neighbourhood form an interesting insight into the early days of the Park District:

> King Street is built upon the margin of an extensive swamp traversed by one or two very filthy ditches. The house drains, and in some cases the privy drains, discharge into this place along the face of a retaining wall. This ground is to be raised for the terminus of the projected railway. In its present state it is a nuisance to the whole of the adjacent portion of the town. It is stated by one of the district visitors that the effect of a north-east wind, coming over this swamp, is to aggravate any febrile disease which may be at that time present.

Each street of the town was described in similarly unhealthy terms. Melcombe's cesspools were draining away into the shingly ground on which the houses were built, quite possibly tainting the resort's salubrious seaside air. Clark pointed out that Weymouth's insanitary crowded tenements were 'but little known to visitors or to the wealthier classes'.

Interesting glimpses of other features of life in mid-19th century

The Backwater dam of 1872. This was the first attempt to control the level of water in Radipole Lake.

Weymouth and Melcombe Regis appear in the Board of Health Report. Many of the houses were stated to be kept very clean internally, and the town appears to have been well swept and well lit. Ashes were removed from each house daily and about £3 a week was spent on watering the streets in the six summer months.

Street lighting was by gas, the lamps being lit for ten months in the year, and half of them lit during the remaining two. They were not lighted for five nights round each full moon.

Nevertheless the Inspector faced an uphill struggle in trying to persuade the inhabitants of the dangers they faced. Shortly before his arrival, at a meeting in the Guildhall, the trustees had congratulated themselves on the 'satisfactory' state of sewerage in Melcombe Regis, suggesting only minor improvements. Clark thought otherwise, and the final paragraphs of his report recommended the application of the Public Health Act to the petitioning parish of Melcombe Regis, and strongly advised that it should apply to the whole borough.

As a result, the Local Board of Health was duly formed and early in 1852 turned its attention to sewage disposal. Having stated that '. . . as the prosperity of the Borough as a watering place mainly depends upon the sands and sea surrounding the town being kept free from all defilement, it is indispensible that neither the soil or sewage of the town be run into the sea . . .' it commenced a search for a suitable method of disposal which lasted into the next century.

Clark's detailed recommendations of 1849 were never proceeded with, neither were those commissioned from Thomas Hawksley in 1864. Only parts of the scheme prepared by John Coode (Engineer-in-Chief of the Portland Breakwater Project) were completed, including the building of a dam across the Backwater. The purpose of the dam was to control the flow of water and maintain a reasonable level in the upper reaches of the Backwater and Radipole Lake, thus obviating the unpleasant smells which arose at low tide. The disused dam can still be seen today, just south of the embankment bridge, which since 1921 has controlled the flow of water by sluices. The second half of his plan, the building of a pumping station and sewage farm, was abandoned and a resolution passed indicating that it was the wish of the Local Board of Health that '. . . the Drainage of the Borough should be carried into the tideway in the least offensive way possible'.

As a result, by late in 1878, the stench from the Backwater was becoming an acute problem. It was blamed variously on seaweed accumulation, the stagnant timber ponds and the fact that some sewage was washing over the

The Esplanade about 1870.

dam and decomposing unpleasantly as it lay trapped in the Lake beyond. There were some residents who asserted that the smell was not as bad as in the days before the dam was constructed. One gentleman who came across the Backwater Bridge four times a day claimed that 'previous to the erection of the dam he had to saturate his handkerchief with Eau-de-Cologne and hold it to his nose, which cost him 2s.0d. (10p) a week, but since the construction of the dam he had never had reason to lay out a penny'. Coode, of course, when advising the erection of the dam, had not envisaged that sewage would be conveyed into the Backwater.

The debate continued, action becoming increasingly necessary as the housing developments of the Park District, Dorchester Road and Westham proceeded apace. Weymouth was even advised not to have such public discussions on the subject for fear that newspapers in rival watering places should publish garbled stories about the problem!

Not until 1891 did the Urban Sanitary Authority, successor to the Local Board of Health, recommend 'The present discharge of crude sewage into the harbour being condemned by modern sanitation and highly detrimental to the interests of Weymouth as a Health Resort, the Surveyor be requested to report within a month on the best means of the sewage disposal of the Borough'.

Finally, just a few years before the close of the century and shortly after the extension of the Borough Boundaries, tenders were accepted for a new Main Drainage Scheme with a sea outfall, on 8th July 1896.

Archer remarked in 1857 that 'The new Water Company is in full and efficient operation, the water good and plentiful'. The original water supply, piped from Boiling Rock near Preston since the end of the previous century, had proved to be inadequate for the growing population, and indeed only the better houses in Melcombe Regis were connected to the supply. This was not the constantly available running water which we know today: it was laid on three times a week for about an hour at each house or court. Here the inhabitants drew sufficient quantities to fill water butts in which the supply was stored to last until the next time water was made available. Elmwood, earthenware and stoneware pipes had conveyed water to Melcombe since 1798, but it was not until the late 1850s that the inhabitants on the Weymouth side of the Harbour received piped water.

Two pumps had been erected to augment the springs and wells on which the Weymouth people depended. One, dating from the 1770s, was sited at West Plains, and can still be seen, preserved in the grounds of Weymouth Fire Station. Here formerly stood the terraced houses of Jockey's Row and Silver

The Town Pump at the end of High Street, first erected in the 18th century. The group of cottages known as West Plain has already been demolished, but Jockey's Row and Silver Street at the rear of the Boot Inn are still in use. The entire area is now covered by the Weymouth Fire Station.

Street, demolished in the 1930s. In 1854 a second pump was built at the top of Boot Hill. The Weymouthians also benefited from two public taps installed on the Melcombe side of the town bridge, where they were allowed to draw water from the piped supply to that side of the town.

Increased supplies of water were obtained when, by Act of Parliament dated 15th July 1855, Weymouth Waterworks Company was authorized to acquire springs at Sutton Poyntz. Water was pumped to a reservoir at Preston, thence to Rodwell Reservoir, from which piped water was made available to the population on the southern side of the Harbour for the first time.

One piece of equipment still in use at Sutton Poyntz pumping station today dates back to a tragic accident in September 1859, when a violent explosion damaged the giant steamship *Great Eastern* in the Channel. Then the largest ship in the world, the *Great Eastern* was on its acceptance trials when the incident occurred. Known as an unlucky ship, Brunel's huge vessel had already added to its troubled reputation a few days earlier, when Brunel himself collapsed after posing for photographs onboard, the victim of a stroke. Now as the trials began, an explosion ripped through the water casing of the forward of the ship's five funnels, horribly injuring fifteen of the crew. Five firemen and stokers died, literally boiled alive by the escaping steam and water.

The *Great Eastern* was brought into Portland Roads for repair. Due to its immensely strong construction, the damage was relatively slight and confined to the funnel, paddle engine-room and the Grand Saloon – by good fortune empty of passengers when the explosion occurred. Brunel, already seriously ill, did not long survive the news of the disaster: he died a week later.

The ship proved to be a great tourist attraction during its unexpected three-week stay at Portland, and more than 20,000 people were shown over the giant

vessel at half-a-crown per head. As the *Southern Times* reported in typically florid prose:

S.S. Great Eastern *in Portland Harbour following the explosion of September, 1859.*

> Monster trains have been organised in every quarter of the compass converging upon Weymouth, and unparalleled crowds, pouring into that favourite marine resort by train after train, rapidly found their way by harbour and other steamers alongside the *Great Eastern* in Portland Roadstead, and these crowds rapidly disappeared into the bowels of the floating city of cabins or diffused themselves over the decks without at all inconveniencing the capacious monster . . .

The local people may have gaped open-mouthed as they toured the ship, but a report in *The Times* was critical of the indifference they displayed during the inquest on the dead seamen. Few Weymouthians attended and those who did paid little attention to the proceedings. The nonchalant attitude of the jury in particular shocked officials from London, but it was perhaps not too surprising since inquests on the victims of shipwrecks and accidents on board ships were all too frequent in 19th century Weymouth.

The *Great Eastern's* damaged 30ft. forward funnel was acquired by the Weymouth Waterworks Company and installed vertically at Sutton Poyntz, where over one hundred years later more than two million gallons of water pass through it every day.

The spill-way at Sutton Poyntz water-works. The basic structure of the cylinder rising from the water is the former funnel of the Great Eastern.

The Market House in St Mary Street, designed by Talbot Bury and opened in 1855.

The 1850s saw the erection of several important buildings in the town. St John's Church, then sometimes referred to as Radipole New Church, opened in 1854 to serve the growing population of Melcombe as it expanded northwards. The 1851 Census figures show that Weymouth and Melcombe Regis now had 8230 inhabitants, an increase of 128% in the 50 years since the first official Census has been carried out in 1801, one of the peak years as a 'Royal resort'.

The architect of St John's Church, Talbot Bury, also designed the Market House in St Mary Street, one of two covered markets which opened in 1855. The second one was the Fish Market on Custom House Quay, still standing today, but now used as a store. The larger general Market House was an ornate building, some 95 feet long with entrances in both St Mary Street and Maiden Street, its facade surmounted by a handsome carving of the Borough Arms. This costly new building replaced the open-air stalls which had crowded the narrow streets behind the quay on market days. It was not well received in the town, and in the following year the local traders called for reductions in stallholders' rents, enlargement of individual stalls and rearrangement of the Market House interior. Some 100 names appear on the petition, 20 butchers (including the appropriately named Josiah Rabbits), 6 dairymen, 10 general dealers, 3 fishmongers and 63 other stallholders, all of whom claimed that the weighing machine provided was not accurate.

There were similar complaints about the new Fish Market, situated in the coal-dust-laden atmosphere of the quayside where the fish displayed soon became grey and gritty. In 1867 the Fish Market was transferred to the general Market House, which survived until the 1930s. One end wall of the original building survived demolition in 1939, and was incorporated into the otherwise featureless design of the arcade and shops, which still bears the name 'Market House' above its St Mary Street frontage.

Archer's guide included engravings of St John's Church and the Market House, together with another of Talbot Bury's works – Holy Trinity Schools at Chapelhay, on the Weymouth side of the harbour. Opened in 1854, and designed to accommodate 600 pupils, 300 boys and 300 girls, these were attractive Portland stone buildings, with a slender spire, Built on the site of the old Chapel Fort of Civil War days,the schools were severely damaged during Second World War air raids. They were later demolished and houses now fill the site.

St John's Church in 1854. The final houses in Victoria Terrace have yet to be built.

In Melcombe Regis, the 1850s had seen the extension of the National Schools by the addition of an Infants School to the already existing Boys (1824) and Girls (1825) departments. In addition to these National Schools on either side of the harbour, a non-denominational British Boys' School had opened some time earlier in Belle Vue. For those able to afford the fees, there were a number of other educational establishments, including Ladies Boarding Schools, Mr Addison's Boarding Establishment for 'sons of gentlemen' at Rodwell, as well as various professors who would instruct in music, language and drawing.

To a certain degree Weymouth had spent much of the first half of the 19th century living off the reputation it had gained in Georgian times. The opening of the railway was to bring a new type of visitor and increased harbour trade, and together with the construction of the Breakwater and the growth of Portland Naval Base was to result in a great expansion of the town in the years between 1860 and the end of the century.

TEN

The Expanding Community

In considering the extensive development which followed the arrival of the railway in 1857, it is worth remembering that the shape of medieval Melcombe Regis had altered little until the spectacular changes which followed its rise to fame as a health and pleasure resort. Prior to 1783, when the first terrace (York Buildings) was built facing the sea, the town had comprised seven streets running north and south, i.e. West Street, St Nicholas Street, St Thomas Street, St Mary Street, Maiden Street, New Street and East Street, and three streets running east and west, St Edmund Street, Petticoat Lane (Lower St Alban Street since 1872) and Coneygar Lane (Lower Bond Street since 1872). There were numerous small courts running between these streets, e.g. Governor's Lane, Steward's Court, Helen Lane, and the town already extended some distance beyond the old limit of Coneygar Lane. Some isolated and quite ancient buildings stood on the northern outskirts – a typical example is the Dove Inn, better known to us today as the 'Black Dog'.

By the 1830s the majority of the Esplanade houses had been completed, the final group, Victoria Terrace and the Burdon Hotel (now the Prince Regent) being finished in 1856. Vacant sites in St Thomas Street and St Mary Street were built on, extending them to the general area of the King's Statue, as today.

The reclamation of land west and then north of the Town Bridge, along the shore of the Backwater had commenced in 1804, extending to the Park Wall of 1834 with further reclamations right up to modern times. Harmony Place (off Lower Bond Street) and Puckett's Stores (later converted to become the Queen's Barracks) had been built on this reclaimed land, much of the infilling being obtained by the removal of a sand-bar across Weymouth Harbour. The Queen's Barracks were later converted into a block of Mechanic's Lodging Houses known as 'Burdon's Buildings', and the site is now occupied by Kennedy's Store.

The early years of the 19th century had seen the construction of the majority of the smaller houses in the area bounded by School Street, Commercial Road, King Street and the Esplanade. The earliest Rate Book which survives is dated 1836, and this lists houses in West Parade (Park Street), Hartford Terrace, Caroline Place, Great George Street and Little George Street (Westham Road). Four years later (1840) there are thirty-three properties listed in Park Street in addition to thirty-five shown as West Parade, and by 1841 Quebec Place, Carter's Cottages (1835), Bath Street and Edward Street had all been constructed. North of King Street, the only development by the mid 1830s was Crescent Street at the rear of Royal Crescent and part of what we know today as Queen Street. Further infilling followed, in the shape of Gloucester Mews (1842), Belvidere Mews (1845), Wesley Street (1852), Turton Street (1860), Terminus Street (1860) and Clifton Place (1861).

1857 saw the arrival of the railway, and by 1865 the line had been extended

Burdon's Buildings, the tall block in the centre of this picture, stood on the corner of Lower Bond Street and Commercial Road. At one time the Queen's Barracks of the Georgian period, it ended its days as a tenement, and was demolished in the 1920s and its residents re-housed in the new council estates at Westham.

Georgian cottages in Bury Street, which survived until the 1970s. Orginally this street led to the old Melcombe Regis Cemetery, but today the entire area is covered by a super-store and car park. The original painting is by Eric Ricketts.

along Commercial Road. Alexandra Terrace at the northern end of Commercial Road was built in 1864, Richmond Terrace (now part of King Street) (1861) and Upwey Street (1861), and with four houses in Wooperton Street built in 1863, eight in Terrace Street (1862) and thirteen in Gloucester Terrace, the infill of the area south of King Street was virtually complete. Smaller developments were Albert Street (1861), Albert Cottages (Westham Road) (1862), and Victoria Cottages (Park Street) all built by 1870. Nearer the town centre, the demolition of the last remains of the old Friary buildings led to the making of Market Street (1870) and Mitchell Street (1873).

Before considering the detailed development of what is popularly known as The Park District, it is worth recalling some of the smaller streets, courts and terraces which have gone from the central town area. Stewards Court and part of Governor's Lane went in the early 1960s to form a car park. West Street and St Nicholas Street are vague shadows of their former selves, the demolitions having been started by German bombs during the Second World War and completed in the 1960s to form a further car park. Seymour Street disappeared many years ago, whilst Bury Street, which once led from St Nicholas Street to the old Melcombe Regis graveyard was demolished in 1975. The long disused graveyard had been emptied in 1974 and the remains re-interred at Westham, and today the site of the graveyard, Bury Street, Seymour Street and much of Petticoat Lane and Coneygar Lane is covered by the multi-storey car park and superstore in Lower Bond Street.

Over the years, many of the old terraces and courts have been re-numbered as part of a main street and the original place-names have dropped out of use. Typical of this change is West Parade in Park Street, but the prime example of long-forgotten terrace names comes in the Park District. The building of the various houses and terraces in this district and on the land adjoining was spread over a number of years, the first developments taking place in the Lennox Street and Walpole Street area. Park Terrace (Melcombe Place) is mentioned in a Corporation minute of 1837 and is really part of an earlier development behind the sea-front, and Lennox House on the corner of Melcombe Place and Lennox Street, is regarded as the first house to be built in this new area. Royal York Terrace (1-5 Lennox Street) dates from 1861 and Walpole Terrace (46-59 Walpole Street) was built in 1863.

By the late 1860s the general layout of the streets was settled and by 1870 we find mention of Brownlow Street, Charles Street, Chelmsford Street, Derby Street, Hardwick Street, Lennox Street, Melcombe Place, Penny Street, Ranelagh Road, Stanley Street, Victoria Street, Walpole Street and William Street. Building was spasmodic and isolated terraces sprang up all over the place. Between them they produced a plethora of place-names, the majority of which were discontinued when the streets were numbered in the early years of this century. How many people today could direct you to Florissant Terrace, Sydney Terrace, Salisbury Terrace, Penman Place or Chalgrove Terrace? – to quote but five out of over sixty such terraces, villas and courts which have been traced in this one area of Melcombe Regis.

The spread of housing north from the Park District into the area of Carlton Road and the various avenues to the west of the main Dorchester Road was to some degree contemporary with the growth of the Park District, although in general a larger type of house was to be the pattern of building in this area. By the 1890s the scheme was well developed, but the bulk of the houses date from the early years of the 20th century. Grosvenor Road, on the site of the old Radipole Barrack field, was adopted as a public highway as early as 1868,

The proposed layout of the Park District as shown on an Ordnance Survey Map of 1864. A Conservative Land Agency, which named streets after Tory statesmen, began building early in 1861. In February that year the Weymouth Telegram *reported that during a gale, the first house in course of erection had been blown down!*

Westerhall about 1870. In the background can be seen the buildings of Weymouth College. The entire area was originally known as Melcombe Common. Today this is a busy one-way main road handling the bulk of traffic entering and leaving Weymouth.

which shows how difficult it is to identify a large group of roads as belonging to one specific period of development.

A comprehensive scheme of development was drawn up by the Johnstone Estate, which owned much of this land, and a 'bird's eye view' of the proposals was produced in 1865. The overall plan was completed only in part, but mass housing and terraces were avoided. Much of the history of the developments along the Dorchester Road and on and around the former Cavalry Barracks near Lodmoor Hill is recorded by Eric Ricketts in his book *The Buildings of Old Weymouth. Part Two: Melcombe Regis and Westham.* (1976).

Argyle Road, between the Dorchester Road and the former Great Western Railway engine sheds was probably developed to provide housing for the former railway workers and with the larger terraced houses on the main road must represent some late Victorian speculative, almost 'ribbon' development, to use a term more associated with the 1920s and '30s. Until the year 1895 the northern boundary of the Borough of Weymouth and Melcombe Regis was at Lodmoor Hill, and much of the Victorian development beyond this point took place in the parish of Radipole. Most of the housing eastwards of the Dorchester Road beyond Lodmoor Hill belongs to the post-World War One era, with the process continuing after the Second World War, but although we tend to think of this as 'modern' Radipole, the first building well away from the old village belongs to a much earlier period. The terrace of cottages which marks the beginning of Spa Road dates from about 1840, when Radipole Spa on the opposite side of the road was a popular centre.

The first G.W.R. bus to operate in Weymouth. Miss Templeman, Mayoress of Weymouth occupies the centre front seat on the inaugural journey.

The buildings of Radipole Spa stood on a site which we can identify today as the corner of Queen's Road and Spa Road, extending over part of the site of the present St Aldhelm's Church. The Spa is shown on a map of 1864 but it is unlikely to have been still in active use. The housing in the area of Spa Road, Queen's Road, King's Road, Icen Road and Roman Road belongs in most part to the very early years of the 20th century. Much of the land had been sold off in plots by the early 1890s but it was to be several years before all the houses were built. Radipole Halt was opened in July 1905, thus providing public transport facilities to the town centre, and it is a good indication that 'modern' Radipole and 'modern' Wyke Regis were developing at much the same time that the first motor bus to be introduced in Weymouth was one from the Spa Hotel at Radipole to the Wyke Hotel at Wyke Regis, also commencing in 1905. This, one of the pioneer road services operated by the Great Western Railway, linked both these new housing areas with the central commercial part of the town. The Spa Hotel was built in 1899, and new public houses are always a good indication of a growing community!

The two roads between Dorchester Road and old Radipole village follow the lines of tracks of a much earlier age, and it is difficult to say whether Spa Road or the Radipole Lane/Manor Road link is the older. It is known that the section of road past St Ann's Church was not built until 1841 and that prior to this Radipole Lane meandered around the site of the modern churchyard to a junction with Spa Lane. Prior to about 1820 the only access for foot passengers from Radipole village to the church was across a narrow timber bridge over the river at the south-east corner of the old rectory garden. Carts and wagons could cross at certain states of the tide by going through the river more or less where the road bridge stands today.

The original town of 'Weymouth' had grown up along the southern bank of the River Wey and by the beginning of the 19th Century consisted of the houses which faced (and in a few cases backed onto) the Harbour between the Nothe headland and the Marsh; Hope Square; the Lookout and the general area of the Red Barracks; Chapelhay and Boot Lane. The main road to Portland followed the route of old High Street, Boot Lane to Clearmount, and then by way of Sandsfoot Castle and the foreshore to Smallmouth Ferry. The main road to Wyke Regis followed the crest of the hill along the line of the Wyke Road of today, whilst a minor lane known as Buxton's Lane was the forerunner of Cross Road and that part of Buxton Road between Blackdown and Foord's Corner. Southwards beyond the line of modern St Leonard's Road was largely farmland.

Towards the end of the 18th century there had been a major scheme of reclamation in the area of Hope Square, when in the year 1781 permission was given to the inhabitants near the Cove to wall it across and fill it up at their own cost. This resulted in a harbour wall at the Cove somewhat shorter than we know it today because at the eastern end there were several houses in Hope Street with direct access to the water. In the early years of the 19th century there were a number of buildings which backed onto the Harbour, both above and below the Town Bridge. The first block to be demolished went as part of the preparations for the Town Bridge of 1824, whilst the Hope Street group was demolished in 1888 as part of a general scheme of Harbour improvement to provide facilities for some new Great Western Railway steamers.

A short distance along the harbourside another major change had just been completed. Holy Trinity Church had been built in 1836 on a site facing the harbour, and in 1884 some old houses alongside the church were removed in order to make an improved access to Chapelhay. Road access from the harbourside to the high land of Chapelhay already existed in the form of steep Scrambridge Hill from Hope Square, at the east end, and the more gentle slope of Chapelhay Street (known as St Nicholas Street prior to 1872) from the vicinity of the Old Town Hall. There was also the steep flight of steps from behind houses in the High Street, which had probably been in use from the 12th or 13th century. The steady increase in the number of houses in the Chapelhay area during the mid 19th century had made these facilities inadequate, and in 1870 the decision was made 'to consider making a better approach to the Chapelhay'. A further ten years was to elapse before a scheme was brought forward, and this involved making a new pathway by removing 'Notley's Houses' and Chapelhay Court at an estimated cost of £1750.

There was a strong movement in favour of building a new street alongside Holy Trinity Church and in April 1884 a tender of £1145 for the construction of the Chapelhay Approach Road was accepted. At the last moment however, the plan was abandoned and a scheme which included steps was adopted. In spite of this the work was completed by December 1884, when the old steps were closed.

At the same time as these improvements were being made, the opportunity was taken to build a major extension to Holy Trinity Church, and this was completed in 1885. Old Chapelhay Steps still survive to this day, overgrown and crumbling, but a visible link with mediaeval 'Weymouth'.

Improvements on the western or landward side of the bridge, i.e. North Quay, were achieved by the construction of a new quay wall which allowed a road to be made between the existing buildings and the harbourside. Part of this new quay wall was built about 1840, with further improvements in 1871 and 1883, resulting in the direct road from North Quay past the gas works to join Newstead Road. Before these improvements there was only a footpath about three feet wide between the houses on North Quay and the Harbour. There is a record that whilst Belfield House was being built in the late 18th century, Isaac Buxton lodged at the old Tudor house (No. 4 North Quay) and used to fish in the Harbour out of the drawing room window.

The physical growth of 'Weymouth' during the 19th century was of necessity southwards and south-westwards (Rodwell) and westwards along Town Lane (Pyehill and the Chickerell Road). Franchise Street is a road of considerable antiquity, but St Leonard's Road was a muddy country lane until well into the 19th century. It has been known at various times as Bazell's Lane, Dixon's Lane, and Butt's Lane, and then as Union Road or Union Place.

Rodwell Avenue did not come into being until the later years of the 19th century and the first houses to be built on the line of what would eventually become this road were those of Spring Place (now Nos. 2-14 Rodwell Road). These houses are shown on Pierse Arthur's map of 1857, which also includes a number of large but somewhat scattered terraces of houses in the area south of St Leonard's Road. Many of these terraces such as Spring Gardens, Oakley Place, Spring Lane and Dorset Place were almost totally destroyed in the air raids of 1940 and 1941 when so much of Chapelhay was bombed. The modern layout of this area bears little resemblance to that of the period 1850-1941. Maycroft Road, Norwich Road and Orion Road are of somewhat later development and survived the devastation of the blitz.

The map of 1857 shows a number of larger houses spaced out along what was then called Longhill Road, as far as Clearmount Corner. This road, from the bottom of Boot Lane as far as Clearmount, was renamed Rodwell Road in 1872 and many of the houses built here in the early years of the 19th century survive today with only slight alterations. Nos 1 & 2 Clearmount, which at one time stood on Clearmount Corner, were destroyed by bombs during the Second World War. Elwell Manor (No. 70 Rodwell Road) stands on the site of an old Dairy House and was rebuilt about 1854. The oldest part of Rodwell House (No. 34) was the first building to be erected in Rodwell and was built by James Hamilton who lived in the house at one time. Later it was occupied by Rev. G. Piers, Vicar of Preston and later again by Rev. George Chamberlaine, Rector of Wyke Regis, who built the rear part of the property.

The earliest development past Clearmount Corner was in the neighbourhood of Connaught Road. Early records do not use this name, but Blackdown is mentioned in the 1860s and most of the larger houses in Connaught Road and adjacent Buxton Road were built during the 1870s and 1880s. Connaught House, or 'Portmore' to use its original name, was built on what was at one time part of the Belfield Estate.

Much detailed information regarding properties in the Weymouth area can be gathered by studying the large scale Ordnance Survey Maps dated 1864. In the case of the village of Wyke Regis, it is possible to compare this with an excellent privately printed map dated 1855 and to assess the changes taking place in the mid 19th century. Wyke Castle, the castellated private dwelling overlooking the Fleet appears to have been built during this period, as does Sandesfort House, the large house (now a private school) at the top of Rylands Lane. There was also a large number of smaller properties being built in the area of Wyke Square and Shrubbery Lane. Several buildings shown on both maps no longer exist today, including Boulton Villa (later renamed Wyke Lodge and demolished 1974), cottages on both sides of Foord's Corner, Wyke House, (later The Wyke House Hotel, demolished 1974), a smithy on the corner of Lanehouse Rocks Road (now part of the cemetery extension) and the Fisherman's Arms Inn on the corner of Chamberlaine Road and Portland Road. By 1866 a Police Station had been established next to the Fisherman's Arms!

The expansion of Wyke Regis into the open countryside between the old village and Ferry Bridge followed closely the establishment of the Whitehead Torpedo Works in 1891. Ferrybridge Cottages were built at the same time as the factory and intended for its own workers, whilst a separate terrace of somewhat larger brick houses some two hundred yards along the Portland Road was provided for more senior employees. Within a few years came the new houses in the Broadmeadow area; Parkmead Road, named after the adjoining farm and one of the oldest place-names in the Wyke Regis area, Gallwey Road, named after Captain Payne Gallwey, first manager of the Torpedo Works, and Victoria Road named to honour the Queen's Diamond Jubilee in 1897. The origins of William's Avenue, Sunnyside and Fair View are not quite as obvious, although they were all built during the same period.

The School in Victoria Road (built by Whiteheads in 1897), The Primitive Methodist Chapel in Gallwey Road (1900), The Wesleyan Methodist Chapel on the Portland Road (1903) and the Wyke Hotel all belong to this period of expansion. The bus service to Weymouth and Radipole dates from 1905, although Wyke Regis Halt on the Weymouth-Portland Railway did not open until 1908. Broadmeadow Road itself, which perpetuates the old field name for the major part of this area, is a later development dating from the early 1950s.

Whilst the development of the Park district of Melcombe Regis was the major new housing project for the second half of the 19th century, it was by no means the only one. Across the Backwater lay the farming lands of Littlefield and Goldcroft, close to the Town Centre as the crow flies, but some distance by road, and administratively an outlying part of the parish of Wyke Regis. The lease granted to the colliery owner and M.P. for the Borough, William Burdon, in 1834 for land adjoining Littlefield as a site for his proposed Gas House and Gasometers, indicates that this was within the borough boundary, but as late as 1857, the only other buildings in this area were a group of four cottages, 'Crocker's Folly', in an isolated position on the line of modern Newstead Road and some distance behind the Gas Works.

Much further to the north lay Goldcroft Farm and a 'Chemical Works' or

The first Backwater or 'Westham' Bridge of 1859, after the removal of its central opening.

Part of the wooden bridge built in 1862 to carry the Weymouth and Portland Railway across the Backwater. The iron viaduct which replaced it has also now been demolished. All the water shown in this photograph has been filled in.

pottery on the shore, more or less in a position at the end of modern Longcroft Lane. The first major move across the Backwater was not so much one for the living as for the dead, as in 1856 a new Melcombe Regis Cemetery was laid out on lands at Goldcroft. Access had to be by way of Gas House Lane (Newstead Road), and the only person to live on this side of the water was Mr J. Gard, the tenant of Goldcroft Farm.

The first bridge over the Backwater, together with the road which was to run in continuation westward, was built under the powers granted by the *Backwater Bridge and Road Act, 1857.* Trustees were appointed and the wooden bridge, together with the new road westwards to its link with Chickerell Road was opened to the public in 1859. A toll of ½d. was levied on each passenger to cross the bridge, and from this levy it earned its old name of 'The 'apenny bridge'. The toll was discontinued in 1879, when it became a county bridge and road.

In 1863 the wooden railway viaduct was built, bringing the new line to Portland across the water from Weymouth station to Littlefield, and then on by way of the new embankment across the Marsh to Rodwell and the south. When the service to Portland opened in 1865 the line still crossed open country until it passed over the Chickerell Road by way of 'Prince of Wales' Bridge, prior to entering the tunnel leading to Rodwell railway cutting.

The first private house, if it can be called that, was a wooden hut on wheels which had been built by a Mr Stagg when he was working at West Lulworth. It was drawn by horse from Lulworth and positioned on land to the north of the new road leading from the bridge, on a spot near where St Paul's Church stands today. It was a familiar landmark for many years with its attractive flower garden and greenhouse. Mr Stagg could not have been very pleased when the Local Board of Health decided to build an emergency isolation hospital on the other side of the road. This was July 1871, when the town was faced with a severe outbreak of smallpox, and the hospital was retained until 1880 when its equipment was sold to the new Port Sanitary Hospital at Ferry Bridge. The site of the hospital was one of the earliest terraces – Rocks Terrace. Later the name was shortened to Rock Terrace and today is better known as Nos. 47-89 Newstead Road.

Abbotsbury Road, at its junction with Holland Road, in the early 1900s.

The first brick house to be built on the Abbotsbury Road was No. 8 Excelsior Terrace, built by Mr F. Dowling and first occupied in March 1880. For six months this house stood alone, and then came the neighbouring house, No. 7 Excelsior Terrace. This particular terrace was sponsored by the Loyal Excelsior Lodge of Oddfellows and is known today as Nos. 72-98 Abbotsbury Road, making the original house No. 86 Abbotsbury Road by modern numbering. Over the crest of the hill, St Paul's Terrace and West End Terrace (156-180 Abbotsbury Road) joined other developments in the general area of modern Franklin Road.

By 1880 the local population had grown enough to warrant the erection of its first Anglican chapel, a day school and a steam laundry, whilst the following year, 1881, saw the opening of the first public house, the Rocks Hotel on a site formerly known as Rocks Close. The chapel, which seated about 190, was erected by Rev. C. Pigou, Rector of Wyke Regis at a cost of £1500. It served until 1896, when the first portion of the new St Paul's Church was completed on the opposite side of the road. St Paul's school served the area until July 1973, when it became the Parish Room, replacing the original chapel building of 1880. This latter has now been demolished and the site redeveloped as a terrace of houses.

A group of local businessmen was responsible for the erection of the steam laundry. It was designed to serve both the newly developing area and also Weymouth itself, and at one time gave the opportunity to some local wag to suggest that this new district be called 'Washington'. The laundry was demolished in the 1970s and a petrol station built on the site. Rockland was yet another name submitted for the new area at a public meeting in 1882, when it was finally decided that the name should be West Ham, now, perhaps inevitably, shortened to the familiar Westham.

The Laundry at Westham advertising in a Weymouth town guide of the 1920s.

It was still very much a rural community, with large tracts of undeveloped land. Twelve Acres, Nine Acres, Rocks, The Turnip Field, Little White Roughet, Knight's Bottom, Knight's Dale, as well as Littlefield and Goldcroft are but a few of the old place-names which disappeared as building advanced. Knight's Dale was developed by Emmanuel Knight and the name survives in Knightsdale Road. Just as the old fields and pasture names have disappeared, so the terrace names, allocated when the area was being built up, have given way to the numbered roads and streets which form the Westham of today. Few people will know the locations of Ashley Terrace, Balmoral Terrace, Diamond Terrace, Gresham Terrace, Laurestine Terrace or Westbourne Terrace, to name a few of the original place-names of the Westham of the 1880s.

During the period between 1880 and the turn of the century, the building of Westham proceeded apace. Much of the development was due to the efforts of John Bagg, a local builder and Mayor of Weymouth in 1900, 1901 and 1902. He held the lease of much of Littlefield from the Earl of Ilchester and sub-leased the lots to various other builders. The Ilchester connection is reflected in the street names Ilchester Road, Melbury Road and Stavordale Road. Stavordale Road was among the last of the side roads to be developed, and many of the larger houses were built during the 1890s by John B. Cole, using bricks from the old Royal Hotel, demolished in 1891. Many of these houses retain a mellow and pleasing appearance, attributable to the fact that at least some of their bricks date from the late 18th century. Stavordale Road reflects the better aspect of Victorian planning, but for the most part the local builders seemed to have but one object, to crowd the largest number of houses into the smallest possible space. The entire length of Abbotsbury Road became a solid mass of brick-built houses, with side roads similarly packed with dwellings large and small.

Union with the Borough of Weymouth and Melcombe Regis came in 1895, a decision forced on the Borough in some ways by the problems of Westham's sewage disposal. The Town Council had pleaded with the Rural District Council who administered Westham to make some improvements in their sanitary provisions, and having failed, concluded that the only sensible thing to do was to bring this new area within the borough boundaries. On 9th

The Esplanade and King's Statue in the 1880s.

November 1895, that part of Wyke Regis Parish known as Westham was added to Weymouth and Melcombe Regis Municipal Borough and to Weymouth Civil Parish. At the same time, parts of Radipole were also incorporated within the Borough. The population of the borough increased by between four and five thousand people, and the area by 452 acres of land and 311 acres of tidal water on the foreshore.

It is not difficult to distinguish between what is generally considered as 'old' Westham, i.e. the area taken over by the borough in 1895, and 'new' Westham, the area largely developed in the wake of the Great War of 1914-1918. 'Old' Westham ends more or less at the 'Adelaide' with a rough boundary along the northern part of Longcroft Road and Longcroft Lane, and to the south along the line of Southview Road and The Marsh. The great expansion to the north and west belongs to a much later period.

Further details of the former terrace names used in the Park District will be found in Appendix H and of those in Westham in Appendix I.

ELEVEN

Resort and Port

The period following the opening of the railway in 1857 saw not only the expansion of the town, but also the birth of a new kind of holiday trade. Towards the end of the 19th century, Weymouth and Melcombe Regis ceased to be an exclusive and fashionable resort catering for the wealthy classes who could afford to spend long summers by the sea. The town began to attract great numbers of ordinary working people, who, through cheap rail travel, could now afford to visit the seaside. It was the new, smaller houses, adjacent to the railway station, which were to provide inexpensive lodgings for many of the hundreds of people seeking accommodation in the town as they streamed off the trains. These years saw the beginning of the 'bed and breakfast' trade, often provided by families who did not necessarily advertise their premises as hotels or boarding houses, but accommodated visitors in 'the season'.

'The season' for wealthy visitors was considerably longer, and these families were still catered for. They could avail themselves of the 'House and Apartment Register' which offered better-class accommodation on the Esplanade and in other fashionable parts of the town, which, in due course, included new villa developments at Greenhill, Westerhall and the area west of the Dorchester Road. There was great interest in the Registrar General's annual report on the mortality figures for the English watering places, resorts vying with each other to maintain the lowest death rate in much the same way as they compete with high sunshine records today. In 1872, Weymouth (despite its drainage and sewage problems) was gratified to find itself a healthier place than Scarborough, Margate, Hastings, Brighton, Torquay, Weston-super-Mare and Tenby.

The beginning of the decline of the upper end of the seaside holiday trade probably dates from the mid 1870s. The passing of the Bank Holiday Act in 1871 gave the Great Western Railway Company the opportunity to lay on many extra trains to bring thousands of day trippers to Weymouth on the new statutory holidays, and a cut in the price of fares in 1873 increased the numbers of visitors still further. Weymouth was losing the 'health' aspect of its earlier resort days and late 19th century holidaymakers began to enjoy shorter seaside holidays, much as we do today. August was becoming the most popular month for these visitors, as reported in the *Southern Times* of 25th August 1877:

> Weymouth at the present time is at the zenith of its prosperity. The long-coveted 'season' which is so anxiously looked forward to from October to August is now at its height and the townspeople consequently in the best of humours. Within the past fortnight, every train has brought a large influx of visitors, until at last really there does not seem any more accommodation to offer. I have seen people going from street to street in search of lodgings, but where they are housed is a matter of speculation . . .

As early as 1880 the Town Council was considering the problem forced on it by the August rush to the seaside, even suggesting that school holidays be staggered to lengthen the season.

In 1845, twelve years before the arrival of the railway, Weymouth Harbour

The leading hotels provided transport to convey Victorian and Edwardian visitors from the railway station. This photograph was taken at the rear of the Royal Hotel.

had suffered a severe setback when the Channel Islands Packet Service was lost to Southampton. It proved only temporary. In 1857 the London and South Western Railway Company's steamer *Express* commenced sailing to Guernsey and Jersey and a week later the rival Weymouth and Channel Islands Steam Packet Company Ltd. began a service using the *Aquila* (264 tons) and the *Cygnus* (245 tons). L.S.W.R. services were short-lived. The *Express* struck submerged rocks on leaving Jersey in September 1859 and was a total wreck. By the end of the year no more L.S.W.R. boats ran from Weymouth.

In 1858 the *Brighton* (286 tons) joined the Packet Company's fleet, operating a new service from Weymouth to Cherbourg. This French service lasted less than a year. Restarted by the G.W.R. in 1878, it continued only until 1885 and was then abandoned until 1974, when the car ferry service between the two ports was introduced. The *Brighton* continued in service at Weymouth until 1887, when she was wrecked in fog off Guernsey.

The local hoteliers must have gained extra overnight guests from the sailings to the Channel Islands, for the *Aquila* and *Cygnus* left Weymouth at 7 a.m. on Tuesdays, Thursdays and Saturdays in 1857 and passengers were requested to be onboard a quarter-of-an-hour before departure!

Developments in services during the latter half of the 19th century were to bring considerable changes to the harbour scene. In 1840 a pile-pier infilled with a mixture of waste Portland stone and shingle'concrete', had been built on the north side of the Harbour. This pier was seen partly as an extension of Weymouth Esplanade, then considered as one of 'the finest marine walks in Europe', and at the same time the promenade was being lengthened northwards from the end of Brunswick Buildings along Greenhill. Other

Horse racing at Lodmoor in the 1860s, where wrestling bouts and a fair added excitement to an already colourful scene.

harbour improvements of 1840 had included extensive dredging to provide a greater depth of water, the construction of a new ballast wharf under the Nothe and new slipways and docks built by local shipowners and repairers.

Weymouth Pier as extended in 1859.

During 1859 and 1860 the pile-pier was rebuilt and extended, and a cargo stage was added in 1877 to facilitate the unloading of Channel Islands' potatoes. During 1888-9 a new passenger stage and baggage hall were built for the Great Western Railway, which planned to take over the ailing Packet Company. The Weymouth and Channel Islands Steam Packet Company had struggled through a number of crises in its thirty years' history, and that the Company survived so long was largely due to the G.W.R. interest, the railway company being ever mindful of possible L.S.W.R. intervention at Weymouth, if they withdrew.

There were also improvements to the south or 'stone' pier, an extension 250 feet long designed to protect the harbour during easterly gales being completed in 1878. This function gave the stone pier its alternative name of 'Weymouth Harbour Breakwater'.

1865 had seen the opening of the Weymouth Harbour Tramway, when the railway line was extended along the quay wall as far as the end of Devonshire Buildings, providing a direct link between the railway station and the Harbour. Entirely horse-drawn in its early days, the steam locomotives that took over in 1880 gave way to diesel traction in 1966 and now mainline locomotives take the trains direct from the main line to the quay. In 1889 the line was extended to the G.W.R.'s new landing stage on the pier, enabling easy access to the Channel Island steamers. Three brand new G.W.R. vessels, the *Lynx, Antelope* and *Gazelle*, all more than twice the size of the Packet Company's ships, were brought to Weymouth soon after the new service

A train on the Weymouth harbour Tramway in 1983. The two photographs show the contrast in rolling stock and scenery – all the water to the right of the lower picture of 1910 has been filled in and laid out as public gardens and car parks.

The Pier and Esplanade in the early 1900s, showing the passenger stage and baggage hall erected for the G.W.R.'s new services in 1889.

commenced on 1st July 1889. A fourth new vessel, the *Ibex* arrived in 1891. The service was fast and the G.W.R. could now offer real competition to the L.S.W.R. service from Southampton. Rivalry was intense and there was constant public interest in the two companies' arrival times in the Islands.

Today, the railway line no longer runs along the Harbour wall, for the vast reclamations from the Backwater in the early 1900s and 1920s have filled in all the water which once lapped against the wall along Commercial Road. The train now rolls slowly through the streets of Weymouth, both a tourist attraction and traffic problem!

The steeply-arched Town Bridge of 1824 photographed about 1860. The newly-built Holy Trinity Schools are in the background, above houses which were demolished in the 1880s. The bow-fronted Town Bridge Buildings on the right were pulled down in 1928.

In 1865 the Weymouth and Portland Railway opened to traffic. To carry the railway across Weymouth Backwater and the mouth of the Fleet two timber viaducts were constructed. The iron replacements for both of them have also now been demolished, following the closure of the Portland Railway in 1965.

In the late 1870s, the two road bridges which carried vehicles and pedestrians across Weymouth Harbour and Backwater were causing problems. The Town Bridge of 1824 and the Backwater (or 'Westham') Bridge of 1859 were both in need of extensive repairs. The Town Bridge, with its raised, arched swing section had steep and inconvenient approaches and a roadway width of 17 feet 9 inches – too narrow for the increasing traffic of the town. A survey of 1879 reported the daily average number of vehicles passing over the bridge as 687 and pedestrians as 10,750. It was decided to alter the bridge substantially, by replacing the central arch with a flat swing section, bearing a roadway 26 feet wide. The cost of these improvements was met by levying tolls on the users of the new bridge until the cost of the alterations was paid in full, and the work was completed in 1881. The tolls remained in force until 1889.

Traffic problems during the period of reconstruction of the Town Bridge must have been considerable. Although a temporary bridge was erected across the Harbour for the use of pedestrians, the Backwater Bridge of 1859 was by now unable to cope with any increase in vehicular traffic. It was, in fact, in a

The Nothe Fort under construction in 1862, drawn by Philip Brannon. (Courtesy Victoria and Albert Museum)

dangerous condition and in 1880 conspicuous notices were posted informing the public of its unsafe state. The timbers had lately been subjected to increased wear due to the numerous heavy wagonloads of bricks which were being taken across the bridge every day to be used in the new building developments in the fast growing suburb of Westham. After lengthy delays, repairs to the bridge were completed in 1882, but they were not satisfactory and the strengthening of the decaying timbers became a continuous process. Replacement bridges were discussed for forty years and it was not until 1921 that a new embankment bridge – the Westham Bridge of today – was finally opened.

A major change in the landscape of the harbour area was to result from the construction of the great Nothe Fort on the headland overlooking Weymouth and Portland Harbours. Work on the Portland Breakwaters was well under way when in 1857 approval was given for the construction of heavy batteries on the Nothe as part of the general scheme of fortifications for the Weymouth-Portland area.

The foundations of the Nothe Fort were begun in 1860, when the land was drained and the sea wall built. The contractor for the project failed in 1862, and the work was completed by men of the Royal Engineers and by convicts from Portland. The new fortifications at Weymouth and Portland were a small part of the extensive system of defence works all along the south coast, which included the forts around Plymouth and Portsmouth, and at Spithead. The Nothe was designed to create a crossfire with the Breakwater Fort, thus guarding the entrance to Portland Harbour. A description published in 1863 described it as:

> . . . a strong casemated battery, in the shape of a horse-shoe, armed with two tiers of the heaviest rifled guns, capable of throwing a projectile of 300 lbs weight to a distance of three or four miles. The lower of these tiers consists of twelve guns in massive casemates, the walls of which are covered by a thick rampart of earth, leaving openings through which may be seen the muzzles of the guns protruding from iron shields of more than twice the thickness of the plating of our most formidable ironclads.
>
> The upper tier of guns is protected by an earthen rampart, the immediate vicinity of each gun being rendered more secure by an iron screen. The foundations are secured by a Cyclopean sea wall, varying in height from 30 to 40 feet, protecting the work from the ravages of the sea and forming the first great obstacle to an attack on the fort. The rear or gorge is closed by a scarp wall, 40 feet in height, and a ditch; the latter crossed by a drawbridge, and flanked by a caponier situated at the south end.
>
> From the further side of the ditch the whole of the Nothe peninsula is gradually sloped down towards Weymouth, so that no cover is afforded to an enemy.
>
> The casemates are fitted up as barrack rooms for about two hundred men, with the usual proportion of officers' quarters, stores, etc. The very ample magazine accommodation is effectually protected by an enormous rampart from any chance of penetration by a hostile shell, and this rampart serves at the same time to hide the interior of the fort from the high ground about Wyke, upon which an enemy might establish himself. Lifts are arranged in different parts of the work, by which the ammunition may be hoisted at once to either tier of guns, and thus the shells etc., may be prepared in perfect safety under cover.

The new fort was much larger than any battery previously sited on the headland, and together with the area occupied by the soldiers during the construction period, robbed the people of Weymouth of a favourite open space. Complaints were frequent, but in 1870 walks were laid out and seats placed on the area outside the fort, which had been leased from the Secretary of State for War at a nominal rent of £1 a year.

One presumes that the account of 1863 must have been based on an official description, but by 1872, when the Fort was completed, it was different both in design and armament. The earthen batteries were not proceeded with and by 1869 it had become a casemated granite fort, designed for ten heavy guns, protected by iron shields and two lighter guns facing landwards. In 1869 the total cost of the project had been estimated as £117,049. By 1872 it was armed with four 9 inch and six 10 inch rifled muzzle-loading guns (RMLs), and in 1887 these were still listed as the main armament supported by two 64 pounder RMLs, all mounted. By 1898 these had been replaced by eight 12.5 inch RMLs and two 10 inch RMLs plus the two 64 pounder RMLs. Traces of the mountings of these guns can still be seen in some of the casemates.

It is a matter of history that these fortifications were never put to the test of combat with a seaborne enemy, but even so the town of Weymouth would, from time to time, reverberate to the blast of the great guns being exercised.

Royal visitors were in Weymouth again on the occasion of the laying of the final stone of Portland Breakwater. Prince Albert, who had witnessed the start, had died in 1861, and it was his son, the Prince of Wales, accompanied by his brother Prince Arthur, who steamed into Portland Harbour aboard the Royal Yacht *Victoria and Albert* on 10th August 1872 to declare the works complete. Following the ceremony at Portland and a review of the assembled fleet, the Princes landed at the Pile Pier. An address was presented, a military band played, the schoolchildren sang, and the royal visitors were then escorted to the Gloucester Hotel for the inevitable luncheon.

The Royal Yacht Victoria and Albert *off Weymouth Pier in 1872, bringing the Prince of Wales to lay the final stone of Portland Breakwater.*

The Mayor of Weymouth who greeted the Prince of Wales in August 1872 was James Robertson. He was still in office on the stormy night of 25th November that year, and holding a banquet at the Royal Hotel, when word was brought to him of a large ship wrecked on the Chesil Beach between Wyke Regis and Portland. The Mayor left his guests and set about organising assistance for some sixty shipwreck victims rescued from the *Royal Adelaide*, an iron ship of 1385 tons, Australia-bound, which was a total loss near Ferrybridge.

It was an eventful night, as were the days which followed. Seven people drowned when the line parted after a heroic rescue attempt, and the ship began to break up. Four more died the following day – not shipwreck victims these, but local men who had discovered that the *Adelaide's* cargo included casks of brandy, rum and gin. On three of these the inquest verdicts were 'died from exposure and wet after drinking raw spirits'; and a boy of fifteen died from 'excessive drinking'.

As was usual on such occasions, hundreds of people arrived on the disaster scene – many taking advantage of the Weymouth and Portland Railway's train service to reach the Beach. All kinds of goods were disgorged by the wreck – bales of cloth, gloves, boots and shoes, hats, cutlery, hams, chests of tea, coffee, figs and livestock. Some items were salvaged under the watchful eye of the Customs officers, but such a huge crowd could not be controlled and much of the cargo disappeared into local homes. The registers of schools show many absences at the end of November 1872, as children joined the treasure-hunting throng.

By this date Weymouth had its first official lifeboat, the *Agnes Harriet*, although this vessel was unable to assist at the wreck of the *Royal Adelaide* where the rescue was carried out by the local coastguards and the people of Portland and Wyke. Weymouth had three oared lifeboats, before, in 1924, the first motor lifeboat arrived on station, the *Samuel Oakes*. Today the R.N.L.I. craft moored in Weymouth Harbour is the *Tony Vandervell*, the eighth lifeboat to serve here. The crews have been provided almost exclusively by the local fishing community. Commercial fishing has never been a major local industry, but there has always been a small group of fishermen at

The naming ceremony of Weymouth's first lifeboat the Agnes Harriet *on Weymouth sands in 1869. Never actually launched from the beach, the lifeboat had been brought through the town on a horse-drawn carriage for the ceremony.*

Weymouth, some with long family traditions in the business. Their knowledge of local waters had been invaluable when on lifeboat duty, and has often been put to a very different use when taking boatloads of summer visitors on short seaborne excursions – a useful supplementary source of income.

Many of the new buildings erected in the town during the latter half of the 19th century were intended for the comfort, convenience and entertainment of residents and visitors. Along the Esplanade, building developments made steady progress northwards on vacant land, but some older properties were pulled down and replaced.

The Gloucester Hotel was enlarged by the erection of the County Club extension. For a few years the site to the north of the Gloucester remained empty following the demolition of the Georgian Royal Hotel in 1891. This charming, but small, bow windowed building was not to the taste of the Victorians, 'The exterior does not display much architectural beauty, and in the interior, comfort has been studied more than splendour' commented a contemporary guidebook dismissively. The second Royal Hotel, far more ornate, was built in 1897 and is described by Eric Ricketts as having 'just that touch of opulence required to season the austere dignity of the earlier terraces'.

Other Esplanade buildings of Queen Victoria's reign are now hotels. The Weymouth Sanatorium, Clarence Buildings, (No. 21 The Esplanade) opened in 1863 and has been converted to holiday flats, having also housed the offices of Weymouth and Melcombe Regis Borough Council from 1903 to 1971. This site was never ideal for a hospital, being close to the noise and bustle of the Channel Islands steamers and the Harbour tramway, and in 1902 patients were transferred to new buildings at Westerhall, now the Weymouth and District Hospital.

More local hospitals were built in the late 19th century. The Weymouth Royal Hospital and Dispensary in School Street, an institution 'for the relief of the sick poor', had occupied various premises in the town since its foundation in 1816. The Weymouth and Dorset County Royal Eye Infirmary moved to purpose-built accommodation in King Street in 1872, whilst at Wyke Regis, a Port Sanitary Hospital, overlooking the Fleet, opened in 1880. Today, all but the 'Weymouth and District' have either closed, amalgamated or moved on: the School Street premises, latterly a Salvation Army Hostel, now stand empty, the site being scheduled for redevelopment; the Eye Hospital has transferred to Greenhill and the Royal British Legion Club occupies the King Street buildings. The Sanitary Hospital buildings at Wyke Regis are now in the heart of a holiday camp complex.

Visitors in hotels and apartments along the Esplanade overlooked a constantly changing scene. Weymouth had once been criticized for its lack of gardens but there were now public walks and gardens at both ends of the promenade. In 1867, George Robert Stephenson, the wealthy owner of one of the large private yachts which were becoming frequent visitors to the harbour, purchased the area of ground near the pier known as 'The Rings' for it to be laid out as gardens for the benefit of the town's inhabitants. A few years later, Sir Frederic Johnstone gave land at the far end of the Esplanade for the same purpose. In 1880 it was decided to name Mr Stephenson's gift 'The Alexandra Gardens', some confusion having arisen since both recreation areas were being referred to as the 'New Gardens'. Johnstone Gardens was dropped in favour of Greenhill Gardens, the name by which they are known today. Sir Frederic

Entertainment in a more leisurely age. Weymouth Town Band and visiting bands and orchestras provided music in the attractive Alexandra Gardens, much changed today.

Johnstone, M.P. for Weymouth 1874-1885, owned extensive property and land on both sides of the Harbour and also presented the site of St John's Gardens, opposite the church. These smaller gardens, laid out with shrubs, lawns and flowerbeds, opened in July 1904. The Nothe Gardens, established during 1888-9 on a much less formal pattern due to their exposed position on the headland, were an extension of the walks laid down in 1870.

Various other improvements followed: the Mayor purchased statuary for the Alexandra Gardens and a bandstand was erected in 1891. The thatched shelters which have gradually disappeared from the Gardens over the last few years were built in 1904, and along the Esplanade itself attractive cast-iron shelters were erected in 1889, some surviving today. Donkeys arrived on the sands in Victorian times, and today, four generations later, the Downton family still provide the donkey rides which thousands of children have enjoyed for a hundred years. Punch and Judy shows were also entertaining visitors on the beach in the 19th century.

One child who delighted in Victorian seaside Weymouth was Llewelyn Powys who recalled his boyhood memories of the town in a nostalgic essay entitled 'Weymouth in the three eights'. The Powys family stayed with their grandmother in Brunswick Terrace and the young Llewelyn's first view of Weymouth Bay – 'a wide field of bright-blue water under a curved and cloudless sky' – was at the end of the short walk from the railway station, along King Street to the Esplanade, a route taken by thousands of holidaymakers before and since.

For this young visitor 'the sea front was always separated into two strict divisions. To the right as I came out of the door was all the gaiety of a Vanity Fair, with varnished pleasure boats, entertainment shows, fairy-story goat-carriages, and white flat happy sands good for building castles. To the left was a more sombre expanse where the sea was rough and had to be kept by banks of heavy pebbles from breaking over into Lodmoor, that wild waste of bird-haunted marshland. It was upon the top of these great beaches to the more serious east that real fishing boats were stabled, true deep-sea fishing boats hollow and benched. Near them I had once seen a draught of fishes brought to land in an encircling net buoyed with corks and strained to breaking-point, a harvest of silver light leaping against the stout black mesh . . .'

The headings of two bills issued by local shops in the 1880s.

Another visitor of this decade was Sir Daniel Gooch, eminent engineer and chairman of the Great Western Railway. On Brunel's death he had taken over as engineer of the *Great Eastern* and had been in Weymouth in the late 1860s and early 1870s superintending the preparations in Portland Harbour for the steamship's cable-laying expeditions. He was to return to Weymouth in later years on a number of occasions, spending Christmas holidays at the Burdon Hotel and finding the hotel and Weymouth much to his liking. Despite the often wet and cold weather and the fact that he and his wife were sometimes the only guests in the hotel, Sir Daniel felt that the climate was beneficial, especially when combined with plenty of exercise (which included walks around the Harbour 'to look at our steamers'). Somewhat surprisingly (or perhaps because the weather had been so windy and cold) Gooch commented acidly on his return to London in January 1885 'The Burdon Hotel has many defects: it is cold and badly furnished and very dear'.

Providing some of the visitors with entertainment, and the town officials with problems, were the bathing machines of Victorian Weymouth. Regulations were in force regarding the use of the machines, and in 1864 alterations to the bye-laws stated:

The Horses to be employed for the purpose of drawing the Machines shall be in attendance on the sands between the first day of May and 31st day of October at six o'clock in the morning and no machine shall be made use of on a Sunday after ten o'clock in the morning and that in case the above regulations shall not be strictly attended to every person so offending shall forfeit and pay any sum not exceeding twenty shillings.

Residents were able to bathe more cheaply than visitors!

For the use of each machine from every inhabitant of the Borough pursuant to ancient custom, not exceeding 6d.
For the use of each machine when occupied by one person (not an inhabitant) 9d.
When occupied by two or more persons not inhabitants, each person 6d.

The bathing machine proprietors had to provide 'a looking glass and a carpet for each Machine and two hand towels for each person and also a pair of drawers for the use of each Gentleman'.

To ensure that Victorian propriety was observed:

Any Male Person not using drawers or other appropriate dress after eight o'clock in the morning will be deemed guilty of indecent exposure of his person and shall forfeit and pay any sums not exceeding twenty shillings.

A Space of not less than 50 yards shall be preserved between the machines appropriated for the ladies and those appropriated for the gentlemen.

All appears to have been in order until the introduction of larger bathing pavilions containing individual cubicles. In 1890 the new 'Gentlemen's Machine' was placed north of the machines then on the beach, and the 'Ladies Machine' to the south. By August there was the first hint of trouble:

In consequence of the indecent exposure of persons using the Bathing Saloons recently placed upon the sands, the proprietors to be ordered without delay to keep the saloons in deep water according to the state of the tide, otherwise the licence to be withdrawn.

But matters continued to deteriorate and the Corporation minutes are scattered with complaints about the distance between the saloons and the wearing of 'proper bathing drawers'. It was all a far cry from the days when King George III, a very moral man, bathed in the sea at Weymouth wearing no costume at all.

Christchurch, opposite Weymouth Railway Station, at the King Street/Park Street junction. It was demolished in 1956.

A little seafront building which has survived the changes in fashion is the Tea Cabin, standing on the edge of the Esplanade near the King's Statue, and surprisingly, dating back as far as 1878, when it opened as a Cabmen's Shelter.

Victorian additions to Weymouth Esplanade – extensions to the Gloucester Hotel in 1862, the Tea Cabin of 1878, the Jubilee Clock, unveiled in 1888 and the new Royal Hotel, opened in 1897.

One of the first applications for the lease of the shelter had come from a Temperance Society, but in the words of one councillor at the time, 'Men would have their dinner there, and he did not see why they should not have a drop of beer with it, of which, if the Society had control of the shelter, they would be deprived' – a sentiment heartily endorsed by another councillor, John Groves, of the long established brewing company.

In the town itself, the great Victorian religious revival had brought about the building of a number of new churches and chapels. Many of these have now been demolished or converted to other uses. Gloucester Street Congregational Church of 1864 has been replaced by 'George Thorne House', a block of flats, the name of which retains a link with the history of Non-conformity in the town. A chapel in Lower Bond Street, replaced by Maiden Street Methodist Church in 1866 disappeared during town centre redevelopment. Weymouth Co-operative Society now uses a former Methodist chapel in Caroline Place, a building which has also housed the Salvation Army and a printing works. Opposite the railway station, Christchurch of 1874 closed in 1939 and has been pulled down – the flats and shops of Garnet Court fill the site. On Weymouth Quay, the Sailors' Bethel, opened by church charities in 1866, has become the headquarters of the Royal Dorset Yacht Club, having been a youth club and a restaurant in recent years.

All the town's Victorian National Schools – St Mary's, St John's, and Holy Trinity have closed or moved to new premises and their sites redeveloped. The 1860's buildings of Weymouth College, a boys preparatory school in Dorchester Road are now surrounded by modern additions since the College (which transferred to Wellingborough on the outbreak of World War II) became a teacher training college – now the Dorset Institute of Higher Education.

Weymouth's second Theatre Royal opened in the 1860s in converted chapel buildings at the lower end of St Nicholas Street. Only the entrance arch survived demolitions in the 1960s.

Weymouth was fortunate in the late 19th century to be represented in Parliament by Sir Henry Edwards, whose generous gifts to the town can still be seen today – ten cottage homes, known as Edwards Avenue, on Boot Hill and 'Edwardsville' in Rodwell Avenue, all designed for elderly inhabitants of the borough. Sir Henry also provided an annual dinner for the old people of

The 1887 Jubilee Clock as first built, erected on a stone base on Weymouth sands.

The stone base of the Clock Tower has been buried beneath the wide Esplanade extension of the early 1920s.

the town and built and furnished new premises for the Working Men's Club in Mitchell Street. A statue of Sir Henry Edwards stands in the grounds of Edwardsville and a memorial was erected by public subscription in Melcombe Regis Cemetery, but the best known tribute to the man who was M.P. from 1867-1885 and who declined the Freedom of the Borough, is the statue outside the Alexandra Gardens, erected in 1885.

Sir Henry Edwards also paid for the clock atop the Jubilee Clock Tower on Weymouth Esplanade, erected to commemorate the Golden Jubilee of Queen Victoria in 1887. Early that year the Town Council were discussing suitable celebrations for the auspicious day – Tuesday June 21st 1887. Following the public reading of the inevitable Loyal Address, and thanksgiving services in the local churches, the day was given over to general rejoicing. There were banquets and luncheons for the leading citizens, an outdoor dinner and tea for the aged poor (the day, though windy, was fortunately fine and transport was laid on to take the elderly picnickers to a field off the Dorchester Road), a street party for the children, sports, band performances and games on the sands. All these activities were set against a background of streets, shops and offices decorated with banners, evergreens, flowers and coloured lights and the effect throughout the town must have been quite stunning.

When all the celebrations had been paid for, the balance of the Jubilee funds was used to provide a permanent memorial of the event, and late in 1887 it was decided that an accurate public clock – a long felt need – should be erected on the Esplanade. That the town was able to build such a landmark as a clock with illuminated dial was due to the benevolence of Sir Henry Edwards and his gift of a fine large clock for the tower. Standing beside it today, it is difficult to envisage that the Jubilee Clock once stood on the sands and has never been moved. The wide sweep of the Esplanade which now stretches in front of it was built in the 1920s, partly to prevent the encroachment of shingle on Weymouth's star attraction, its fine golden sands.

Jubilee Year also saw the erection of the Jubilee Hall in St Thomas Street – a new theatre for Weymouth, which some twenty years later was the first establishment to show moving pictures in the town. The building still stands, much enlarged in the 1920s, when it re-opened as the Regent Theatre and Dance Hall, but its days as a cinema are long over. More local celebrations followed in 1897 on the occasion of Queen Victoria's Diamond Jubilee.

An unusual gift to the town during the Victorian period was the presentation in 1891 of a footbridge over the railway lines at the end of Hanover Terrace (now Hanover Road), leading to what was then the Western Esplanade along Radipole Lake. The donor was W.H. Alexander, a generous contributor to many causes, who later resided in Weymouth. His gift was much appreciated by the people living in the area who had previously walked across the railway tracks, a dangerous procedure in view of the many trains then using Weymouth station. Western Esplanade, a popular walk along the shore of the Lake, has now been absorbed by the 20th century reclamations which provided a new lakeside road – Radipole Park Drive, and the gardens behind it, and which necessitated the doubling in length of Mr Alexander's original bridge.

A Victorian view of the Crown Hotel, at the lower end of St Thomas Street. The building was altered and extended in the late 1920s at the same time as the Town Bridge was under reconstruction.

On the Weymouth side of the Harbour, the Sidney Hall was presented to Holy Trinity parish in 1900 by Sir John Groves, in memory of his son Sidney, who died in 1895. The building was intended for the use of the Church Lads' Brigade, of which Sidney Groves had been a member.

Along with such improvements as these, there were also the schemes which came to nothing. Some got no further than the discussion stage – a pleasure pier opposite the end of King Street was proposed more than once and there were plans for a large Winter Gardens at the southern end of the Esplanade. A proposal to construct a tramway line along the Esplanade and up the Dorchester Road as far as Lodmoor Hill was put forward in 1884 but was soon abandoned. Another major transport project was actually begun at Newton's Cove in the 1890s: it was here that the Great Western Railway Company wanted to develop a new port.

A branch railway line was scheduled to leave the main line near Upwey station, sweep round in a great bend and pass under the high land between Weymouth and Wyke Regis by means of a tunnel, emerging just above the Old Castle Cove, and then along what we know today as Underbarn ending up in the new docks. The scheme received no support from the Town Council who stood to lose their harbour dues, and was finally abandoned in 1913, but not before much preliminary work had been done. The approach road to Bincleaves Torpedo Testing Establishment was part of the railway project, as well as much of the reclaimed land on which the Establishment stands today. A surviving link with this project is the Railway Dock Hotel at the foot of Rodwell Avenue. It was named in anticipation of the completion of the scheme.

The St Thomas Street frontage of V.H. Bennett's shop as built in late Victorian times. Over a long period he was able to acquire all the adjoining properties and form Weymouth's largest departmental store.

The 1890s also saw the start of the second stage of the enclosure of Portland Harbour by the construction of the two breakwaters nearest to Weymouth, one of which joins the mainland at Bincleaves. Although the stone was again quarried by convict labour on Portland, the actual construction was carried out by a firm of civilian contractors, and this second stage of the project had none of the ceremony of the first. No massive overhead railway carried the stone out to sea; instead it was transported from the Island in specially constructed barges which emptied their contents directly into the water on site. These final two breakwaters replaced a temporary arrangement of dolphins

Christmas 'Show Night' was one of the eagerly awaited annual events in the days before World War I. On this evening, shops stayed open until late, pubs did a roaring trade and crowds thronged the streets to 'shop gaze' at the special displays such as this one by butcher Andrews of St Mary Street.

and cables which had been erected to combat the threat posed by the newly invented torpedo.

At the same time as these works were in progress, a new Ferrybridge was under construction, replacing the timber structure of 1839. Built by the Dorset County Council to the plans of Sir John Coode, the first half of the bridge opened in September 1895 and the completed bridge was fully opened to traffic the following year.

The closing years of the Victorian era in Weymouth were marked by a major financial disaster. In March 1897, the Weymouth Old Bank, also known as Messrs. Eliot, Pearce and Co.'s Bank, collapsed. The failure of this institution shocked not only Weymouth, but also Portland, Dorchester and Bournemouth where the bank had long-established branches and where it was considered to be as secure as the Bank of England itself. There were creditors large and small ranging from the Borough Treasurer, the Gas and Water companies, and Cosens and Company, to individual savers and the children of the National Schools whose school banking account was deposited with Messrs. Eliot. It was to be over six years before the affairs of the Bank were finally wound up and the last of three dividends paid out to the creditors, the total repayment being only 7s.11¼d. (40p) in the £1.

As Weymouth entered the 20th century the long reign of Queen Victoria was drawing to a close: sixty-three years which had seen great changes in the town so much enjoyed by her grandfather a century before. The Queen died in January 1901 and the statue of Her Majesty which stands at the northern end of the Esplanade became the third 'Royal' monument on Weymouth sea-front.

TWELVE

The Twentieth century

The extensive reclamations from the Backwater and Radipole Lake, which during the 19th and early 20th centuries had completely changed the shape of Melcombe Regis, led eventually to consideration being given to how Radipole Lake itself could be developed. A comprehensive scheme was produced in 1933 to include sports facilities, boating lakes and ornamental walks, but it was never proceeded with, apart from the infilling between the Park Drive and the railway line to make Radipole Park Gardens, the enlarged railway sidings, and the playing fields at Radipole. The only other reclamations have been the large car parks near the former Melcombe Regis station, filled in during the 1950s and those carried out along the western shore of the lake during the years following the Second World War, anticipating the new main road to Redlands by-passing the town and Esplanade traffic. Since 1948 the lagoons and reed beds of Radipole Lake have been a bird sanctuary, a peaceful and attractive wildlife haven, although close to the town centre.

The complete reclamation of Weymouth Marsh, the large open area west of the railway embankment on the Portland line, has been a long process. By 1928, some six acres, rather more than half the total area, had been drained and improved, being given the new name of Westham Playing Fields. The completion of the scheme was not achieved until well after the end of the Second World War, with the building of the Youth Activities Centre in 1964, followed by the construction of running tracks and other facilities. Finally, in 1974, the transformation of the former 'marsh' was further enhanced by the building of the long awaited Swimming Pool.

All these changes had been linked directly or indirectly with the River Wey, and come as a reminder that the river was still a vital factor in the development of the area. It was because of the river that Weymouth had first developed as a trading port, and the commercial harbour continued as a major contributor to the local economy. Throughout the 20th century the Great Western Railway steamers and later those of British Railways, have provided the bulk of the trade passing through the harbour. During the years prior to 1933 there were only minor changes in the harbour facilities; passengers used the landing stage on the pier, built in 1889, whilst the goods were loaded and unloaded at the cargo stage adjacent to the rear of Devonshire Buildings. Apart from a short-lived service to Nantes during 1909-11, the entire G.W.R. service out of Weymouth was with the Channel Islands, with the annual build up of passengers during the summer and the seasonal peaks when thousands of tons of early potatoes and tomatoes passed through the port. Occasional trade with ports along the French north-west coast was forthcoming as the result of the efforts of private and continental ship-owners, but for all practical purposes it was the Channel Islands Service which was the backbone of the local sea-borne trade.

A detail from a photograph of Templeman's Mill in 1900. The Mill was destroyed by fire in 1917.

Some of the largest independent vessels to use the port in the years before the First World War were the grain boats serving Templeman's Crown Flour

A typical quayside scene during the G.W.R.'s long association with the port of Weymouth. This photograph was taken some years prior to a major extension of the pier, opened in 1933 by H.R.H. The Prince of Wales (Later King Edward VIII).

Between the wars there was a considerable trade in French broccoli, brought in to the port on non-railway vessels. Scenes like this were also a familiar sight at the old cargo stage in the days when the Channel Islands steamers unloaded huge cargoes of potatoes, tomatoes and flowers.

Mills, close to Custom House Quay. One of the disasters of the Great War period was the destruction of these buildings by fire. Templeman's had been working non-stop during the war years supplying flour to all the local bakeries, and the blaze which gutted the mills in December 1917 wiped out a small but important industry in the town.

The import of coal by sea was another long established part of the Harbour trade and continued until 1939, but the unloading was a dusty process and all attempts to revive the trade in subsequent years have been fiercely opposed by those living and working near the harbourside. Another seaborne trade to disappear was that of the importing of cement. London, or sprit-sail barges would bring in their cargoes from the Medway, but although many thousands of tons arrived in this way, the barges and their cargoes are a thing of the past. Timber boats from the Baltic were regular visitors up to the end of the 1930s. These were the last of the great sailing ships to trade into the port of Weymouth, and their tall masts provided an attractive addition to the Weymouth skyline, in sharp contrast with the smoke and steam of the cranes dotted along the cargo stage.

A graceful sight in Weymouth Harbour in the 1930s – the timber ship Yxpila. *One of the attractions when this vessel was in port was the acrobatics of one of her Finnish crew who dived from the rigging to entertain the crowds.*

Throughout this period the tramway had provided the rail link with the Harbour, but with the steady growth in the overall length of railway vehicles, especially passenger stock, the sharp bend at Ferry's Corner presented serious operational problems. In 1938 land was reclaimed from the Backwater at this point and the tramway re-aligned on a more generous curve, passing under the outer of the two archways beneath the new Town Bridge.

The Town Bridge had been completely rebuilt during the years 1928-1930, when the first stone bridge was dismantled. The new bridge had one wide, two-arm central opening to enable larger vessels to pass up harbour. The irony is that apart from paddle-steamers passing up river for refit, or to lay-up

4th July 1930. The Town Bridge has been officially opened by H.R.H. the Duke of York (later King George VI) and Cosens paddle-steamer Empress, *crowded with Weymouth schoolchildren, is the first vessel to steam through.*

Waste Portland stone being tipped behind the new retaining wall at the start of reclamations to form Westwey Road, opened to traffic in 1932.

during the winter, and some small tankers and tar vessels, no large ships have ever used the upper reaches of the harbour.

Whilst the bridge was being rebuilt a temporary wooden bridge was erected for pedestrians, but all other traffic had to be routed via Newstead Road, Abbotsbury Road and Westham Bridge. This alternative route would have been impossible but for the fact that in 1921 the old wooden bridge to Westham had been replaced by the Westham Bridge of today, the separate footbridge being added in 1973. Westham Bridge is in reality a dam, with sluices which control the level of the water in Radipole Lake, rendering the old dam of 1872 redundant. If only Westwey Road had been completed before the Town Bridge was demolished, the re-routing would have been far less inconvenient.

Between 1949 and 1952 the cargo stage was completely reconstructed and eventually linked by one continuous harbour wall with the passenger facilities on the pier. The years following the Second World War saw a considerable growth in passenger traffic using the port, partly as a result of the decision made in 1960 to make Weymouth the premier passenger port for the Channel Islands at the expense of its old rival Southampton. Competition from air travel had made serious inroads into the numbers crossing to the Islands by sea, but concentrated on one port only, they still produced some very busy summer Saturdays on Weymouth Quay!

But methods of passenger and cargo handling were changing, and late in 1972 the Corporation decided to convert the Harbour Pier to accept car ferries on the 'roll-on-roll-off' principle. The first service, to Jersey only, began in 1973, but with the completion of handling facilities at Guernsey, a full Channel Islands car ferry service became possible. April 1974 saw the commencement of a new cross-Channel ferry service to Cherbourg, and it soon became obvious that the days of the traditional passenger and cargo vessels at Weymouth were numbered.

The railway steamers have always been an integral feature of the Weymouth scene, and the retirement of an ageing vessel and its replacement by a new one a matter of considerable local interest. The *Roebuck* and *Reindeer* joined the fleet in 1897, the *Reindeer* remaining in service until 1928 although her sister ship was lost during the First World War. The *St Julien* and *St Helier* arrived from the builders in 1925 and were the backbone of the service from then until the early 1960s, apart from war service between 1939 and 1945. The last of the traditional passenger ships were the *Caesaria* and *Sarnia* which took over the service in 1960 and 1961 and continued until made redundant by the advent of the car ferries in the 1970s. Of the relief or 'summer only' vessels, the two *St Patricks* are the best known, the original being a casualty of the Second World War when operating in the Irish Sea. In addition to these there have been a number of cargo vessels, the best remembered being the *Sambur* and *Roebuck,* contemporaries of the legendary ships the *St Julien* and *St Helier*.

Servicing the cross-Channel steamers has always been a major influence on the railway provision at Weymouth, and the introduction of the car ferries has been accompanied by a matching decline in the passenger and goods traffic arriving at and leaving Weymouth Quay by rail. Long before the car ferries arrived the traditional handling of Channel Island perishables at Weymouth had virtually disappeared, much of the traffic being carried by private shipping companies operating into rival English ports. Railway goods traffic to and from Weymouth ended early in the 1970s, not only for the port but also for the town itself, and today the only goods trains seen at Weymouth are the

Reclamations in 1909 provided the site for Melcombe Regis Station and enabled the new iron viaduct to be considerably shorter than its timber predecessor. The Weymouth and Portland Railway closed in 1965. This station was demolished the following year and the viaduct was dismantled in the mid-1970s.

occasional rake of oil tankers servicing the car-ferries. Passenger services at least, to and from London, have greatly improved since 1967 when the main line from Waterloo to Bournemouth was electrified, but the old Great Western main line from Paddington has been a shadow of its former self since the Boat Train was moved to Waterloo in 1959.

The two local branch lines were closed as part of the general reduction in railway provision. First to go was the Abbotsbury Line, opened in 1885, with hopes of mineral traffic to supplement the passenger services, but which had never been more than a typical small branch service. This closed in December 1952. The Portland Line which opened in 1865, had been extended to Easton on the top of the Island in 1900, and following the completion of the new iron viaduct across Radipole Lake, a new station, named Melcombe Regis, was built on reclaimed land to the north of the bridge. Prior to the construction of this additional station, Portland trains went into the main station yards and then reversed back into Weymouth Station, reversing the routine for the return trip to Portland. Melcombe Regis station was demolished in 1966, and the site used for the construction of a warehouse.

During its life-span, the Portland Line acquired three intermediate halts, Westham, Wyke Regis and Sandsfoot Castle, and one station, Rodwell. From the time it was built until the coming of the motor bus, the line provided the main system of public transport to and from the Island. It served not only the people of Portland, but also the Naval dockyard, established after the building of the breakwaters, and also had a revolutionary effect on the export of finished Portland stone. It also transported thousands of sailors on shore-leave when the Fleet was in port, although the majority of liberty-men were landed direct at Weymouth. The Portland Line closed to passenger traffic in 1952 and for all traffic in April 1965. Although there may have been some argument for retaining this line as a link with the Portland Naval Base, the high cost of replacing the two decayed iron bridges across the Weymouth

Backwater and the Fleet was one of the major factors in the decision to close the line. The bridges remained for some years after the closure of the branch, but have now been demolished.

Weymouth in the early years of this century advertised itself as 'The Naples of England' and boasted numerous attractions. For those who preferred a sea trip, Cosens steamers went to every place of interest on the coast between Brighton and Start Point. An excursionist with sea legs and a season ticket could take advantage of a varied weekly programme which also included occasional Channel crossings. In the early 1900s the Cosens' Fleet comprised eight impressively named paddle-steamers, the *Majestic, Monarch, Brodick Castle, Victoria, Empress, Premier, Queen* and *Albert Victor*.

Also on offer were sports such as tennis, golf and bowls as well as the usual seaside attractions of boating, fishing and swimming. The Bathing Saloons which had brought the beach into such disrepute during the late 19th century, offered cheaper facilities than the individual machines, and it was also possible to bathe at Greenhill for free, at certain stated times. All the old bathing machines, many of which dated back to the Georgian era were sold off during the First World War, to be replaced in the 1920s by more modern cabins, which although fitted with small wheels, were no longer drawn out into the sea. In 1930 the Weymouth Bathing Saloon Company owned six of the large Saloons and 32 separate machines.

The wicker-work carts drawn by goats which once took children for rides on the beach and around the town.

Yachting, too, was well established and the town's reputation as a sailing centre was much enhanced when Sir Thomas Lipton brought his America's Cup contenders, *Shamrocks I* and *III* for racing trials in the Bay. It was also the age of the large private steam yachts, which added to the harbour scene.

There were horse-drawn vehicles lined up at the King's Statue, to take visitors on outings to such favourites as Abbotsbury, Upwey (the Wishing Well and strawberry teas), and Osmington Mills (for lobster teas). These carriages later gave way to motor charabancs of the 1920s – open seaters with canvas hoods, many with solid tyres to give the tripper a thorough jolting *en*

'The best sand in the world for making models' according to Weymouth's sand modeller Fred Darrington. These Edwardian children certainly made good use of it.

Horse drawn transport lined up at the King's Statue waiting for passengers in about 1910.

route for the beauty spots. Photographs show these open 'charas' filled to capacity with smiling cloche-hatted ladies and their escorts, all set for a day out at a time when cars were a luxury item and this far more sociable form of travel prevailed.

The Great Western Railway abandoned its bus service between Radipole and Wyke Regis in 1909, after only four years service, but re-introduced it again in 1912, and between 1921 and 1923 experimented with additional services to Upwey, Chickerell and Preston. The National Omnibus and Transport Company arrived in Weymouth in 1923 with services between Weymouth and Swanage, Sherborne, Yeovil and West Bay, whilst the service between Weymouth and Portland Victoria Square was commenced by a rival firm, the Road Motors Ltd. In 1925 the 'National' bought out the Weymouth Motor Co. and the Road Motors, and by 1927 this company controlled all but a few private coach owners. Edward Street Bus Station was built in 1927, adjacent to the railway station and from 1929 the fleet name Southern National was adopted for the buses in this area, incorporating the G.W.R. service from 1934.

By the 1920s, motor charabancs had replaced the carriages. Today this area in front of the Statue is the site of gardens, although regular bus services still commence their journeys from stops in the vicinity.

Although there have been considerable variations in the frequency of operation, the general scheme of local bus services has remained almost unaltered since the 1930s apart from some re-routing to serve modern housing estates and the abandonment of certain 'summer only' services which were a popular feature during the years prior to the Second World War. Among these were services from the Pavilion Theatre to Bowleaze Cove, using open-sided 'toast-rack' buses, one from the King's Statue to Sandsfoot Castle, another from the Statue to the Nothe Gardens, and one which ran along Radipole Park Drive to Icen Road in Radipole. None of these special services were re-started after the war, although open top double-deckers have been operating on popular holiday routes in recent years.

It was in 1905, the same year that the first motor omnibus service had started in Weymouth, that the enclosure of Portland Harbour was completed. The new breakwaters provided a safe anchorage for the largest warships, and a growth in the importance of Portland Dockyard. The early years of this century were to see the great naval armaments race between Britain and Germany, and the presence in Portland Harbour and Weymouth Bay of the latest additions to the Royal Navy's battle-fleets was a source of great interest to the ever growing numbers of summer visitors. The first of the great Naval Reviews of the 20th century took place in Weymouth Bay in 1912, when King George V spent three days with the Home Fleet, accompanied by his second son, Prince Albert, then a Dartmouth cadet and unaware of his future destiny. As King George VI he too would review the Fleet at Weymouth, and in very similar circumstances, in 1938 and 1939, the period before the outbreak of World War II.

The Fleet Review in May 1912 was an impressive show of strength in the arms race. It was deafeningly impressive in Weymouth, the *Southern Times* reporting '. . . That the biggest guns of the dreadnoughts and super-dreadnoughts were being employed under the critical eye of the King was rather uncomfortably demonstrated to Weymouthians at noon when the whole town shook with the reverberation of the heaviest armament in the British Navy'.

An ever increasing number of naval personnel were being brought ashore by liberty boats, and catering for the entertainment of 'Jack Tar' on shore leave became an increasing part of the local economy. There were occasional arguments between the locals and the sailors, and more often than not, between the sailors themselves, but the Navy was always welcome. For the comfort of these special visitors, the Royal Navy Sailors Home was erected in St Nicholas Street in 1907, but in the early 1960s it was demolished as no longer needed.

One summer evening at the end of July 1914, thousands of sailors on shore leave in Weymouth were suddenly recalled to their ships. Theatre and cinema performances were interrupted to announce the 'return to ships' order and as the word spread the streets filled with men hastening to board the waiting liberty boats. There were tearful farewells at the pier, and the following morning the Battle Squadrons slipped out of Portland Harbour to join the rest of the fleet. They left behind a general air of unrest and apprehension, increased by a flurry of troop movements in and around the town.

August Bank Holiday Monday lacked the gaiety of previous years and most of the numerous excursion trains to Weymouth were cancelled. War with Germany was declared on 4th August 1914.

The interior of the Sidney Hall, converted for use as a Military Hospital in 1914.

During the first months of the Great War, Weymouthians adjusted to the inevitable changes which war brought. The holiday industry was immediately affected when the takeover of the railways by the military authorities led to the cancellation of many trains and the temporary stranding of thousands of seaside visitors. Sporting and entertainment fixtures were abandoned and soon Weymouth was plunged into the gloom of the black-out. Great recruiting campaigns and rallies in the area brought hundreds of local volunteers ready to enlist for King and Country, and it was not long before the columns of the *Southern Times* began recording the long lists of names of Dorset men killed on active service.

From now on the town was to see great numbers of soldiers, as well as sailors, on its streets. Huge army camps sprang up around Weymouth, at Wyke Regis, Westham and Littlemoor. Local vessels from both the G.W.R. and Cosens fleets went on war service. Refugees from Europe began arriving at the quay, including numbers of Americans stranded on the Continent when war broke out. As time went on, the landing of shipwreck victims became a familiar occurrence in Weymouth, their vessels sunk by enemy action.

The Princess Christian Hospital at Greenhill and the Royal Hospital in School Street were requisitioned for military casualties, as was the Borough's Isolation Hospital. Ambulance trains began arriving with patients from casualty stations at the Front and during the war years thousands of wounded men were to be treated at Weymouth. More hospital and convalescent home accommodation became an urgent necessity and among the buildings taken over in the town for this purpose were the Sidney Hall, Burdon Hotel (now the

Prince Regent Hotel), St John's Mission Hall, The Convent of the Sacred Hearts and private houses such as 'Massandra' at Greenhill and 'Ryme' overlooking Portland Harbour.

In 1915 the War Office required camps to which Australian troops could be sent when they were discharged from hospitals in England and the first of these soldiers to arrive in the Weymouth area were received at 'Monte Video', Chickerell. The wounded Australians were retrained for return to the Front, or sent home if unfit. Soon great numbers of Australian and New Zealand troops began arriving in the town and the Kursaal building in the Alexandra Gardens was used as their reception centre. The area where they encamped at Westham was built on after the war and the street names there commemorate these Antipodean visitors – Queensland Road, Melbourne Street, Sidney Street, and others. Recently-built housing developments at Littlemoor have continued this tradition.

After the Victory celebrations in 1918, the post-war problems of poverty, depression and unemployment led to the setting up of special schemes to provide work. Amongst the earliest was the construction of the new Westham Bridge, followed by the extension of the Esplanade around the Jubilee Clock and the widening of the roadway in the vicinity, further widening of the Esplanade and improvements in Greenhill Gardens.

Other changes were taking place. In 1927 the old Royal Baths at the top end of St Thomas Street and St Mary Street were demolished, making way for the Clinton Arcade development of Edwin Jones and Co. The arcade of small shops on the ground floor with restaurant and dance hall above was a long accepted 'short cut' between the main streets, but it was never a public right of way, the owners being mindful to close the arcade one day every year – Good Friday – to maintain their own rights. Debenhams later took over the Clinton building and when the company left Weymouth in 1982, the ground floor was redeveloped as three separate units.

Westham Embankment Bridge, opened in 1921. Reclamations on the far side of the bridge were to provide the sites for Westwey Road, Weymouth Central Library and the Public Health Centre.

St Thomas Street in 1954. The shops in the foreground adjoining the Clinton building have altered little since the days when the Royal Baths stood on the site.

The Gloucester Hotel ablaze in 1927.

13th April, 1954. The Pavilion Theatre of 1908, renamed 'The Ritz', goes up in flames – the largest fire in Weymouth since the Second World War. (Courtesy of G. H. Woollatt).

The possibility of amalgamating the Weymouth Police Force with that of the County had been rejected on a number of occasions, but eventually, in 1921 the local force was disbanded and the County took over. One of the more unusual duties which had been allocated to the Weymouth Police Force in its early days was that of acting as the Fire Brigade. It was not until 1888 that consideration was first given to the formation of a Volunteer Fire Brigade for Weymouth, but within two years the decision was made that fire-fighting should be one of the tasks of the Police. However, a Voluntary Fire Brigade was eventually founded in 1895, and in 1897 the Corporation acreed to appoint an 'Efficient Fireman from the Metropolitan Fire Brigade' to act as instructor to the Volunteer Force. He was also responsible for maintaining the equipment, which at that time consisted of two hose carts with about 600 feet of hose and one 30 feet fire escape, and was supplemented two years later by the purchase of the town's first fire engine. For many years the Fire Station was on the corner of St Edmund Street and Maiden Street in the old 'House with the cannon ball' dating from the Stuart period, but in 1939 it moved to new headquarters on North Quay.

One of the largest blazes ever tackled by the Weymouth Brigade was that of the Gloucester Hotel on the Esplanade, which caught fire on 3rd March 1927, and was extensively damaged. The crowds who gathered watched spellbound as the hotel's 'boots', William Dicker, climbed a series of drainpipes and edged across a narrow parapet sixty feet up to escort two terrified ladies (one an invalid) to safety from the top floor rooms. Much of the damage to the historic former royal residence was internal, and Thomas Hardy was one of

The glass Kursaal of 1913 in the Alexandra Gardens. The theatre which replaced it in 1924 operated until after the present Pavilion opened in 1960, but two summer shows proved uneconomic in Weymouth and it is now an Amusement Centre.

those who came to see the ruined interior. The facade of the Gloucester was not damaged and although it was rebuilt with an additional storey, the building retains its original appearance.

Another great fire in Weymouth during the present century was that of the Ritz Theatre. Originally named the Pavilion Theatre, it had been built by the Corporation on reclaimed land adjoining the pier, and opened in 1908. It was almost entirely of wood, and served both for the summer shows and as a second theatre in competition with the Jubilee Hall in St Thomas Street. After closing throughout the Second World War, the Pavilion re-opened as 'The Ritz' only to be destroyed by fire on 13th April 1954. Thousands of spectators, their numbers swelled by Weymouth schoolchildren at home for the Easter holiday, watched the fire reduce the attractive and typical seaside pier building to a mass of ash and tangled girders in little more than an hour. The site remained vacant until a new Pavilion Theatre opened in 1960.

The Pavilion was not the only source of local entertainment in the early 20th century. There were concert parties on the sands and a variety of music could be enjoyed in the Alexandra Gardens. Brass Band concerts had been a regular seasonal feature at the bandstand since 1891 and in 1913 'The Kursaal' was erected around this original bandstand to provide shelter for the audience in inclement weather. Somewhat glowingly described as 'The Miniature Crystal Palace', this was the building used as a reception centre for troops during the First World War, and it was completely demolished and replaced by the Alexandra Gardens Theatre in 1924.

In 1909 a regular programme of moving pictures commenced at the Jubilee Hall which adopted the new name of 'Royal Victoria Jubilee Hall and Picture Palace'. More cinemas followed: the Belle Vue Cinema opened in 1910 and lasted until 1956, the building being converted to the present Elim Church. In 1912 the Palladium Cinema opened on the Town Bridge: it now houses a club. The Regent Theatre replaced the Jubilee Hall in 1926 and after a number of name changes is today a bingo hall. The only cinema remaining in Weymouth is the Classic, which commenced business much later than the others, in 1933, opening originally as the Odeon Cinema in a converted building in Gloucester Street.

One of the great annual events in the Weymouth calendar was 'Swindon Week' (later extended to 'Swindon Fortnight'). Every year in July a massive contingent of railway workers from the G.W.R. works at Swindon would descend on Weymouth for their annual holiday. The transport of more than 20,000 people to a variety of holiday resorts (of which Weymouth was the most popular) was a major feat of logistics. Typical are the figures for 1930, when 21 special trains left Swindon in less than 2½ hours, the last one being away by 7.05 a.m. The Weymouth trains delivered over 5000 holidaymakers at a very early hour, who then streamed out into the town to find restaurants open ready to serve breakfast, and a welcome waiting from old friends of many years standing.

'Swindon Fortnight' continued as an annual event until well after the Second World War, but the popularity of foreign travel and the growth of family excursions by car, rather than group excursions by train, marked the end of this long tradition.

Westham Road, formerly called 'Little George Street', photographed in 1938, shortly before the shops on the right-hand side were demolished and a new block built.

The boundaries of Weymouth as set out in 1895 remained unaltered until 1933 when a major extension took in the surrounding villages of Broadwey, Preston, Radipole, Upwey and Wyke Regis. The population rose from 19,843 in 1901 to 42,349 in 1971, and one of the major tasks of the Corporation during the 20th century has been the provision of council houses. The earliest council estates were at Pyehill and Granville Road, erected just before the First World War, to be followed by the original Westham estate, completed during the 1920s. This first Westham estate, approximately the area between Kitchener Road and Abbotsbury Road, was further extended in the 1930s into the Norfolk-Sussex Road area, and again, after the Second World War, into Hereford and Bedford Roads. A further massive growth in the provision of council estates followed the Second World War, with new housing projects at Lanehouse, Radipole Lane, Downclose, Chapelhay and Littlemoor. Some 500 additional houses had been completed by 1952.

Private enterprise housing has been a major feature between the two World Wars, with extensive estates at Wyke Regis, Southlands, Goldcroft, Radipole and Southill, whilst following the Second World War there were further developments at Preston, Broadwey, Radipole and in the Field Barn area of Southill. The last of these resulted in a new road being built across Chafey's Lake in 1961, giving more direct access to Southill and old Radipole village.

As the housing estates, both municipal and private, spread out over the surrounding countryside, new schools, churches and other public amenities were established, details of which are set out in Appendices C, D and E.

Prior to the Second World War, the majority of local residents were employed in the Portland Naval Base and Dockyard, the Whitehead Torpedo Works and the local service industries, as well as in the annual rush to serve the summer visitors. Many naval families who made temporary homes in the Weymouth area whilst 'Dad's ship' was attached to Portland, came back to settle permanently after he left the service.

The oldest local industry of all has remained firmly rooted in the area of Hope Square adjoining the Harbour and town centre. Brewing by ale-house keepers of the town is as old as the town itself, and the results of the failure to abide by the regulations have already been mentioned. Although William Devenish did not purchase his local brewery until 1824, it is known that the business he acquired had been operating in the mid-18th century. As early as 1742, Mary Fowler, a previous owner of what was to become Devenish Brewery, had leased a piece of ground 'on which heretofore stood a Brewhouse' – a sure indication that Hope Square had been the home of brewing for a very long time.

The rival brewery of John Groves and Sons Ltd had been largely rebuilt in the early 1900s on its site adjoining the Devenish establishment, and the two firms operated in competition until their merger in 1960. In spite of the business rivalry, Groves had come to the aid of Devenish when the latter's brewery was badly bombed in the air raid of August 1940.

The Pier Bandstand, as opened in 1939. In the foreground stands Weymouth's War Memorial.

The 1930s saw a return to relative prosperity. There was full employment in the Dockyard and at Whiteheads as a programme of re-armament got into its stride, and there were visitors in plenty with money to spend. But there were clouds on the horizon. In November 1938, Councillor John Thomas Goddard M.C., took his oath of office as Mayor of Weymouth and Melcombe Regis, little thinking that he was to create an all-time record for the length of his tenure of office – seven years of continuous service.

During the months prior to the outbreak of war, the people of Weymouth had been watching with interest the building of the new Pier Bandstand, a short pier, intended solely for use as an open air theatre. It opened in 1939, but the design came in for considerable criticism, as to many it spoilt the long continuous sweep of the Bay, and was a 'fair weather' building of little use on a wet day.

Early in August 1939, the Reserve Fleet assembled in Weymouth Bay and the town was packed with sailors enjoying a run ashore. On August 9th King George VI was at Weymouth to review his assembled squadrons, and such was the public interest that it is estimated that 45,000 people passed through Weymouth station on that one day alone. Many local men were already in uniform, reservists called back to the colours, and when the fleet sailed there was a general air of expectancy. War was declared on 3rd September 1939, and the Civil Defence organisation was placed on full alert, but nobody had any idea just what to expect.

The Second World War brought change and damage to Weymouth. The capture of the Channel Islands early in the war caused the loss of the long established Harbour trade, and most of the local vessels went on war service. Following the evacuation from Dunkirk in 1940, hundreds of troops and

May 1944, and Weymouth holds its breath! The unexploded bomb in Melcombe Avenue is finally lifted.

The scene after the air raid in November, 1941, which trapped Mayor Goddard for several hours beneath his home, The Royal Adelaide, Abbotsbury Road. It was rebuilt after the war.

1944, and the Invasion of Europe has begun. United States 'G.I.s' on the Esplanade, prior to embarking for Normandy.

evacuees were landed at Weymouth and the local schools and halls became emergency clearing centres.

In July 1940, the town suffered its first air raids, and No. 12 Russell Avenue had the doubtful honour of being the first house in Weymouth to be demolished by bombs. In all six bombs were dropped in that raid, and in addition to the one house demolished, two were seriously damaged and fourteen others slightly damaged, but only two people were wounded. The first large scale raid on Weymouth came on 11th August 1940, when a total of 463 houses were damaged, mainly in the Hope Square, Chapelhay, Rodwell, Newstead Road and Westham Cross Roads areas. Both local breweries were hit, causing extensive damage.

The Southern National Garage was wrecked on 21st October 1940, together with ten houses in the immediate vicinity. Chapelhay was badly damaged on the night of 17th November 1940, and what few buildings did escape damage were almost all hit during a further raid on 9th May the following year. There were heavy casualties on both occasions.

Mayor Goddard suffered the fate of being buried under the ruins of his home, The Adelaide Hotel, Westham, during a raid in November 1941. He was entombed for several hours, but was retrieved undamaged and able to express his disapproval of the entire matter in no uncertain terms! A raid on 2nd April 1942 badly damaged the offices of the *Dorset Daily Echo* as well as numerous other properties in St Nicholas Street. The *Echo* had to be printed at Bournemouth for the remainder of the war. It was during this same raid that the Methodist Chapel in Newstead Road was almost destroyed.

Raids of a smaller nature followed, but it was after a comparative lull of over two years that Weymouth was hit again. Allied forces were gathering in the neighbourhood for the invasion of Normandy, and it is almost certain that this raid was designed as an attempt to disorganise the preparations. The most serious damage was in the Melcombe Avenue district, with the Weymouth and District Hospital taking a severe knock. Patients had to be evacuated to the adjoining buildings of the Weymouth College whilst repairs were effected. Three members of the Rescue and Casualty Service were killed by a bomb whilst on their way from the Cranford Avenue Depot, and several houses and the Christian Science Church were very badly damaged. An unexploded bomb penetrated 28 feet below ground and the work to remove it lasted a week.

Weymouth and Portland were among the major loading ports for the invasion of Normandy, and from 6th June 1944 to 7th May 1945, 517,816 troops and 144,093 vehicles embarked from these harbours. For weeks prior to sailing they were encamped in the woods and valleys of the Dorset countryside, waiting for a brief visit to Weymouth and then on across the Channel to Normandy. The event is commemorated in a special memorial erected on the Esplanade opposite the Royal Hotel, the local headquarters of the American Forces at this stage of the war.

Although it was generally believed that the air raids on Weymouth came partly because of its close proximity to the Portland Naval Base and partly because it lay on the direct flight path of German bombers heading for Bristol and the Midlands, a detailed German photographic survey of Weymouth made during the months prior to the outbreak of hostilities indicated the port installations, gasworks and electric power station, as well as defences.

Whilst the air raids and consequent damage remain the most vivid recollection of the war, the people of Weymouth contributed to the war effort in a variety of ways. Local men were in all branches of the armed forces, local factories produced war weapons whilst service clubs and canteens endeavoured to provide a welcome for the thousands of servicemen who were stationed in the area during the five years of war. One well-remembered forces canteen occupied the premises adjoining the Town Bridge – at one time the Palladium Cinema. Another, 'The B.W. Club', occupied St John's Church Hall in the Park District. Christchurch closed early in the war, and saw service as a British Restaurant. For the various branches of the Civil Defence organisation it was a dangerous and exacting five years, and several of its members were casualties, some fatal.

The European War came to an end, and on 10th May 1945, U.249, the first

U.249, the first German U-Boat to surrender, is escorted into Weymouth Bay, on 10th May 1945.

German U Boat to surrender, was escorted into Weymouth Bay. Slowly life returned to normal, or what passed for normal at a time when there were shortages of everything. The G.W.R. steamers returned from war duties and a limited service to the Channel Islands was re-started in September 1945, using the cargo vessels *Sambur* and *Roebuck*. The full passenger service was re-opened in June 1946 by the *St Helier*, joined later in the year by her sister ship, *St Julien*. The *Roebuck, St Helier* and *St Julien* had all been present at the evacuation from Dunkirk. Later *H.M.S. St Helier* undertook a variety of war-time duties, including that of an assault landing ship, whilst the *St Julien* spent the majority of the war as a hospital ship, including service in the Mediterranean.

All the Cosens paddle-steamers returned to be rebuilt and refurbished, and eventually all the normal day-cruises were back in operation; Portland Harbour, Lulworth Cove, Swanage, Bournemouth and the Isle of Wight. But rising costs and the fact that most of the paddle-steamers were long past their efficient operating age meant that this very pleasant feature of a holiday at the seaside was to come to an end. One veteran of the fleet, the *Monarch*, was to be replaced by an ex-Southern Railway paddler, which was renamed *Monarch* to continue the local tradition, but by 1967 the last of the local paddle-steamers had gone to the scrap yard. The *Consul, Embassy, Emperor of India, Empress*, two *Monarchs* and the *Victoria* will all be remembered by Weymouthians for many years to come. Although no longer ship-owners, Cosens and Co. Ltd. are still part of industrial Weymouth, operating from their general engineering works on the same site where for more than a hundred years they serviced and maintained their fleet of paddle-steamers. The Commercial Road area is still very much the centre of the boat-building and repair industry of Weymouth, conveniently sited for the extensive system of yacht moorings which have been installed in recent years.

The need to encourage light industries to set up in this area has led to the Corporation establishing industrial estates on the borough boundaries at Lynch Road in 1947, extending to the adjoining Granby Estate during the 1960s. The manufacture of torpedoes at Wyke Regis has long ceased and the

The Town Bridge opens to permit the departure of the Paddle Steamer Monarch, *on her way to the breakers' yard in 1950. Although this vessel was replaced, the entire Cosens fleet had gone by 1967. Primarily pleasure-steamers, these ships had also served as liberty-boats when the Fleet was in the Bay, as salvage-vessels, and as tugs when sailing ships still visited the port of Weymouth.*

former Whitehead Factory is now owned by the light engineering company of Wellworthy.

The creation back in 1885 of the South Dorset Parliamentary Division had brought a new look to the local political scene. Weymouth now had to share a single M.P. with a large area of South Dorset, but the town still represented the strongest political influence in the new constituency. By the end of the 19th century the seat was no longer dominated by the Liberals, and their only victory this century was in the election of 1906. The Labour Party had first contested the seat in 1918, but apart from a brief period in the early 1960s when a Labour member was elected, it has remained solidly Conservative since 1910.

Many aspects of life in Weymouth during the years following the Second World War have already been described. Most changes take place as the result of careful planning, but occasionally other factors are involved, as in 1955 when Weymouth experienced the most severe floods ever recorded. On the night of 18th/19th July, 11 inches of rain fell in the area of Hardy's Monument on the hills above Portesham, and the following day the floods hit the valley of the River Wey. There was extensive destruction from Upwey down through Nottington, Broadwey and Radipole, with a build-up against Westham Bridge which flooded the car parks and Melcombe Regis Gardens. Nothing like this had been seen in living memory and the 11 inches of rain which fell that night still stands in the *Guinness Book of Records* as the greatest rainfall in 24 hours in the United Kingdom.

The floods of 19th July 1955 trapped coaches parked overnight at Westham whilst Edward Street Bus Station was being rebuilt. Both of the churches which dominate the skyline have now been demolished.

North Quay, Weymouth in 1961. The area behind these buildings was once the heart of the old Borough of Weymouth of pre-union days, the one remaining link being the old Tudor House close to the parked cars. The entire area was cleared in the early 1960s and today is the site of the Municipal Offices.

Apart from the improvements to the port facilities, including the construction of new passenger terminal facilities on the pier, opened in 1967, the Weymouth Corporation has been responsible for another major alteration to the Harbour area – the building of new Municipal Offices on North Quay. The various departments of the Corporation had been brought together under one roof in 1904 when the Corporation purchased the former Weymouth Sanatorium in Clarence Buildings. In the years which followed, the responsibilities and staff of the local authority grew to the point where additional accommodation was needed and an adjoining house was purchased. A new Public Health Centre was built in the early 1930s on the site of Stavordale House, near Westham Bridge, but the need for new Municipal Offices was a regular item on the agenda of the Corporation for many years. It was not until the 1960s that a decision was made to build on the North Quay site. Many of the properties in this part of old Weymouth had been damaged during the war and eventually the remaining ones were purchased by the Corporation and demolished. The most notable building to go was what was known as 'The Old Tudor House', an interesting link with Weymouth's past, but almost inevitably a victim of 'progress'.

The new Municipal Offices were opened by H.R.H. Princess Anne on 1st June 1971, the four hundredth anniversary of the union of Weymouth and Melcombe Regis into one Borough. For the first time in all that period, the administration of the borough was centred on 'Weymouth' and not its ancient rival 'Melcombe Regis'. Throughout the four hundred years of the union and on until the amalgamation with Portland in 1974, the official name of the borough had always been 'The Borough of Weymouth and Melcombe Regis', but known to everyone by the shorter version of 'Weymouth'.

As part of a national scheme of local government reorganisation, Weymouth and Portland were amalgamated into one authority as from 1st

The Municipal Offices, opened on 1st June 1971, the Quatercentenary of the 1571 Act of Union.

April 1974, under the title of The Borough of Weymouth and Portland. This amalgamation introduced a new chapter in the continuing story of Weymouth, and would seem to be a very suitable place at which to bring this record to its conclusion.

The passing centuries have seen many changes. The Harbour, once the lifeblood of the twin towns (and the cause of their rivalry), lost its importance, and then once more conditions changed as trade with the Channel Islands built up. In recent years, the basic method of handling the traffic through the port has changed, and the classic type of passenger vessel has given way to the modern car ferry.

The 'crazes' of each decade have come and gone: traditional seaside entertainments such as Punch and Judy shows and donkey rides have outlived them all. Before the First World War roller skating was all the rage, and rinks were constructed at the Jubilee Hall and the Pavilion. The Skee Ball Pavilion on the beach near the Alexandra Gardens was enjoyed in the late Twenties and Thirties, and a Vaudeville Theatre flourished on a specially designed stage erected on the sands. The Go-Karts and Bingo of today will no doubt make way for a new fashion before long, for the seaside must be ever mindful of pleasing its visitors in order to survive.

Weymouth means many things to many people: one thing to the family which makes it their home – quite another to those who choose it for their annual holiday. For all of them change is inevitable, for without change there could be no progress – and no history to record. It is our hope that we have been able to convey at least something of the many centuries since man first settled in the mouth of the River Wey.

A symbol of the future: the Coat of Arms of the new Borough of Weymouth and Portland, established 1st April, 1974.

Appendices

APPENDIX A

THE LOCAL GOVERNMENT OF WEYMOUTH

The Borough of Melcombe Regis	1280-1571
The Borough of Weymouth	1318-1571
The Borough of Weymouth and Melcombe Regis	1571-1974

Since the charter of 1571 uniting the two boroughs, the rights and privileges of the new Borough have been confirmed by numerous royal charters, the last being that of King George III granted in 1804. Under the Municipal Corporations Act a newly constituted Corporation took office on 1st April 1836.

The Boundaries of the Borough have been extended on three occasions, 1836, 1895 and 1933.

Certain specialized aspects of local administration have been controlled by: Weymouth Local Board of Health, 1851-1876; Weymouth Urban Sanitary Authority, 1876-1895; Weymouth Urban District Council, 1895-1915.

Prior to 1933 the villages of Broadwey, Radipole, Preston, Upwey and Wyke Regis had their own Parish Councils, and were also represented on the Weymouth Rural District Council.

The Dorset County Council was established in 1888, and eventually many local services formerly administered by the Weymouth Corporation became the responsibility of the County, e.g. police, roads and education.

On 1st April 1974, the Borough of Weymouth and Melcombe Regis was amalgamated with the Urban District Council of Portland, forming the Borough of Weymouth and Portland.

APPENDIX B

CENSUS RETURNS, 1801-1981

Year	Weymouth	Melcombe Regis	Weymouth & M.R.	Broadwey	Preston	Radipole	Upwey	Wyke Regis	Population TOTALS
1801	1267	2350	3617	210	385	151	363	451	5177
1811	1747	2985	4732	264	447	173	398	570	6584
1821	2370	4252	6622	282	508	226	485	914	9037
1831	2529	5126	7655	385	555	382	618	1197	10792
1841	2669	5039	7708	498	672	487	619	1911	11895
1851	2957	5273	8230	610	711	609	637	1898	12695
1861	3515	6498	10013	614	723	691	646	2025	14712
1871	3828	7533	11361	712	747	1154	694	2365	17033
1881	3630	7920	11550	761	689	1322	729	2748	17799
1891	3591	7626	11217	774	678	1925	752	4182	19528
1901	10031	9812	19843	821	664	301	812	1910	24351
1911	11372	10952	22324	854	691	310	871	2330	27380
1921	12486	12070	24556	904	886	328	920	2397	29991
1931	11612	10576	22188	960	855	340	910	4378	29631
1951	Commencing with the Census for 1951 the Returns are based on the new Wards of the enlarged Borough,								37099
1961	the boundaries of which differ from those of the old Parishes. Accurate comparisons are therefore								41045
1971	impossible, and only totals are given. There was no Census in 1941. Figures for 1901 reflect								42349
1981	the boundary changes of 1895.								46260

APPENDIX C

PUBLIC UTILITIES AND AMENITIES

WATER. The Company of Proprietors of the Weymouth Waterworks was established in 1797 to bring water from the Boiling Rock, Preston, the initial supply being to Melcombe Regis only. In 1855 an Act was obtained to take water from Sutton Poyntz, one of the main sources still in use today, whilst in 1935 additional supplies were obtained from West Knighton. The Company joined with others to form the Dorset Water Board in 1969, and since 1974 has formed part of the Avon and Dorset Division of the Wessex Water Authority.

GAS. The first Weymouth Gas Works was erected by W.W. Burdon in 1836, who remained the sole proprietor until the formation of the Weymouth Gas Consumers Company Ltd. in 1867. The Gasworks was enlarged between 1928 and 1933, when 3 acres of mudland were reclaimed from the Backwater, and further additions were made after the Second World War. Nationalised in 1948 it today forms part of Southern Gas.

ELECTRICITY. Supply commenced from Sunnybank Power Station, Westham on 26th September, 1904. Power was first taken from the National Grid in 1932. Owned and operated by the Weymouth Corporation from first introduction until nationalisation in 1947. Today it forms part of the Yeovil/Weymouth District of Southern Electricity.

PUBLIC LIBRARY. Public Libraries Act adopted by Weymouth Urban Sanitary Authority, 1893. First Public Library opened in Electric House, 1944 – Reference only. Full lending library service commenced Westwey Road, 1948. Wyke Regis Branch Library opened 1962. Amalgamated with County Library Service, 1974.

LOCAL HISTORY MUSEUM. Established by Weymouth Corporation in former Melcombe Regis School in 1971, as a temporary 'Local History Exhibition'. Re-opened 1972 as a Museum, and amalgamated with Portland Museum in 1974 to form Weymouth and Portland Museum Service.

APPENDIX D

LOCAL CHURCHES AND CHAPELS

12th Century*	St Nicholas Church, Broadwey. Much enlarged and restored during the 19th Century.
13th Century*	St Ann's Church, Radipole. Dedicated to St Mary until 1927, when the Parish of Radipole was re-formed.
1298	Christchurch Chapel, Melcombe Regis. First mentioned as 'Melcombe Chapel'.
14th Century*	St Andrew's Church, Preston. Replaced a Norman Church.
1377	St Nicholas Chapel, Weymouth. Chapel of Ease to Wyke Regis Church. Destroyed during the Civil War.
15th Century*	St Laurence's Church, Upwey. South aisle and gallery, 1838; clerestory and roof, 1841.
1455	All Saints Church, Wyke Regis. Replaced at least two earlier churches, probably of Saxon foundation.
1605	Christchurch, Melcombe Regis. Later re-dedicated to St Mary. Demolished 1815.
1802	Congregational Chapel, Dorchester Road, Upwey.
1804	Congregational Chapel, West Street, Melcombe Regis. Closed 1864 when replaced by Gloucester Street Church. Later converted to Theatre Royal. Demolished 1968.
1805	Wesleyan Methodist Chapel, Coneygar Lane, Melcombe Regis. Closed 1867, when replaced by Maiden Street Church. Demolished 1975.
1809	Independent Meeting House, Church Street, Upwey. Later a Primitive Methodist Chapel, closed c1932.
1814	Baptist Chapel, Bank Buildings, Melcombe. Stone facade added 1859, with further improvements in 1928.
1816	Methodist Chapel, Preston. Closed.
1817	St Mary's Church, Melcombe Regis. On site of church of 1605. Interior re-designed, 1975.
1822	Hope Congregational Church, Trinity Street, Weymouth. Enlarged and rebuilt, 1862. Combined with Gloucester Street Church, 1971, as United Reformed Church.
1835	St Augustine's Church, Dorchester Road. Roman Catholic. Facade added 1900.
1836	Holy Trinity Church, Weymouth. New Parish formed, 1836. Church enlarged 1885.
1839	Methodist Chapel, The Grove, Broadwey. Closed 1928.
1841	Primitive Methodist Chapel, Hope Square, Weymouth. Closed 1876 when replaced by St Leonard's Road Chapel.
1842	Methodist Chapel, Collins Lane, Wyke Regis. Closed 1903, when replaced by Portland Road Chapel.
1854	St John's Church, Dorchester Road. New Parish formed.
1864	Congregational Church, Gloucester Street, Melcombe Regis. Closed 1971, on amalgamation with Hope Congregational Church as United Reformed Church. Demolished 1980.
1867	Methodist Church, Maiden Street.
1869	United Free Methodist Chapel, Caroline Place, Melcombe Regis. Later used by the Salvation Army. Closed.
1870	Wesleyan Methodist Chapel, Elwell Street, Upwey. Closed 1971.
1871	Wesleyan Mission, Derby Street, Melcombe. Rebuilt 1902.
1874	Christchurch, King Street, Melcombe. Chapel of Ease to St Mary's. Closed 1939. Demolished 1956-7.
1876	Primitive Methodist Chapel, St Leonard's Road, Weymouth. Closed 1962.
1880	St Paul's Chapel, Abbotsbury Road, Westham. Chapel of Ease to Wyke Regis Church. Served as Parish Room of St Paul's Church, 1895-1973. Now demolished.
1888	Salvation Army. First met in Warehouse in Maiden Street, Melcombe Regis.
1888	Gospel Hall, George Street, Melcombe. Now known as Bethany Hall, Westham Road.
1894	St Nicholas Church, Buxton Road, Rodwell. Chapel of Ease to Holy Trinity Church. Completely rebuilt, 1964.
1896	St Paul's Church, Abbotsbury Road, Westham. Completed 1913. New Parish formed 1901.
1900	Primitive Methodist Chapel, Galwey Road, Wyke Regis. Closed 1932. Sold to Wyke Regis Women's Institute.
1902	Wesleyan Mission Hall, Newstead Road, Westham. Destroyed by bombing, 1942. Rebuilt, 1955.
1902	Wesleyan Methodist Chapel, Derby Street. Closed 1980.
1903	Ebenezer Hall, Abbotsbury Road, Westham.
1903	Salvation Army Citadel, Westham Road, Melcombe.
1903	Wesleyan Methodist Chapel, Portland Road, Wyke Regis. Amalgamated with Primitive Methodist Chapel, Galwey Road, 1932.
1905	Congregational Church, Spa Road, Radipole. Completely rebuilt, 1953-54.
1908	St Martin's Church, Chickerell Road, Weymouth. Chapel of Ease to Holy Trinity Church. Closed.

1928 Methodist Chapel, Dorchester Road, Broadwey.
1929 Christian Science Church, Melcombe Avenue, Melcombe Regis.
Dedicated 1962, when free of debt.
1934 St Joseph's Church, Abbotsbury Road, Westham.
Roman Catholic.
1940 St Aldhelm's Church, Spa Road, Radipole.
Sister Church to St Ann's, Radipole.
1954 St Edmund's Church, Lanehouse Rocks Road, Weymouth.
New Parish formed.
1954 Church of the Holy Family, Chapel Lane, Upwey.
Roman Catholic.
1955 St Charles' Church, Sunnyside Road, Wyke Regis.
Roman Catholic.
1958 Elim Church, Belle Vue, Melcombe Regis.
Formerly the 'Belle Vue Cinema'.
1962 Downclose Gospel Hall, Doncaster Road, Wyke Regis.
1968 Methodist Church, Lynch Lane, Weymouth.
Replaced a temporary church built in 1949.
1973 Emmanuel Church Centre, Southill, Weymouth.
Associated with St Ann's and St Aldhelm's Churches, Radipole.
1978 Kingdom Hall, High Street, Weymouth.
Meeting place of the Jehovah's Witnesses.

*The Church is of earlier foundation. The date given is that of the oldest surviving part of the building.

APPENDIX E

SCHOOLS AND COLLEGES

1824 Melcombe Regis National Schools, School Street. – Boys. (Earlier school known to exist 1812).
Rebuilt 1883. Also known as St Mary's Schools. Closed 1982.
1825 – Girls.
Rebuilt 1883. Also known as St Mary's Schools. Closed 1982.
1839 St Nicholas School, Broadwey.
Known to exist 1839, extended in 1871, 1894 and 1904. Closed 1972.
1840 Radipole School, Radipole Lane.
Closed 1965.
1840 Upwey School, Church Street.
Closed 1972.
1850 Preston School.
Enlarged. Now St Andrews C.E. Primary School.
1853 Holy Trinity Schools, Chapelhay.
Damaged by enemy action, 1939-45. Not used again, site redeveloped.
1860 Middle School, Commercial Road.
Became Weymouth Engineering and Technical School, 1918-1939. Now Weymouth Arts Centre.
1864 Weymouth College, Dorchester Road.
Originally known as Weymouth Grammar School.
Closed 1939, now part of Dorset Institute of Higher Education.
1864 St John's Schools, Dorchester Road.
Closed 1974. Site sold and redeveloped as flats.
1880 St Paul's School, Abbotsbury Road.
Closed 1973. Now used as Parish Room.
1897 Wyke Regis Schools, Victoria Road, Wyke.
Built by Whitehead Torpedo Co.
1905 St Augustine's Roman Catholic Schools, Walpole Street.
Replaced temporary school in Horsford School founded 1857 and another in Queen Street (1870). Closed 1964.
1906 Cromwell Road Schools.
1909 Convent High School, Carlton Road.
1911 Melcombe Regis Boys School, Westham Bridge.
Closed 1970. Now Weymouth Local History Museum.
1913 Victoria Secondary Schools, Alma Road.
Later known as Weymouth Secondary School, and from 1927 as Weymouth Grammar School. Moved to new premises at Charlestown 1964-1967. Now part of South Dorset Technical College.
1939 South Dorset Technical College, Newstead Road.
Now includes premises of former Weymouth Grammar School.
1946 Teachers Training College, Dorchester Road.
Former Weymouth College buildings, now enlarged.
Renamed Weymouth College of Education, 1965, and became part of Dorset Institute of Higher Education, 1976.
1948 Broadwey Modern School, Dorchester Road.
1952 Wyke Regis County Infants School, Portland Road.
Known as 'The Rainbow School'.
1952 Holy Trinity Church of England Infants and Junior Schools, Cross Roads.
1954 Westhaven County Infants and Junior Schools, Radipole Lane.
1957 All Saints Church of England Modern School, Sunnyside Road, Wyke Regis.
1963 Wyvern Training Centre, Chickerell Road.
1964-67 Weymouth Grammar School, Charlestown.
Replaced former building in Alma Road.
1964 St Augustine's Roman Catholic Primary School, Hardy Avenue.
Replaced former buildings in Walpole Street.
1965 Radipole County Primary School, Manor Road.
1969 Westham Modern School, Charlestown.
1972 St Nicholas Church of England Primary School, Broadwey.
Replaced Upwey and Broadwey Schools.
1973 Southill County Primary School, Radipole Lane.
1974 St John's Church of England Primary School, Coombe Avenue.
Replaced former buildings in Dorchester Road.
1975 Westfield Special Day School, Littlemoor Road.

APPENDIX F

DATES OF THE VISITS OF KING GEORGE III TO WEYMOUTH, 1789-1805

The King was accompanied by Queen Charlotte on all fourteen occasions he stayed in Weymouth. All of their thirteen surviving children also paid visits to the town at some time or other during the period of Royal Weymouth, (the King's two youngest sons, Prince Octavius and Prince Alfred, had died in infancy before 1789).

1st visit.	30th June 1789	– 14th September 1789. (See Note B)
	1790 – no visit.	
2nd visit.	3rd September 1791	– 15th October 1791.
3rd visit.	17th August 1792	– 1st October 1792.
	1793 – no visit.	
4th visit.	15th August 1794	– 27th September 1794.
5th visit.	17th August 1795	– 3rd October 1795.
6th visit.	1st August 1796	– 17th September 1796.
7th visit.	31st July 1797	– 18th September 1797.
8th visit.	1st September 1798	– 22nd October 1798.
9th visit.	17th August 1799	– 14th October 1799.
10th visit.	30th July 1800	– 8th October 1800.
11th visit.	3rd July 1801	– 1st October 1801.
12th visit.	3rd July 1802	– 1st September 1802.
	1803 – no visit.	
13th visit.	25th August 1804	– 29th October 1804.
14th visit.	13th July 1805	– 4th October 1805.

NOTES

A. The dates quoted are those when the Royal Family arrived at and departed from Weymouth, and do not include time taken on journeys between Windsor and Weymouth.

B. During the visit of 1789 the Royal Party was absent from Weymouth between 13th and 28th August, whilst on a tour to Plymouth and the West of England.

APPENDIX G

THE ESPLANADE – DETAILS OF ORIGINAL TERRACE NAMES

Present Day Number	Original Terrace Name and numbers
1-6	Devonshire Buildings (1-5)
7-15	Pulteney Buildings (1-9)
17 and Edward Court	Bank Buildings (1 and Weymouth and Dorsetshire Bank)
19-30	Clarence Buildings (5-12)
31-34	Grosvenor Place (1-3B)
35-40	Augusta Place (1-6), Victoria Hotel and
Victoria Hotel and Weymouth Hotel	Weymouth Hotel.
47A-51	Charlotte Row (1-6)
53-57	York Buildings (2-6)
59	Chesterfield Place (Seacroft)
65-66	Johnstone Row (1-7)
68-84	Royal Terrace (1-17)
85	Gloucester Hotel
86-89	Gloucester Row (1-4)
90-91	Royal Hotel
92-99	Gloucester Row (7-14)
101-115	Royal Crescent (1-15)
116-131	Belvidere (1-16)
132-138	Victoria Terrace (1-7)
139	Hotel Burdon (now Hotel Prince Regent)
140-146	Victoria Terrace (8-14)

APPENDIX H

THE PARK DISTRICT – INDEX OF ORIGINAL OR PROPOSED TERRACE AND VILLA NAMES

Original/Proposed Name	Present Location
Adelaide Place/Court.	Queen Street.
Augusta Place.	27-29 Walpole Street.
Avenue Villas.	39-48 Avenue Road.
Belvidere Cottages.	27-32 Crescent Street.
Belvidere Court.	Crescent Street.
Belvidere Mews.	18?-26 Crescent Street.
Bristol Terrace.	1-6 Brownlow Street.
Cambridge Terrace.	6-8 Lennox Street.
Chalgrove House.	1 Walpole Street.
Chalgrove Terrace.	38-48 Ranelagh Road.
Charles Terrace (5-1).	28-31 Hardwick Street.
Cheam Terrace.	36-39 Derby Street.
Chelmsford Terrace.	35-50 Chelmsford Street.
Clifton Villa.	42 Hardwick Street.
Crescent Court.	Between 8 & 9 Crescent Street.
Derby Cottages.	1-3 Derby Street.
Derby Terrace.	4-10 Derby Street.
Devon Cottage.	34 Walpole Street.
Ebenezer Villa.	Brownlow Street.
Elsie Villas.	26a, 26b, Lennox Street.
Ethel Terrace.	31-33 Chelmsford Street.
Fairview Terrace.	37-43 Walpole Street.
Farwell Cottages.	1-3 Charles Street.
Florissant House.	40 Brownlow Street.
Florissant Terrace.	12-16 Brownlow Street.
Grange Terrace (9-1).	4-12 Grange Road.
Hardwick Cottages.	8-9 Hardwick Street.
Hardwick Row.	34-38 Hardwick Street.
Hardwick Terrace.	4-7 Hardwick Street.
Holland Villa.	41 Hardwick Street.
Howard Place.	30-36 Walpole Street.
Langholme Street.	Avenue Road.
Melborne House	26c Lennox Street.
Myrtle Villa.	24 Lennox Street.
Nuneham Terrace.	50-54 Ranelagh Road.
Osborne Terrace.	26-35 Brownlow Street.
Oxford Terrace.	60-65 Walpole Street.
Park Cottages.	39-40 Hardwick Street.

Park Terrace.	1-4 Melcombe Place.
Park View.	2-? Queen Street.
Park Villa.	25 Lennox Street.
Penman Place.	16-20 Hardwick Street.
Portland Place.	43-46 Lennox Street.
Queen Court.	Prior to 1 Queen Street.
Ranelagh Street (Prior to c1900).	Ranelagh Road.
Ranelagh Terrace.	1-8 Ranelagh Road.
Royal York Terrace.	1-5 Lennox Street.
Salisbury Terrace.	25-31? Derby Street.
Seaton Terrace.	33?-37 Ranelagh Road.
Southwick Terrace	24-31 Ranelagh Road.
Stanley Terrace.	3-10 Stanley Street.
Surrey Terrace (21-1).	23-42 Charles Street.
Surrey Villas.	83-84 Walpole Street.
Sydney Terrace (1-9).	4-12 Charles Street.
Victor Terrace.	42?-57 Brownlow Street.
Victoria Arcade.	Between 12 & 13 Crescent Street.
Victoria Villa.	47 Lennox Street.
Vine Cottages.	7-8 William Street.
Walpole Cottages.	66-70 Walpole Street.
Walpole Place.	75-82 Walpole Street.
Walpole Terrace.	46-59 Walpole Street.
Waterloo Cottages.	3-5 William Street.
Waterloo House.	48-49 Lennox Street.
Wellington Cottage.	Lennox Street.
Wilton Terrace (11-1).	13-23 William Street.
Windsor Terrace.	17-24 Brownlow Street.

APPENDIX I

WESTHAM – INDEX OF ORIGINAL OR PROPOSED TERRACE AND VILLA NAMES

Original/Proposed Name	Present Location
Albert Cottages.	58-64 Newstead Road.
Albert Terrace.	134-140 Abbotsbury Road.
Alexandra Terrace.	2-8 Franklin Road.
Alma Terrace.	1-29 Alma Road.
Andover Road	*
Arch Cottages.	30-34 Newstead Road.
Ashley Terrace.	17-27 Cromwell Road.
Auckland Terrace.	1-19 Ilchester Road.
Balmoral Terrace.	*
Balmoral Villas.	50-52 Abbotsbury Road.
Bedford Terrace.	29-37 Cromwell Road.
Beresford Lodge.	132 Abbotsbury Road.
Bournemouth Terrace.	*
Cheriton.	Stavordale Road.
Clifton Terrace.	*
Corney Terrace.	18-28 Newstead Road.
Cromwell Cottages.	Cromwell Road.
Cromwell Villas.	104-106 Abbotsbury Road.
Cygnet Cottages.	71-75 Abbotsbury Road.
Devon Terrace.	*
Diamond Terrace.	100-128 Newstead Road.
Dodbrooke.	Stavordale Road.
Eldon House.	1 Cromwell Road.
Eldon Terrace.	3-9 Cromwell Road.
Elmslea.	3 Essex Road.
Emmadale Cottages.	3-21 Emmadale Road.
Emmadale Terrace.	2-42 Emmadale Road.
Eppingdale.	1 Essex Road.
Excelsior Terrace.	72-98 Abbotsbury Road.
Fairfax House.	11 Cromwell Road.
Franklin Villas.	Franklin Road.
Glendale.	51 Abbotsbury Road.
Goldcroft Terrace.	*
Gordon Terrace.	6-34 Melbury Road.
Gresham Terrace.	64-70 Abbotsbury Road.
Grove Cottages.	Grove Terrace, Cromwell Road.
Hampden Villas.	46-48 Abbotsbury Road.
Harman Terrace.	*
Hartley Terrace.	*
Heathfield.	Stavordale Road.
Helmsley.	Stavordale Road.
Holly Terrace.	1-5 Holly Road.
Holyrood Cottages.	24-42 Holly Road.
Hooperne Villas.	110-112 Abbotsbury Road.
Ilchester Terrace.	2-24 Ilchester Road.
Ilchester Villas.	17-27 Abbotsbury Road.
Ingleside.	Stavordale Road.
Jubilee Terrace.	27-39 Newstead Road.
Kellaway's Cottages.	1-4 Kellaway Terrace.
Kelso Terrace.	87-101 Abbotsbury Road.
The Knoll.	16 Franklin Road.
Landale Terrace.	21-35 Ilchester Road.
Laurestine Terrace.	Part of the terrace formerly known as Rose Cottages or Rose Terrace, and finally as 103-117 Abbotsbury Road.
Linden Terrace.	*
Linden Villas.	Stavordale Road.
Lingdale Villas.	54-56 Abbotsbury Road.
Littlefield Villas.	2-8 Alma Road.
Melrose Villas.	100-102 Abbotsbury Road.
Milton Terrace.	Milton Road.
Miramoor.	15 Cromwell Road.
Myrtle Cottage.	118 Abbotsbury Road.
Newstead Villas.	93-101 Newstead Road.
Olivet.	14 Franklin Road.
Oxford Terrace.	120-130 Abbotsbury Road.
Prospect Terrace.	1-27 Melbury Road.
Rock Cottages.	43-45 Newstead Road.
Rock(s) Terrace.	47-89 Newstead Road.
Rockland House.	65 Abbotsbury Road.
Rockland Villas.	57-59 Abbotsbury Road.
Rose Cottages/Terrace.	Later part of Laurestine Terrace, which is now 103-117 Abbotsbury Road.
St Paul's Terrace.	156-174 Abbotsbury Road.
Shirley Terrace.	Cromwell Road.
South View.	44 Abbotsbury Road, & 91 Newstead Road.
Southdown View.	*
Stavordale House.	2 Abbotsbury Road.
Stavordale Villas.	Stavordale Road.
Summerland.	Stavordale Road.
Sunnybank.	Stavordale Road.
Surrey Terrace.	66-98 Newstead Road.
Victoria House.	142 Abbotsbury Road.
Victoria Terrace.	79-85 Abbotsbury Road.
Waverley Terrace.	*
Westbank Villas.	53-55 Abbotsbury Road.
Westbourne Terrace.	Cromwell Road.
West End Terrace.	176-182 Abbotsbury Road.
West End Villas.	161-171 Abbotsbury Road.
Wykeham Villa.	13 Cromwell Road.

*Known to have existed in, or been planned for the Westham Area, but the exact location not identified.

Bibliography

CORPORATION ARCHIVES

The prime source of information on municipal affairs is the collection of minute books and archive material preserved by the Weymouth and Portland Borough Council. This includes the 'Sherren Papers', a large collection of official documents discarded early in the 19th Century, but preserved by James Sherren, and, now returned to municipal ownership, forms the basis of the town's collection. For more details apply to The Curator, Local History Museum, Weymouth.

Abstracts from the archives have been published:

Moule, H.J., (editor). *Descriptive catalogue of the charters, minute books and other documents of the Borough of Weymouth and Melcombe Regis. 1251-1800.* (1883).

Weinstock, Maureen B., (editor). *Weymouth and Melcombe Regis minute book 1625-1660.* (1964).

Wolff, Henry and West, Jack A.C., (compilers). *Weymouth and Melcombe Regis in the nineteenth century: abstracts from the minute books of the Weymouth Corporation, the Local Board of Health, the Urban Sanitary Authority and the Urban District Council, 1800-1899.* (1972).

SERIAL PUBLICATIONS

Proceedings of the Dorset Natural History and Antiquarian Field Club, 1877-1928

Proceedings of the Dorset Natural History and Archaeological Society, 1928 to date

Somerset and Dorset Notes and Queries. 1890 to date

The Dorset Year Book, 1904 to date

The Weymouth Red Book, for 1905

GENERAL BOOKS
(All include major sections on Weymouth).

Gerard, Thomas. *Survey of Dorsetshire* (Written 1620s, published 1732 as by John Coker)

Good, Ronald. *The Old Roads of Dorset* (1966)

Good, Ronald. *Weyland: the story of Weymouth and its countryside* (1946)

Hutchins, John. *The History and Antiquities of the County of Dorset.* 3rd edition, 1861-1870. 4 volumes. (Volume II contains Weymouth)

Leland, John. *Itinerary* (1535-1543)

Lloyd, Rachel. *Dorset Elizabethans* (1967)

Mills, A.D. *The Place-Names of Dorset, Part I* (1977)

Payne, Donald. *Dorset Harbours* (1953)

Royal Commission on Historical Monuments. *An Inventory of the Historical Monuments in the County of Dorset. Vol. 2. South East* (in three parts). (1970)

Sellman, R.R. *Illustrations of Dorset History* (1960)

The Victoria History of the County of Dorset. Vols II (1908), and III (1968)

Weinstock, Maureen B. *Studies in Dorset History* (1953)

Weinstock, Maureen B. *More Dorset Studies* (1960)

Weinstock, Maureen B. *Old Dorset* (1967)

WEYMOUTH AND MELCOMBE REGIS
General History.

Barrett, William Bowles. *Contributions to the History of Weymouth.* (Manuscript notes). 4 volumes.

Cosens, E.S.L. *A Short History of Weymouth for the Use of Schools* (1927)

Ellis, George A. *History of the Borough and Town of Weymouth and Melcombe Regis* (1829)

Ricketts, Eric J. *The Buildings of old Weymouth and Portland. 4 vols* (1975-1979)

WEYMOUTH AND MELCOMBE REGIS
Stuart Period

Bayley, A.R. *The Great Civil War in Dorset, 1642-1660* (1910)

Cade, John and MILLS, John. *The last speeches and confession of Captain John Cade and John Mills, Constable, who were hanged at Weymouth for endeavouring to betray that garrison . . .* (1645)

Ince, Peter, *A brief relation of the surprise of the forts of Weymouth: the siege of Melcombe, the recovery of the forts and raising of the siege* (1644)

WEYMOUTH AND MELCOMBE REGIS
18th Century

Dodington, George Bubb. *The Diary of . . .* (edited by) Henry Penruddocke Wyndham (1823)

Dodington, George Bubb. *The Political Journal of . . .* edited by John Carswell and Lewis Arnold Dralle (1965)

KING GEORGE III AT WEYMOUTH

Boyce, Benjamin. *The Benevolent Man: a Life of Ralph Allen of Bath* (1967)

Broadley, A.M. *Royal Weymouth, 1789-1805* 4 volumes (1907)

D'arblay, Madame. (Fanny Burney). *Diary, 1778-1840.* Vol. 4 (1904)

Ham, Elizabeth. *Elizabeth Ham by Herself, 1783-1820.* (1945)

Landmann, George T. *Adventures and Recollections, Vol II* (1852)

WEYMOUTH AND MELCOMBE REGIS
19th and 20th Centuries

Acutt, Douglas G.F. *Brigade in Action* (1946)

Gooch, Sir Daniel. *Memoirs and Diary,* edited by R.B. Wilson (1972)

Lucking, J.H. *The Great Western at Weymouth* (1971)

Lucking, J.H. *Dorset Railways* (1982)

Powys, Llewelyn. *Dorset Essays* (1935)

Robens, J.E. *Old Weymouth: some recollections of a nonagenarian* (1914)

MISCELLANEOUS

Weymouth guidebooks and directories.

Local newspapers.

Index

The names 'Weymouth' and 'Melcombe Regis' are only included in this index where they refer to the independent towns prior to 1571, or where they form part of the official name of an organisation or geographical location.
Churches and Schools are listed in Appendices D and E, and details of Terraces on the Esplanade, in the Park District and at Westham are given in Appendices G, H, and I.
Illustration numbers are printed in italics.